Bert Cardullo, Editor

# What Is Dramaturgy?

**PETER LANG**
New York • Washington, D.C./Baltimore • San Francisco
Bern • Frankfurt am Main • Berlin • Vienna • Paris

**Library of Congress Cataloging-in-Publication Data**

What is dramaturgy? / edited by Bert Cardullo.
p. cm. — (American university studies. Series XXVI, Theatre arts; vol. 20)
Includes bibliographical references.
1. Theatre—Production and direction. 2. Drama—Technique. I. Title.
II. Series. III. Series: American university studies. Series XXVI, Theatre arts; vol. 20
PN2053.C316   792'.023—dc20   93-2357
ISBN 0-8204-2177-4
ISSN 0899-9880


**Die Deutsche Bibliothek-CIP-Einheitsaufnahme**

Bert Cardullo:
What is dramaturgy? / Bert Cardullo, ed.
–New York; San Francisco; Bern; Frankfurt am Main;
Berlin; Baltimore; Wien; Paris: Lang.
(American university studies: Ser. 26, Theatre Arts; Vol. 20)
ISBN 0-8204-2177-4
NE: American university studies / 26

Cover design by George Lallas
Photo on the front cover by David Smith

The paper in this book meets the guidelines for permanence and durability
of the Committee on Production Guidelines for Book Longevity
of the Council of Library Resources.

© 1995, 2000 Peter Lang Publishing, Inc., New York

Printed in the United States of America

# What Is Dramaturgy?

# American University Studies

Series XXVI
Theatre Arts

Vol. 20

PETER LANG
New York • Washington, D.C./Baltimore • San Francisco
Bern • Frankfurt am Main • Berlin • Vienna • Paris

# Table of Contents

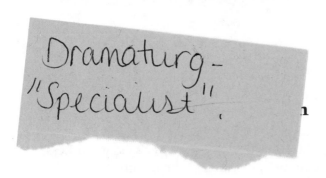

It has often been charged that a dramaturg is really a director or dramatist *manqué*. Perhaps the blame lies with the first official dramaturg, Lessing, a talented man who probably could have assumed any role in the theatre and performed it superbly. Today's dramaturg finds himself in the position of defining his role—one that is either expanding or shrinking, depending upon your point of view (and your theatre!).

The problem of definition is not merely academic or theoretical but one that goes to the heart of the creative process of theatre both in Europe and the United States. The dramaturg, many people in the theatre agree, can play a vital role, but what that role is, what it should be, and whether in fact the dramaturg alone should perform it, have yet to be clearly established. These were the considerations that led me to reprint or commission essays, interviews, and statements that explore the state of dramaturgy from the late 1970s to the present day. My rationale for reprinting pieces from the 1970s and 1980s, as opposed to publishing a volume consisting entirely of new material, is simple: the dramaturgical "explosion" in the United States, if not on the Continent, occurred at this time, and these documents from the period capture the excitement and profundity of Americans' discovery/Europeans' rediscovery of the idea of a dramaturgical theatre. In addition, these articles provide a valuable glimpse into the birth of a "new" theatrical profession and, what is more important, the concomitant rebirth or reimagining of much contemporary theatre.

The contributors to *What Is Dramaturgy?* take one or more of the following into account: (1) the role of the dramaturg in the theatrical life of the writer's country; (2) the dramaturg's function in his own theatre; (3) the differences and similarities between the functions of the dramaturg and the literary advisor; (4) the ideal qualifications for a dramaturg, including education and background; and (5) the future as well as the history of the dramaturg and dramaturgy. Part I attempts to answer the question "What is dramaturgy?" from a historical, theoretical, and practical standpoint, as does Joel Schechter's essay on Lessing in Part II, "Dramaturgy in Germany," the country where the practice began. Part II also includes an interview with a practicing dramaturg, a descriptive analysis of the dramaturg's role in European theatre in general, and an account of the work of the eminent dramaturg/dramatist Bertolt Brecht. This pattern—of analysis, interview, and documentation—is repeated in Parts III and IV of *What Is Dramaturgy?*, which are concerned with dramaturgy in America and Eastern Europe respectively. Part IV is limited to, but not limited by, interviews with the two best known literary managers in the history of the English theatre, Kenneth Tynan and John Russell Brown, while Part VI consists of an exhaustive bibliography of dramaturgical studies in English. Throughout the book, the reader will note an alternating, and sometimes dual, emphasis on new-play dramaturgy and classical-play dramaturgy: Art Borreca's essay, for instance, is concerned with the former kind, Richard Pettengill's with the latter, and C. J. Gianakaris' with both kinds of dramaturgy.

As the idea of dramaturgy grows, so too does the dramaturg's potential sphere of influence. Once relegated to the back of the rehearsal hall, he can now be in the forefront of almost all the activities of the theatre: including selection of the repertory, translation and editing of texts, explication of the social, cultural, and political connotations of a given play, design of programs and posters, collaboration with the director in selecting a cast as well as with the scenic, costume, and lighting designers in creating a visual metaphor for the drama in question. In fact, the drama*turg* remains only a step away from becoming a drama*tist*—or from being expelled from our overspecialized theatre precisely because he combines so many functions in one person. His is a creative situation to be envied or deplored, again depending on your perspective. Certainly the dramaturg's dilemma is one that Lessing would have understood, and even applauded.

Bert Cardullo

# Acknowledgements

I'd like to express my gratitude to the following journals for permission to reprint articles and interviews from their pages: *Theater, Slavic and East European Arts, Performing Arts Journal, Callboard,* and *Theatre Quarterly.* Thanks to Leon Katz, Art Borreca, and Carol Rosen for contributing previously unpublished material to this volume. And special thanks to Michael J. Flamini of Peter Lang Publishing and William C. Kelly of the University of Michigan's Office for Research for supporting this project, and thus helping to promulgate the idea of a dramaturgical theatre.

B.C.

# I

# WHAT IS DRAMATURGY?

"The goal of dramaturgy is to resolve the antipathy between the intellectual and the practical in the theatre, fusing the two into an organic whole."

—Leon Katz

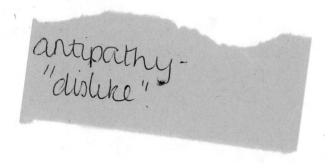

# Enter Dramaturgs

Bert Cardullo

If you consult a dictionary, the meaning of the word "dramaturgy" you find there is "the craft or the techniques of dramatic composition considered collectively," and a "dramaturg" is defined simply as "a dramatist or playwright." Now we know that a playwright is a "maker" or "worker" of plays, not merely a writer of them (as a shipwright is a maker of ships and a wainwright a maker of wagons). This meaning of "playwright" is reinforced by the Greek word *dramaturgy* (and its back formation, *dramaturg*), which is made up of the root for "action or doing" (*drame*) and the suffix for "process or working" (*-urgy*). Here we may helpfully think of the words "metallurgy"—the working of metal—and "thaumaturgy"—the working of miracles.

But let us venture on another meaning of the word "dramaturgy," which has come into usage in the American theatre fairly recently. As a result of our belated acknowledgement of European theatre practice, "dramaturgy" today denotes the multi-faceted study of a given play: its author, content, style, and interpretive possibilities, together with its historical, theatrical, and intellectual background. This study is conducted by people called "dramaturgs" in the European repertory theatre, most conspicuously in Germany, where each of the approximately 120 municipal theatres has a dramaturgical department. The dramaturg's profession was instituted in the United States during the rise of the regional theatre movement and continues to be important in ensemble theatres as well as in those regional theatres that have remained non-commercial. As critics-in-residence (also known as literary managers or literary advisors), dramaturgs perform a variety of tasks. Broadly speaking, the dramaturg's duties are (1) to select and prepare play-texts for performance; (2) to advise directors and actors; and (3) to educate the audience. To fulfill these duties, dramaturgs serve as script readers, translators, theatre historians, play adaptors or even playwrights, directorial assistants or sometimes apprentice directors, critics of works-in-progress, and talent scouts.

After selecting a play for production in collaboration with his theatre's artistic director, the resident dramaturg prepares the text for performance by translating or editing it, researching the play's production history if it has one, and collaborating with its director on textual interpretation. If a play is new and the playwright is present at rehearsals, the dramaturg discusses cuts, rewrites, and the reordering of scenes with the author. Dramaturgical preparation of a classic need not be entirely different from collaboration on a new play. Research into the production history, textual variants, and sociopolitical background of a classic can increase the accuracy with which a past playwright's language, stage conventions, and world view are realized on stage, if the director wants his work to be true to the original text. However, an old text can also be turned into a "new" one—that is, invested with a contemporaneity of language (through a new translation or adaptation), a topical "concept" (more on this later), and/or a novel staging.

Dramaturgs assist as well in the casting of a play, and during rehearsals they offer in-house criticism of productions-in-progress for the benefit of cast, director, and dramatist. To inform the director, the cast, and the audience about a play's past history and its current importance, dramaturgs assemble "protocols" (or casebooks consisting of written and found materials toward a theatrical production), prepare program notes, lead post-performance discussions, write study guides for schools and groups, lecture in the community as well as the academy, and publish scholarly essays and books. Through collaboration with a resident dramaturg/in-house critic, then, the director is able to integrate textual and acting criticism, performance theory, and historical research into a production *before* it opens, instead of simply receiving post-mortems afterwards from journalists and avid theatregoers.

Arthur Ballet, former dramaturg at the Guthrie Theatre in Minneapolis, once said that dramaturgs must constantly ask themselves and the people with whom they work, "Why are we doing plays at all and why are we doing *this* play, *here, now?*" Although it is not an easy role to play, the dramaturg must be the artistic conscience of his theatre; he must help in the formulation of that theatre's aesthetic policy and ensure its faithfulness to its articulated aims.

To return the discussion to a practical level, John Lahr, now the theatre critic for *The New Yorker,* reports that *his* job at the Guthrie in the 1950s and early 1960s was primarily to bring new plays to the theatre and do the program notes. Later, however, when he was literary manager under Jules Irving at Lincoln Center, he did what he calls the "more satisfactory work" of collaborating with directors in rehearsal, writing lyrics for new songs in some plays, adapting such classics as Molière's *The Misanthrope,* and performing general advisory work, in addition to writing program notes and bringing new plays like Pinter's *Landscape* and *Silence* to the theatre. Says Lahr:

> It's very important that theaters have a dramaturg, preferably who can combine his critical intelligence with practical theater work. . . . Critics have something to give the theatre. They need not be enemies. . . . If theaters want better critics, they must open their doors. . . . I think that critics must . . . learn about the craft from the inside so they can serve the art they purport to love.

As defined thus far, dramaturgy has two dimensions: organization of the many facets of repertory theatre activity, and specific production research. In addition to the functions described above, German dramaturgy departments, writes Martin Esslin, have the job of planning the performance schedule:

> Not only do the plays have to be selected, but they have to be selected to suit the character of the particular company, providing a fair share of good parts for all the principal actors. . . . The working out of the very complex casting rosters in companies that may be playing in two different houses at the same time, while often keeping a road company touring in neighboring, smaller cities, demands great ingenuity in adjusting the repertoire, planning rehearsals for understudies, etc. . . . [In the dramaturgy department also] the repertoire is carefully planned to provide a balanced diet [of classics and new plays, both foreign and domestic] for the requirements of the public of the city served by the theater in question.

Esslin concludes that "in most German theaters the chief Dramaturg holds a position of considerable power and often dominates even the top man, the artistic director."

But none of these definitions or job descriptions has yet revealed the root importance of dramaturgy. To do so, we must ask ourselves two questions: (1) in what sense is the practice of dramaturgy by resident theatrical "critics" similar to its practice by the dictionary-defined "dramaturg," the playwright or maker of plays?; and (2) where did the idea of dramaturgy, in its multiple meaning of making, studying, and explaining the play-in-production, come from?

The second question is easier to answer, so let's start with it: the modern sense of dramaturgy comes from the time of the German Enlightenment, after about 1765, particularly from the writing and work of Gotthold Ephraim Lessing. A leading intellectual figure in Germany's growth into national-literary prominence during the last forty years of the eighteenth century, Lessing was the first dramaturg of modern Western theatre. After studying theology early in life, he turned to literary and dramatic studies, wrote plays, traveled extensively, served in the Seven Years' War (1756-1763), and worked as resident critic (or dramaturg) between 1767 and 1769 for the Hamburg National Theatre, Germany's first permanent, subsidized repertory company. As dramaturg for the Hamburg theatre, Lessing supervised the selection of plays, advised in their staging, and translated some French and English works, in addition to writing criticism of each play performed. Though the permanence of the Hamburg National Theatre is questionable, since it lasted only about two years, its plan to develop a repertory of new plays led the theatre to hire Lessing, a playwright-critic who both carefully evaluated new scripts and wrote them himself. This commitment to new plays, and to theatre freed from commercial pressures, is shared by a number of theatres in America that employ dramaturgical advisors: the O'Neill Theater Center, the Mark Taper Forum, the Yale Repertory Theatre, the Guthrie Theater, and the Manhattan Theatre Club, among others.

Lessing's essays on productions staged at his own theatre were collected in the *Hamburg Dramaturgy* (1767-1769), a highly influential document that laid the groundwork for the German theatre's break from the rigid prescriptions of French neoclassical theory, with its concern for "rules" and "decorum." In the *Hamburg Dramaturgy* Lessing articulated his own important theory of drama based on his reading of Aristotle, Plato, Horace, Quintilian, and other classical authors. He championed Shakespeare in particular and English literature in general against the French, thus paving the way for the revolt of the Storm-and-Stress writers against the past, as well as for the monumental translations of Shakespeare's plays by A. W. Schlegel, Ludwig Tieck, and his daughter Dorothea in the early 1800s. The achievements of Lessing, a multiple-threat man of letters, scholar, dramatic theorist, and playwright, can instruct every modern theatre. His tradition continues into twentieth-century European theatre, where we find illustrious figures making theatre history through a combination of radical creativity and critical intelligence.

In the German theatre, Brecht is preeminent. His Berliner Ensemble, from 1949 to the present day, offers one of the best illustrations of collaborative learning and criticism at work on theatrical production. And we must not forget that Brecht's early career as a playwright and theorist included a good deal of dramaturgical work—first for his own Munich production of *The Life of Edward II of England* (which he co-wrote with Lion Feuchtwanger), then continuing in Berlin during the mid-twenties when he was dramaturg for Max Reinhardt and subsequently Erwin Piscator. Two of the leading theatres of Europe today—West Berlin's Theater am Halleschen Ufer (under Peter Stein) and Milan's Piccolo Teatro (under Giorgio Strehler)—include an elaborate dramaturgical dimension. As previously stated, most municipal theatres in Germany boast dramaturgical staffs. And in England the formidable National Theatre has had the first-rate critical collaboration of Kenneth Tynan and later John Russell Brown.

Lessing was not only the first important dramaturg but also, to repeat, the first to be critical of his own theatre and its role in society. From Lessing to Brecht a tradition of "oppositional" dramaturgy can be traced: beginning with Lessing's advocacy of middle-class drama over decadent, aristocratic plays, and culminating though not ending in Brecht's politically engaged concept of epic theatre, which he tried to implement when he was dramaturg at Reinhardt's Berlin theatre in 1925. (American dramaturgs, for their part, have fostered new drama that was not immediately popular or widely accessible.) Not all dramaturgs have been members of this "oppositional" tradition. Many were conservative, or at least complacent, simply following the orders of superiors (a longstanding practice among other German civil servants!). But the most influential European dramaturgs have been men of ideas (few women until recently) who advanced their ideas of theatre by recommending plays and also by writing as well as directing them. Dramaturgs such as Lessing, Tieck, Brahm, Ibsen, Brecht, Kipphardt, and Heiner Müller are now known primarily as playwrights and/or directors, a fact that should be noted by their American successors. The dramaturg's position has frequently been a transitional phase of his life in the theatre; a young playwright or critic often served as dramaturg while writing essays and plays less remunerative than script reading and rehearsal watching. Perhaps, then, the dramaturg's work should be regarded not as an end in itself but as part of a collaborative creation, and a source of training for future play directors, artistic directors, playwrights, and critics.

Future dramaturgs need to be trained too, of course. Without prior study of theatre history, criticism, theory, and dramatic literature their usefulness to a theatre would be severely limited. William Ellwood noted in 1970 that "very few [American] graduate programs in theater are capable of turning out Dramaturgs for the repertory theater." The situation has changed somewhat over the past twenty-five years or so: the Yale School of Drama, the University of California at San Diego, the University of Massachusetts at Amherst, and the State University of New York at Stony Brook have initiated actual dramaturgy training programs. However, most American dramaturgs are working, not at (regional) repertory theatres, but at theatres that produce new plays. Even if our universities are now turning out dramaturgs trained, as dramaturgs in Europe are, for repertory theatres, the question remains: who will start turning out repertory theatres for our dramaturgs?

This leads us back to that first question: "In what way is the work of the in-house theatrical critic like that of the playwright, both defined by the word 'dramaturg'?" The answer to this question will also establish the reasons why dramaturgy is necessary for the resuscitation of theatre art in our time.

If a dramaturg is a playwright, a maker of plays; and if we agree that a "play" is an elusive *thing* whose existence we cannot surely point to in the text alone or in any one production by a theatre company, then the definition of the synonyms "dramaturg" and "playwright" becomes slippery. If we cannot say with certainty what *the play* is, how can we say what the *playwright* makes? One thing at least is certain: the playwright (or dramaturg) makes the text—that is, he writes the words that characters will say. This bare fact impels many to declare that a play's text can be interpreted in limitless ways. There are even some theatre artists who believe that a play's text is something closer to *raw* than *formed* material, and therefore must be formed—*interpreted*—by them, primarily through the creative agency of the director. Taken to its extreme, this view makes the director the creative equal—and sometimes even superior—of the playwright. And so we often see productions of plays that bear the names of authors, but that in fact carry the interpretive definitions of other "authors," namely directors. This other authorship, this meta-creation of the playtext through production, makes the production itself into a singular, sovereign work of theatre art, of which we must say in each instance: "I saw an *Othello*," or "I liked that *Mother Courage*," or "Andrei Serban's *Cherry Orchard* troubled me."

The key word used by many of today's theatre artists to designate the creative singularity of this or that production of a particular dramatic text is "concept." The "production concept" is the creation of a director (or a consort of director, designers, and occasionally a lead actor) who aspires to the same authorial status as that enjoyed by the playwright. Each—the playwright, on the one hand, and the director, on the other—would claim to have "made" the play (whatever that is). So we find ourselves these days thinking about plays as if they had two necessary authorships: the "literary" by the writer, and the "theatrical" by the producing artists. But hardly ever does anyone bother to investigate the origin of this assumption. The few who do inquire into the matter seriously are usually regarded, alternately by literary people and theatre practitioners, as troublemakers. They are critics (nasty folks!).

Or they are dramaturgs, some of whom are themselves the "authors" of production concepts that transcend the plays from which they originate. But a dramaturg is also the guardian of the text (presuming there is a text worthy of guarding) as opposed to its "author," a stand-in for the playwright. His job is to know (insofar as this is possible) as much as the playwright—about history, society, culture, and politics as well as drama—when he set about writing this or that play, and his goal is thus to ensure the theatrical transmission of the *playwright's* vision, the "making" of the play on stage. And it is here that the dramaturg is caught, straddling the fence between the director as superstar and the dramatist as wordsmith, or conversely between the director as traffic cop, merely the stager of a text, and the playwright as *auteur*. That is, faced with the alternative of a directors' theatre that bears little relation to playwrights' texts and a directors' (stage managers'?) theatre that is overliteral or unimaginative in its transmission of those texts, the dramaturg is compelled to forge a compromise between the two. It is just such a compromise—arduously achieved and precariously balanced—that is necessary for the elevation of the drama to its rightful status as artistic pulse of the nation (as opposed to New York City), for the return of "repertory" to our (regional) theatres, and thus for the revival of theatrical art in our time. Not *dramatic* art, not an *imagistic* theatre, and not *performance* art, but *theatrical* art, which compellingly weds word to image and act.

The dramaturg is spokesman for the word if not a creator of words himself; he is the champion of ideas in a theatre—and a world—increasingly devoid of them; and he is a believer in the elusive if not ineffable spirit of well-wrought dramatic texts, which he helps to embody in beautifully shaped, infinitely shaded, and piercingly heard theatrical productions. Without the dramaturg, in fact, there is no real theatre. He is its true architect and archaeologist, the discoverer, transmitter, and interpreter of playtexts both ancient and modern, a kind of playwright for all ages or crossroads of dramatic tradition. A dramaturg is to a play as a mechanic is to an automobile: he may not have built it, but he knows what makes it work, and this enables him to rebuild it as the theatrical occasion warrants. Playwrights—and directors as well as audiences—should be grateful, and should take advantage.

1994

# The Compleat Dramaturg

Leon Katz

These are the skills, knowledge, and experiences I believe a dramaturg should have when he enters the profession:

1) A critical sensibility, together with the ability to write mature essays and reviews addressed not merely to professionals and scholars, but also to reasonably intelligent, generally aware readers and theatregoers.

2) A thorough knowledge, in depth, of the dramatic repertory based on a wide range of reading in dramatic literature, scholarship, and criticism in all periods and genres of drama, with special areas of expertise of his own.

3) The ability to do scholarly research, plus practical experience in tracking down scripts, options, copyright information, and publication as well as production histories of plays.

4) The ability to read and translate plays from, ideally, several foreign languages but as a minimum one, and the even more valuable ability to adapt the translated text into stageworthy dialogue in English.

5) The ability to read new scripts intelligently, and to write summaries and appraisals of them with professional competence.

6) The ability to cut scripts knowledgeably, with an understanding of how to do so without destroying their logic or losing their essential dramatic and theatrical values.

7) Experience in preparing a dramaturg's protocol—a five-part pre-production study of a play—together with a glossary of the text, for the information of the director and possibly the rest of the company. The parts consist of (a) the historical, cultural, and social background of the play; (b) relevant biographical information concerning the playwright, plus a history of the writing of the play and an assessment of its place in the author's

*oeuvre;* (c) a critical and production history of the play, including a report on the textual problems (if any) of the original and an assessment of the major translations (if the play was written in a language other than English); (d) a comprehensive critical analysis of the play, including the dramaturg's suggestions for a directorial-design concept for a new production; and (e) a comprehensive bibliography of materials on the play: editions, essays, articles, reviews, interviews, recordings, films, videotapes, etc.

8)  The ability to prepare useful background study guides— often a digested version of the protocol or parts thereof—to be made available to student or "group" audiences.

9)  Experience and expertise in collaborating with directors and designers to create a production concept, or, if a specific "concept" is not to be employed, an approach to the play and an articulation of its goals in production.

10)  Based on the dramaturg's intimate knowledge of a play, and on pre-production discussion with a director about his approach to the play, the expertise to contribute significantly to a play's casting and design.

11)  Expertise in taking dramaturgical rehearsal notes (which can be of crucial value to a receptive director), knowing at what points in the rehearsal process his notes are of value, what *sort* of notes are useful at different stages of the rehearsal process, and what sort of notes have constructive value together with what sort do not.

12)  A thorough awareness of dramaturg's rehearsal decorum. It is most important for the dramaturg to take notes during rehearsal as inconspicuously as possible. He must be aware that the very sight of someone vigorously writing notes can be unnerving to directors and actors, who may feel that premature judgment is being made upon them. What helps most in allaying this source of irritation is the dramaturg's creation of the feeling in the company, as early as possible in the rehearsal process, that he is part of the same team and anxious for the same, good result. The courtesies and parameters that guide the dramaturg are these: he avoids interrupting of his own volition the director's work or the rehearsal; he does not show his notes to, or discuss them with, any member of the company

without the request or consent of the director; in manner and in conversation, he avoids exhibiting negative responses toward the director's or the company's labors. The dramaturg, as much as any member of the company, shares the responsibility for creating an atmosphere of mutual trust and respect during rehearsals.

13) Knowledge of the do's and don'ts governing the dramaturg's conduct during consultation sessions with the director. However discussion between the two occurs, whether regularly and formally or only occasionally and informally, the dramaturg suggests his opinion to the director but does not force it on him, and understands that the final decision on all matters raised in discussion is necessarily the director's.

14) In working with playwrights, the ability to break down a script, analyzing its structural strengths and weaknesses, and make constructive suggestions for revision.

15) Training and experience in appropriate writing styles and formats for program notes (which should reflect the director's concept of the play and production and provide audiences—even critics—with a relevant context for viewing the play-in-production), newsletter articles, interviews, and publicity releases.

16) Experience in keeping notes for, and writing up, post-production records: production logs, season histories, post-production critical evaluations.

17) The experience of an apprenticeship in a professional theatre, working within the framework of its particular procedures and policies, and gaining familiarity with its overall administrative and budgetary set-up.

18) Above all, to have developed his individual "idea of a theatre" out of which he would, if this earth were heaven, map out seasons of repertory to advance that particular idea; and even if this earth is not heaven, to have developed the determination to work tirelessly toward advancing such a theatre, or orienting a theatre in which he works toward his artistic goal. Concomitantly, to have developed enough common sense to recognize that a theatre in which he is employed will not normally adapt itself overnight to his particular aesthetic orientation, but to retain enough idealism to yearn and plan for the

existence of his ideal theatre, some day, somewhere. For dramaturgy as a profession ultimately looks toward the shaping of the artistic policy of a theatre, the formulation of its artistic policy being evidenced in its choice of repertoire, its approach to productions, and the cultural and aesthetic orientations of the artists it employs.

1984

# Ten Dramaturgical Myths

David Copelin

Lately, a lot of nonsense has been written (and, of course, spoken) about dramaturgs and literary managers. From the *Dramatists' Guild Quarterly* to *The Drama Review* by way of *Can Play*, *Theatre Times*, and even *American Theatre*, playwrights and those who pretend to support their interests have taken some pretty hefty swings at our emerging professions. To hear some commentators tell it, most literary management is inept, and most dramaturgy, however well-meaning, is bad dramaturgy. Are literary managers and dramaturgs negative influences on our stages *by definition?*

"If they would just crawl back through the crack in the theatrical sidewalk that spawned them," goes the argument, "then things could get back to 'normal.' Remember the good old days when real artists like us created dramatic masterpieces with no taint of 'play development'? If only these stupid literary managers, these obtuse dramaturgs, these theatre nerds, these (God save us) *intellectuals* would take a hint and vanish! Oh, wouldn't that be heartwarming?"

Sorry. Wrong scapegoats.

We literary managers and dramaturgs are ready to define the nature and quality of the services we offer to playwrights, directors, producers, and audiences. Too often, people who are primarily looking after their own interests, their own territory, have made such choices for us. Too often, the result has been dramaturgical passivity, dissatisfaction, and dreary theatre. But enough is enough. Let's correct both bad press and bad practice. Let's explode some myths about our misunderstood professions.

MYTH #1: *Literary managers and dramaturgs tell playwrights how to rewrite their plays.*

REALITY #1: No literary manager or dramaturg with any sense or sensitivity would do this. Yes, we ask questions. Yes, we point out the consequences of the choices that a playwright makes. We care about themes, resonances, a play's context. We may suggest alternative structure, the rearrangement of scenes, the *dramatic* (not economic) need for more or fewer characters. But our response or advice is based on one crucial principle: the script belongs to the playwright. Copyright is moral right. Changes can only be made by the author, or with the author's consent.

Once a playwright feels that this principle has in fact been accepted by all his coworkers, the playwright's fabled paranoia, suspicion, and resistance vanish, and real collaboration can begin. It is part of the dramaturg's job to see that the principle is mutually agreed to and mutually adhered to. In other words, the only person who can "develop" a play is its playwright. Director, dramaturg, actors, and designers are resources for this process, but do not control it.

MYTH #2: *Since dramaturgs have raised staged readings to an art form, playwrights have been encouraged to develop their plays to death.*

REALITY #2: We all know by now that readings of scripts have limited usefulness. In many theatres, dramaturgs have organized and run readings of plays for subscribers and even for those artistic directors who don't have time to read scripts, but that is more a way of carving out an area of responsibility than it is evidence of some deep-seated belief in readings as a substitute for productions.

Readings are, however, the cheapest way for a theatre to respond positively to a playwright's work. "We'll give your script a reading, which will enable you to hear it and develop it further, with our guidance." It's a sort of trial marriage, a way for the theatre to assure funders, playwrights, and audiences that it is seriously interested in new plays, without making the ultimate commitment of production. It's a managing director's dream. *But does it help the playwright?* How many playwrights' resumés have you seen that list five or six staged readings for the same play, but no productions?

This is what Steven Dietz meant when he coined the phrase "developed to death." After too many readings, some scripts get so accessible that there is no longer any reason actually to stage them. Everything in these over-developed scripts becomes too clear. There's no more mystery. Inevitably, the reason we were attracted to the script in the first place disappears along with the lumps, the odd corners, the specific voice.

I think that most literary managers and dramaturgs now heed the Dead End sign on this road. The staged reading is not and cannot be an art form, because it explicitly denies the discoveries made in extended rehearsal as well as those values which can only be communicated by performance. Ironic, isn't it, that the rise of the staged reading as a way to "develop" plays occurred just as performance itself was becoming less verbal and more visual? Ever tried to do performance art in a staged reading? And theatre is, after all, performance art.

MYTH #3: *Literary managers and dramaturgs function as "objective voices" in rehearsal.*

REALITY #3: Underlying this notion is the unspoken hope that we won't be around often enough to have any serious influence on production choices. But staying away from the process, pretending Olympian detachment, deigning to attend a run-through with a yellow pad in order to give the director a sheaf of notes, causes resentment and resistance. The objectivity born of ignorance of the day-to-day creative rhythms of rehearsal is not nearly as valuable to any production as is an *informed subjectivity*.

After all, no matter how insightful we may be, someone has to be ready to listen to these insights for them to do any good. Our credibility as observers is based, not on our title, but on our function. When the other artists see us there from the first concept meeting right through opening night, they come to accept us as part of the creative process, instead of as interlopers in it. As Gordon Davidson put it, "You've got to get your hands dirty." As Woody Allen said, "Ninety percent of success is showing up." Either sitting behind a pile of scripts or writing subscription brochure blurbs is not a terribly interesting alternative. Should we see ourselves as artistic consultants? Or as bureaucrats? In which mode are we more valuable to a theatre?

MYTH #4: *As intellectuals, literary managers and dramaturgs want to replace warm human emotions in the theatre with cold abstract ideas.*

REALITY #4: Sentimental blather. Haven't you ever been excited by an idea? Aren't you fed up with the peculiar notion that audiences, let alone dramatic characters, can't both think and feel at the same time? Sometimes ideas and emotions agree; sometimes they conflict with each other. So what's the problem? Are emotions really deeper and truer than thoughts? America sometimes seems to take that for granted, but it's actually just a habit reinforced by bad TV. Didn't glorifying emotion at the expense of thought give the world Adolf Hitler? Barry Manilow? *Steel Magnolias?*

No, literary managers and dramaturgs don't want to replace human emotions with abstract ideas, and we certainly don't accept the common error that human emotions are necessarily "warm" while abstract ideas, or any ideas, are necessarily "cold." We know how many crimes have been committed under that phony standard. We'd rather recognize the joy of ideas as embodied in and by works of dramatic art, and their concurrence and compatibility with emotions. We're not afraid to have ideas if they are presented in truly dramatic form (not like raisins dropped into oatmeal). Patronizing an audience, assuming its stupidity or lack of interest in ideas, is the worst kind of elitism. Such elitism is not just anti-intellectual, it's inhumane. It's poison.

MYTH #5: *Literary managers and dramaturgs are no more than powerless, stage-struck "Ph.D. gofers" with no real artistic talents of their own, reduced to working as underpaid readers and clerks.*

REALTY #5: Oh yeah? What about Robert Blacker and Walter Bilderback at LaJolla? Mark Bly and Michael Lupu at the Guthrie? Ann Cattaneo at Lincoln Center? Amlin Gray and Mame Hunt at Berkeley Rep? Morgan Jenness all over the place? Lots of others. And then, of course, there are those who began as literary managers and dramaturgs, and are now producers: André Bishop at Playwrights' Horizons. Oskar Eustis at the Eureka. Rocco Landesman and Jack Viertel at Jujamcyn. Russ Vandenbroucke at Northlight. Do you begin to see the true pattern?

Besides, the issue isn't power. *It's influence.* At a recent gathering of literary managers and dramaturgs, someone raised the question of whether or not we are "handmaidens" to other theatre artists. We are not. We may be, if we're lucky, handmaidens to artistic *visions,* to ideas, to perspectives, to the goal of ensuring that our theatres remain essential as both makers and reflectors of our culture. Are literary management and dramaturgy service jobs? I guess they are. And what service!

MYTH #6: *Dramaturgs interfere with the "natural" relationship between the director and the playwright (of a new play), and between the director and the text (of an older work).*

REALITY #6: "Natural?" Or merely habitual? It's interesting that European directors, accustomed to working with dramaturgs on translations, adaptations, the formation of production concepts, of creative theatrical *thinking,* have a lot less trouble using us properly than do many directors and playwrights raised in the American theatrical tradition. The conflicts that arise are sometimes artistic in nature, which is healthy; sometimes, though, they are merely territorial.

Many American directors and playwrights have been trained to think of themselves as solitary creators whose idiosyncrasy would be subverted if they allowed anyone else too far into their process. Good old rugged individualism! But really, is the John Wayne school of drama the most productive model for any theatre artist?

Happily, a number of director-playwright-dramaturg teams have been formed, primarily among the younger and less tradition-bound generation. The ideal partnership probably has four components, with a playwright, a director, a dramaturg, and a designer working together over a longer period of time than just one project. While the current structure of our theatres often precludes this long-term collaboration, that structure is not immutable.

No, the real interference in the creative process comes from fear. I know playwrights who refuse to allow a dramaturg into pre-production conferences, then claim that no dramaturg has ever been of any use to them. How's that for a self-fulfilling prophecy? I know some talented directors who apparently feel so inferior about their inability to say what they are thinking that they distrust those who are more articulate, more "intellectual" than they. Such directors don't realize that, given the choice between the many artists who are more glib than gifted, and the few whose productions are consistently more effective than their rhetoric, any true dramaturg would prefer to work with the latter.

MYTH #7: *Literary managers and dramaturgs don't like most American theatre the way it is. They want our scripts and productions to be more theatrical, more resonant, less naturalistic, less trivial, more aware of the world, better. Can't they appreciate how wonderful things are?*

REALITY #7: No.

MYTH #8: *Literary managers and dramaturgs are just critics in very thin disguise. They're not team players, they have little sense of performance, and they're always demanding instant results.*

REALITY #8: When Samuel Beckett's Estragon uses the epithet "Crritic!" to silence Vladimir, the moment is hard to resist. Who wants to be criticized? But there is a difference between in-house critics, process critics, which is what all good literary managers/dramaturgs are, and what Michael Feingold calls "out-house critics." Journalistic reviews and dramaturgical input into rehearsal and performance choices obviously differ in significant ways. Whatever our background, we soon learn what process means from a practical point of view.

At our best, we are the ideal audience for a production. We are connoisseurs of text, staging, production values, acting choices, a play's philosophy and its place in its artistic context. We also retain our sense of performance, to recognize the unique nature of theatre. But this comes with experience.

As for instant results: beginning dramaturgs, like beginning playwrights and directors, have been known to demand them. But has anyone ever gotten them? This behavior is self-extinguishing.

MYTH #9: Dramaturg *is such an ugly word!*

REALITY #9: Yeah, we know. The German dramaturgical tradition, while of immense interest to us, is of limited use because our society, our economy, and our theatres are very different from those in Europe. And we suffer from this job title. Zelda Fichandler once told me that the word *dramaturg* reminded her of "someone with a big book in one hand and a big stick in the other." Zelda herself has great dramaturgical skills—I shall always treasure her decision to spell Brecht's mythical city *Setzuan* because "*Szechwan* looks like a sneeze"—but she dislikes being called a dramaturg. So, we're stuck with a name that is hard to pronounce, impossible to define, downright un-American, and which the *Dramatists' Guild Quarterly* refuses to spell correctly. But there *is* a bright side: my mother still has no idea what I do for a living.

MYTH #10: *There will always be literary managers, because someone has to read all those plays, but dramaturgy is a nasty fad that will go away.*

REALITY #10: Don't hold your breath. Or better yet, do.

1989

# II

# DRAMATURGY IN GERMANY

"For a dramaturg, the production's the thing."

—Michael Feingold

# Lessing, Jugglers, and Dramaturgs

Joel Schechter

"It was Lessing, the most eminent of dramatic critics (so I am told by persons who have read him), who was reproached by Heine for not only cutting off his victims' heads but holding them up afterwards to show that there were no brains in them. The critical profession, in fact, is cruel in its nature, and demands for its efficient discharge an inhuman person like myself."

—George Bernard Shaw

Gotthold Ephraim Lessing was so financially impoverished by January, 1767, that he agreed to serve as a resident critic at the Hamburg National Theatre. He would have preferred to be a librarian at the Royal Library in Berlin, but Frederick the Great denied him that opportunity in 1766. King Frederick hired a Frenchman instead of a German. Lessing had to settle for a position in Hamburg. In this casual, almost accidental manner, the dramaturgical profession began.

While at the Hamburg National Theatre, Lessing wrote *Hamburg Dramaturgy*, a collection of essays on theatre which popularized dramaturgy as both a word and a practice. Today Lessing's successors—resident theatre critics throughout Germany and Austria—are called Dramaturgs. Lessing, like many modern Dramaturgs, was a playwright who advised his theatre's management on play selection, and offered his theatre continuous, sometimes adverse, criticism of its productions. Since Lessing's day Dramaturgs have also been known to direct plays, translate foreign drama, commission works, prepare essays for inclusion in theatre programs, and usher. Nearly all Dramaturgs read plays, though one notable exception is the Dramaturg in Brecht's *Messingkauf Dialogues*; he stays out of his office because "it would mean sitting under the reproachful eyes of all those scripts I ought to have read."

While the dramaturgical profession is largely an Austrian and German phenomenon, comparable positions exist for a

Literary Manager at the National Theatre of Great Britain, and for a Play Advisor at the Royal Shakespeare Theatre. In the past few years, as permanent American theatre companies have increased in number, a few of them—the Yale Repertory, the Mark Taper Forum—have also hired Literary Managers.

Despite these recent developments, the history and function of the Dramaturg remain relatively unknown in the United States. Our commercial theatres have had no need for Dramaturgs; even Lessing found his dramaturgical advice ignored once art had been, in his words, "degraded . . . to the level of a trade." As Lessing's career suggests, salable theatre and Dramaturgs are often at odds. This and other problems that Lessing encountered two centuries ago in his role as first Dramaturg still trouble the profession. The new profession gave rise to controversies that can now be "considered proverbial for the fate of the man of letters who rashly interferes in the business of the theatre," as Edwin Zeydel notes in his biography of Germany's second major Dramaturg, Ludwig Tieck.

Lessing's reputation as a man of letters in the theatre rests on several well-received plays and a few volumes of criticism. *Hamburg Dramaturgy*, written between April, 1767, and April, 1769, has been carefully analyzed by Lessing scholars and historians. Their analyses usually focus on the German critic's preferences for Aristotelian theory and for Shakespearean plays over French Neo-Classic theory and drama. The book's relevance to the origins of the dramaturgical profession deserves closer attention. While the *Dramaturgy* offers no detailed reports or complaints about Lessing's professional role at Hamburg, it includes numerous clues about his dramaturgical influence, or lack of it. From the book an intriguing if incomplete biography of the theatre's first Dramaturg can be reconstructed.

## Theatre Pays Lessing
## To Write Unfavorable Notices

Lessing's dramaturgical career began when he was asked by a consortium of twelve Hamburg businessmen and their theatre's managing director, J. F. Löwen, to serve as Theatre Poet. The consortium of financial backers expected Lessing to write new plays for them, and to lend their enterprise the prestige of his already respected name. Lessing initially balked at the invitation; he could not promise to write plays on a regular basis. Löwen, who had once been a theatre critic himself, then thought of paying Lessing to publish criticism of National Theatre performances in a consortium-sponsored journal. Lessing accepted this offer, and in April, 1767 he began writing biweekly sheets of criticism which sold for a shilling per copy, and sold by subscription for five Hamburg marks a year. While the journal's contents and its title, *Hamburg Dramaturgy*, were wholly Lessing's creations, the consortium's sponsorship of the journal invites suspicion. Why would the National Theatre publish Lessing's commentary on its plays, and pay the critic, unless it expected favorable notices? Lessing's employers undoubtedly thought that, besides acquiring the prestige that his reputation as playwright and critic already carried with it, they would attract an audience through his printed commentaries. As J. G. Robertson has noted, the Hamburg consortium expected Lessing "to act as a kind of publicity agent." Robertson adds that these expectations were never fulfilled; Lessing "declined to praise the work of the theatre and the pieces it produced, declined to laud indiscriminately the actors—in fact, he did everything that he was not wanted to do."

Instead of inviting the public to Hamburg's National Theatre, Lessing's essays occasionally attacked the taste of spectators already there, comparing eighteenth-century Germans unfavorably to ancient Athenians. Far from seeing himself as a publicity agent, Lessing assumed the role of public educator; he wrote, as he declared any good author would write, to "enlighten the mass and not confirm them in their prejudices or in their ignoble mode of thought." This Age-of-Enlightenment missionary stance, which underlay Lessing's Hamburg essays and caused most of his difficulties with actors at Hamburg, was not his alone. At least in theory, the managing director of the theatre, Löwen, also planned to educate German audiences, first by having Lessing publish information about plays and their authors, along with a running commentary on performances, in his journal. Löwen also proposed to develop the country's first permanent repertory company by offering prizes for new German plays and by staging the new drama in repertory with standard, already popular French works.

As it turned out, the prizes were not awarded; the theatre's managing committee, of which Lessing was a member, chose to produce mainly well-established plays by Frenchmen. Perhaps the National Theatre, with its avowed aim of producing German plays, was misnamed. It certainly was mismanaged. The "permanent repertory company" lasted about two years, ending in bankruptcy. Mismanagement and disputes led both Löwen and Lessing to resign from their positions in the summer of 1768. Lessing issued further installments of the *Dramaturgy* after his break with activity at the National Theatre, but these later essays were less a running commentary on performances than an exegesis of Aristotle's *Poetics* and obituaries for a failing repertory theatre. Objections from actresses compelled Lessing to record virtually nothing about acting at Hamburg after the twenty-fifth of his one-hundred and four essays in the *Dramaturgy*. The journal reported on most productions long after they had opened, and only the first fourteen weeks (fifty-two nights) of the theatre's productions were covered by the *Dramaturgy* in two years.

### Lessing Stays in the Theatre's Buffet Between Intermissions

Lessing's duties at the Hamburg National Theatre were never well-defined by the management, so it cannot be said that he violated his contract by publishing irregularly. He offered both plays and critical essays to his employers. Four of Lessing's plays were eventually staged at Hamburg. The management held him to no schedule, but his work as critic and advisor was regulated somewhat by company actresses, who exercised far more influence over theatre policy than their Dramaturg did. One actress, Madame Mecour, received a promise that the paid critic would never mention her in print, before the first installment of *Hamburg Dramaturgy* had been published. Although Lessing praised another actress, Madame Hensel, for her performance in the title role of his play, *Miss Sara Sampson,* she was far from pleased with his performance as critic. Lessing apparently saw nothing wrong with praising a production of his own play. Nor was Madame Hensel especially upset by such praise. Instead she complained that Lessing stepped out during his theatre visits, missing whole acts, and that he frequented the theatre's buffet entirely too much. Perhaps if he had not failed to see the merit of her leading roles in nine other plays, including a few Voltaire roles for which she was famous, the lady would not have complained about Lessing's negligence. In any case, rather than leave it up to the critic whether her name would be mentioned in his essays, Madame Hensel forbade Lessing to write about her anymore. Persuaded by the two actresses and by other considerations to be mentioned shortly, Lessing ceased to discuss all acting at Hamburg after June, 1767.

## Lessing Suppresses Scandalous Anecdotes

T. W. Rolleston contends that Lessing "would speedily have wrecked the enterprise" at Hamburg if his commentaries on acting had not ceased with Essay #25. While it is heartening to suppose that Lessing exerted enough influence to wreck the enterprise, it is more probable that the actors and actresses who dominated Hamburg's National Theatre would have shortened his stay there had his comments on acting continued. In the repertory of plays at Hamburg can be found one measure of the management's respect for its performers; plays by Voltaire and other Frenchmen whom Lessing disliked were frequently staged, so that Madame Hensel and Director Löwen's wife and other cast members could repeat the roles for which they had received acclaim under other managements.

Madame Hensel exerted considerable influence over the consortium's business manager and chief financial backer, Abel Seyler. Through Seyler his mistress directed National Theatre policies to her own advantage, and the performer-dominated system of production left Director Löwen at her mercy. Lessing makes only one allusion to the Hensel-Seyler scandal in his *Dramaturgy*; he subtly, humorously suggests that Madame Hensel's affairs are not his.

> In truth I pity my readers who promised to themselves in this journal a theatrical newspaper as varied and manifold, as amusing and comical, as a theatrical newspaper should be. Instead of containing the story of the plays performed, told in short lively and touching romances, instead of detailed biographies of absurd, eccentric foolish beings, such as those must be who concern themselves with writing comedies, instead of amusing, even slightly scandalous anecdotes of actors and especially actresses, instead of all these pretty things which they expected, they get long, serious, dry criticism of old well-known plays, ponderous examinations of what tragedy should or should not be, at times even expositions of Aristotle. And they are to read this? As I say, I pity them.

Instead of recording scandal in his journal, Lessing repeatedly asserts through his long, serious, dryly humorous criticisms the moral, instructive force of theatre—the antithesis of scandal—that he found in important plays and dramatic theory. He intended his own criticism to have this force; like the playwrights that he praised, Lessing as Dramaturg wrote to improve the aesthetic and moral sensibilities of his audience.

## Lessing Discovers That Actors Are Vain;
## Their Plays, Mediocre

Since Lessing eschewed scandalous anecdotes, *Hamburg Dramaturgy* offers no narrative account of actor resistance to his criticism. The criticism that offended performers at Hamburg survives in his book's first twenty-five essays. He rarely accuses a specific cast member of a specific fault, possibly because Madame Hensel warned Lessing not to abuse her name. But references to the vanity of unnamed performers recur. Explaining why mediocre plays have been included in the Hamburg repertory, Lessing notes:

> Some mediocre plays must also be retained on account of their containing excellent parts in which this or that actor can display his whole strength.

> Mediocrity always fares better with the actors. Perhaps because they can put more of themselves into the mediocre; perhaps because the mediocre leaves us more time and repose to observe their acting.

These comments on mediocre drama could be construed as a defense of the genre. Another, more cynical comment by Lessing would have been more offensive to the cast at Hamburg. In praising Herr Borchers, the resident critic distinguished this actor "from many other young actors who want forever to shine on the stage, and whose petty vanity to be seen and admired in nothing but gallant, amiable parts often constitutes their foremost and only vocation on the stage." Lessing, naming no offenders here, permitted every young actor and actress to suspect the accusation was aimed at him or her alone.

He also wrote about the acting company's fear of being criticized:

> I only know one way in which to flatter an artist of my own or of the other sex; and this consists in assuming that they are far removed from all vanity that art is above all else in their estimation, that they like to be judged openly and freely, and would now and then be criticized falsely rather than seldom. Whoever does not understand such flattery, in him I must confess myself mistaken and he does not deserve that we should study him.

After these remarks and the protests of cast members, Lessing ceased to study the acting at Hamburg.

His assertion that "art is above all else," especially above vanity, suggests that Lessing regarded theatre as an endeavor through which the artist subordinates himself to a collaborative work. The Dramaturg thought that "the true masterpiece fills us so entirely with itself that we forget its author over his work," and he wondered how a performer or author could be offended when artistic works, not personalities, were being scrutinized by the critic. In writing criticism, Lessing implemented his classicist's attitude by starting outside himself, searching first "for someone from whom he can differ, . . . and then gradually approaching his subject," confident that "the rest will follow of its own accord."

Lessing devoted less and less space in his journal to actual performances after Essay #25, concentrating instead on aesthetic theory and textual criticism. He had planned from the start to supplement the running commentary on plays with discussions of dramatic theory, to benefit actors, playwrights, and spectators. The actors and, through them, the selection of plays had eluded his influence, however; the critic was left with mainly theory, play texts, and public taste to address.

### Lessing Is Visited By Jugglers And Acrobats

A Dramaturg who does not confirm the public in its prejudices, and instead challenges popular taste, invites a decline in attendance and risks becoming, in Zeydel's phrase, "the man of letters who rashly interferes with the business of the theatre." Lessing argued that criticism never discourages a serious playgoer; he was "firmly convinced that criticism does not interfere with enjoyment and that those who have learned to judge a piece most severely are always those that visit the theatre most frequently." Unfortunately, not many Germans visited the Hamburg National Theatre with frequency; subsidies ran out, company tours were insufficiently remunerative, and the permanent repertory company was bankrupt by March, 1769. It is doubtful that Lessing's adverse criticism dissuaded any readers from seeing Voltaire or Corneille, since most of his essays were published long after the plays under discussion had opened. Still, Lessing clearly had preferences that differed from those of both the Hamburg management and the public, and he said so in print.

In his essays Lessing never urged the management to produce a specific play, but it is difficult to agree with J. G. Robertson that "Lessing himself gives us no reason to think that he was particularly dissatisfied with the repertory." Dissatisfaction is strongly evident in his reference to Hamburg's staging of "wretched stuff" by Corneille, and in his unequivocal advice "to leave all existent Christian tragedies [including the one by Cronegk under discussion] unperformed. This advice . . . deprives of nothing more than very mediocre plays." Another Christian tragedy, Voltaire's *Zaïre*, was performed five days after Lessing published his advice against the genre, which may indicate how little his remarks altered policy. Lessing wrote only about the plays, however, not about Hamburg management policies, even when the management began hiring jugglers and acrobats to draw spectators. He had anticipated this and other concessions to low popular taste by noting, in the *Hamburg Dramaturgy* preface, that "the best managers have degraded a free art to the level of a trade."

Would trade have declined even further had the Hamburg management implemented Lessing's preference for Shakespeare over Voltaire? Robertson questions "whether Lessing or anyone else on the continent in his time would have countenanced such an experiment [introducing Shakespeare to the Hamburg stage] before Duci, in a series of adaptations between 1769 and 1792, had pointed out how Shakespeare could be rendered practicable for the eighteenth-century theatre." Yet Lessing had recommended Shakespeare to the German public *prior* to 1769. In Essay #15 he reminded "the public what it seems purposely to have forgotten. We have a translation of Shakespeare." (Lessing himself needed no translation; he knew the English language well.)

## Lessing Invites The Audience
## To Hiss At An Actor

The German public's neglect of Shakespeare was nearly excusable, since only Wieland's translation of twenty-two plays was available. Perhaps they were awaiting the superior Tieck-Schlegel translations. Lessing was far less forgiving when it came to the German public's neglect of its own nation's poets. He angrily noted that the French public

> . . . convinced of the worth of a poet and the influence of the theatre upon morality and manners, does not reckon the one among its useless members, or the other as an object concerning only busy idlers. How far in this respect are we Germans behind the French. To say it right out, compared with them we are true barbarians! Barbarians more barbaric than our oldest ancestors who deemed a minstrel a man of worth.

Not only did the public lack respect for its poets, and fail to see theatre as a moral force, it also showed far too much respect for some German actors, in Lessing's view. He urged spectators to stop applauding the "sleepy actor [who] will rouse himself towards the end of the scene, when he is to make his exit, raise his voice and overload the action, without reflecting whether the sense of his speech requires this extra exertion." Those watching the sleepy actor "should hiss at him!" advised Lessing, adding that "alas, the spectators are partly not connoisseurs, and in part too good-natured."

## Lessing Arrives Two Thousand Years Too Late

These comments may have offended both audience and actors at Hamburg, but the remarks would not have offended ancient Greeks, not if Lessing's account of Greek behavior is accurate. He praised the audience sophistication of ancient Athens, where "the mob has moral feelings so fine and delicate that actors and authors run the risk of being driven from the stage on account of impure morality." "Compared with this [Athenian audience] how indifferent, how cold is our people towards the theatre," complained Lessing. Since eighteenth-century Germans had no genuine Aristotelian tragedy to lure them to Hamburg, and to excite their pity and fear, he argued that most of his contemporaries "go to the theatre from idle curiosity, from fashion, from ennui, to see people, from desire to see and be seen, and only a few, and those few very seldom, go from any other motive." Lessing felt that not only great tragedy, but also intellectually provocative comedy was absent from German culture. He wrote that "whoever desires to be amused beyond mere titillation, whoever wishes to laugh with his reason, he goes to the theatre once and never goes again." An audience member sharing Lessing's attitudes would hardly ever have been seen sitting in the Hamburg National Theatre, which may explain why Madame Hensel complained that Lessing himself could not sit still there.

Lessing's final essay in the *Dramaturgy*, written when he knew that the Hamburg enterprise had failed financially as well as aesthetically, includes one more strong blast at the German public:

> Out on the good-natured idea to procure for the Germans a national theatre, when we Germans are not yet a nation! I do not speak of our political constitution, but only of our social character . . . We are still

the sworn copyists of all that is foreign, especially are we still the obedient admirers of the never sufficiently admired French.

German Francophilia extended to the throne of Frederick the Great, as Lessing learned in 1766 when the monarch chose a Frenchman over Lessing to fill a librarianship at Berlin's Royal Library. "That a German should . . . have the audacity to doubt the excellence of a Frenchman, who could conceive such a thing?" asked Lessing while conceiving such a thing in his *Dramaturgy*. To counteract the excessive German admiration for French drama, the Hamburg Dramaturg repeatedly disputed the aesthetics of Voltaire and Corneille, contending that "no nation had more misapprehended the rules of ancient drama than the French." Ironically, while he condemned fellow countrymen for admiring French drama, Lessing himself admired Diderot along with Shakespeare and the ancients.

Neither he nor his contemporaries could admire German playwriting when so little of it was not inferior to, or clumsily derived from foreign drama. Goethe, Schiller, Lenz, Tieck, Grabbe, Büchner, Kleist, and Hebbel had not yet arrived; to a small extent, Lessing's admiration for Shakespeare, which the great German Romantic and Post-Romantic playwrights subsequently shared, inspired many important German plays.

### Lessing Bequeaths His Troubles To Tieck, Immermann, Brecht, Kipphardt, and Ritz

Small as Lessing's influence at the Hamburg National Theatre may have been, his effect on later criticism and on the dramaturgical profession was far from negligible. Publication of others volumes of dramaturgy followed soon after his. In 1775 von Gemmingen, a playwright associated with the state-supported theatre in Mannheim, wrote *Mannheimer Dramaturgie*. Von Knigge published *Dramaturgische Blätter* in 1789. Albrecht compiled *Neue Hamburgische Dramaturgie* in 1791. The word "dramaturgie" seems to have been in vogue among German critics after Lessing. (Incidentally, this German word should not be confused with the French term for playwright, which is "dramaturge.")

The hiring of Dramaturgs continued despite the objections to Lessing's profession that had been raised by his associates at Hamburg. Dramaturgs brought to theatres not only the prestige of having a "Lessing" on the staff; they also possessed a knowledge of playwriting and dramatic theory with which new plays could be expertly screened prior to production, assuming that the management was interested in new plays. At Hamburg, Löwen had initially vowed to produce new German plays, and being a former theatre critic himself, he knew that a man with Lessing's background could both locate the plays and write them. As the number of subsidized repertory theatres increased in Germany, more productions of untried plays could be risked by managements no longer wholly dependent on popular taste or box-office success for their financial backing.

Dramaturgs after Lessing not only recommended "new" playwrights such as Shakespeare for production, but also saw their advice implemented. Ludwig Tieck's dramaturgical influence brought premieres of Goethe's *Torquato Tasso* and *Faust,* Shakespeare's *Henry IV,* Calderón's *Dame Cobold* (at which the audience hissed), and Kleist's *Broken Jug* to Dresden after 1825. Karl Immermann, Dramaturg at Düsseldorf in 1835, prompted the staging of Shakespeare, Calderón, and other "experiments." Otto Brahm's dramaturgy led to premieres of Ibsen, Strindberg, Zola, and Gerhart Hauptmann in Berlin toward the end of the nineteenth century. In an essay on Brahm, Schlenther suggests that Brahm's visits to the theater in Hamburg while he was still a young bank clerk resulted in a direct line of descent from Lessing's dramaturgy to Brahm's.

Later Dramaturgs exerted more influence than Lessing over play selection, but it should not be thought that Lessing's disputes with actors and with audience and management taste were simply the birth pangs of the dramaturgical profession. The same disputes recurred half a century later, during Ludwig Tieck's tenure as Dramaturg, and echoes of the disputes can still be heard in German theatre today. Edwin Zeydel's account of Tieck's tenure at Dresden practically sums up Lessing's dramaturgical career as well. Tieck was appointed Dramaturg at Dresden in 1824. Then, as Zeydel reports,

> . . . it soon developed that his strong opposition to the prevailing low
> standards of taste would make his position very difficult . . . The
> bureaucrats in the theatre were deaf to his suggestions. The public
> resented the 'despotic' manner in which he foisted his taste upon
> them. The actors . . . grumbled about the unabbreviated performances
> of Shakespeare's plays, and were indignant over his plain-spoken criti-
> cism of their work . . . And the Dresden playwrights could not forgive
> him the severe judgment of their feeble efforts . . . It is clear, then, that
> Tieck was not spared the indignities and intrigues which have always
> been the lot of men with exquisite literary taste who venture to oppose,
> with their own artistic standards, the indolence and commercialism of
> the existing stage, the public's witless love of pleasure, and the venal
> criticism of the day.

Artistic standards as high as Lessing's or Tieck's, along with almost comic arrogance, led one twentieth-century Dramaturg to demand that the theatre management transfer all its decision-making power to him. Bertolt Brecht made this demand in 1925, while he was one of several literary editors and advisors at Berlin's Deutsches Theater. According to Carl Zuckmayer, Brecht asked the management to cede its control so that "he could mold the repertoire entirely according to his own ideas and rename the Reinhardt theatres [such as the Deutsches Theater] 'epic smoking theatres,' for he was of the opinion that people might be more inclined to think if they were allowed to smoke in the theatre. As these demands were rejected, he confined his activity to occasional appearances to collect his salary." Brecht, like Lessing, had a far longer and more active career as playwright than as Dramaturg.

Dramaturgs now reside at permanent theatres throughout Germany, and they have been holding national conferences annually since 1952. Their adversary stances toward audience and management prejudice still occasionally provoke strong reactions. The left-wing political views of a few West German Dramaturgs have resulted in their dismissal. In 1971, Dramaturg Heinar Kipphardt (author of a documentary play about J. Robert Oppenheimer) was dismissed from the Kammerspiele in Munich for trying to publish an objectional program. The program, which pictured the heads of West German businessmen, politicans, and other modern dragons, was to be distributed at performances of *Der Dra-Dra*, a play by East German poet Wolf Biermann that suggests there is something totalitarian about dragons. The play was postponed by Kipphardt's superior (the *Intendant*, or Managing Director), and many Kammerspiele actors resigned to protest Kipphardt's dismissal.

Jorg Wehmeir, former Dramaturg at the Stuttgart Staatstheater, resigned from his post a few seasons ago because he was annoyed by the hundreds of letters he received demanding mere entertainment. In 1974 Peter Ritz, a left-wing Dramaturg, was dismissed by the Burgomaster of Memmingen after staging Nestroy's 1848 parody, *Freedom in Krahwinkel*, a play which ends with a corrupt Burgomaster being expelled by the citizens he governs. Also in 1974, three Dramaturgs at Stuttgart's Kleines Haus threatened to resign after they provoked considerable protest by distributing sex-education manual excerpts at a revival of Wedekind's sex-tragedy, *Spring's Awakening*.

Lessing himself might have been shocked by some of the ideas for which modern Dramaturgs risk dismissal; but in a sense, these modern controversies uphold the first Dramaturg's resolve not to confirm audience or management in their prejudice. Not every Dramaturg is an iconoclast. Lessing revered Aristotle, after all, and one Düsseldorf Dramaturg resigned a few seasons ago because he was not radical enough to please his audience; presumably the audience wanted more controversy. Lessing never had that problem.

Despite the opposition that Lessing and other Dramaturgs encountered, or perhaps because of it, these critics have played a far more active role in their country's intellectual life, and in the theatre's life, than most American theatre critics. The absence of Dramaturgs or their equivalent from American theatres may be one measure of our culture's deficiency. Not only are Literary Managers new to the American theatre scene; so, by German standards, are residential theatre companies. While German residential companies have been subsidized since Lessing's lifetime, America lost its closest equivalent to Europe's permanent theatres when touring companies drove stock companies out of business a century ago. Only since 1950 have residential companies returned as an important force in American theatre.

Germany's dramaturgical profession, in the two centuries since it began, has proven itself integral to the development of repertory theatres—theatres committed, as the Hamburg National Theatre purportedly was, to staging new plays and building a permanent acting company. For much of the past century, American theatre has been dominated by commercial enterprises formed to produce a single hit or star vehicle instead of a full season's repertory. While these American enterprises may have needed a market researcher on their staff, they had little use for a Lessing or his opposition to popular prejudice and other complacencies that inhibit the development of repertory theatre art. Due to the overriding commercialism of our theatre, American theatre criticism has been an art of one-night stands; the critic sees a play the night it opens, writes a consumer's report on it, and forgets it. We have few critics with memories, critics who stay with a play from the first rehearsal to the last performance, or stay with a repertory company all season, as Dramaturgs do. For the dramaturgical profession to achieve recognition in America, it must persuade our theatres that critics, besides selling plays through reviews, can also collaborate on productions: By advising the playwright or director during rehearsals; by recommending to producers plays that challenge both actors and audience; by offering theatre companies standards of achievement based on past theatre history and criticism; by helping companies to surpass earlier achievements, and to create the Utopian theatre of which Lessing wrote in his *Dramaturgy*: a theatre where even the lighting technician (or "candle-snuffer," in Lessing's words) is a Garrick.

1975

**Acknowledgements**
Sources quoted in my essay include Helen Zimmern's translation of the *Hamburg Dramaturgy* (Dover, 1962), J. G. Robertson's invaluable book, *Lessing's Dramatic Theory* (Cambridge, 1939), and Edwin Zeydel's *Ludwig Tieck, The German Romanticist* (Princeton, 1935).

# The Role of the Dramaturg
# in European Theater

Martin Esslin

The recent trend among American theaters towards the appointment of literary managers or "Dramaturgs" has, I believe, awakened interest in this function, which, in most countries of Europe with established companies, is regarded as being as essential to the smooth running of their operation as the work of directors and designers. The function of Dramaturg is organically linked to the existence of theaters with long-term artistic policies, permanent companies, and a planned repertoire. The absence of the Dramaturg, until relatively recent times, in the theater of the English-speaking world, was intimately connected with a commercial system which precluded the development of a long-term repertoire policy, as each production was planned as a separate commercial venture unconnected to any previous ones except, perhaps, by the personality of the producer.

In the original Greek meaning of the term, a Dramaturg is simply a playwright. He was, originally, in the theatrical companies of the eighteenth and early nineteenth century, the resident playwright who wrote his own plays for the actors in the troupe, or found foreign plays which he translated, say, from the French or Italian, or produced cut versions of classical plays that required a cast too large for the restricted number of actors available to his particular troupe.

From this function there developed the contemporary job of the Dramaturg, most clearly defined today in the German theater. The German pattern of theatre is dominated by the existence of highly subsidized permanent companies in all cities of above, roughly, fifty thousand inhabitants. There are some 120 such theaters. These theatres, National, State, or Municipal, all have a system of genuine repertoire. In other words, a visitor staying in one of the cities with such a theater for a few days will be able to see two or three different plays within the same week. Moreover, these theaters all have a subscription system which guarantees their "Abonnenten" (subscribers) six to eight performances each season.

It is clear that the planning of the performance schedules of such theaters (most of which also have a smaller house which they run as a studio or workshop theater for more experimental work) is a very complicated task: not only do the plays have to be selected, but they have to be selected to suit the character of the particular company, providing a fair share of good parts for all the principal actors. Also, the production and rehearsal schedule will have to be carefully dovetailed so that the subscribers will get their monthly or bi-weekly offering with the right variety and in the right sequence. This is the main task of the *Dramaturgie* (as the Dramaturg's department is called in the German theater). Such a department will have a *Chefdramaturg* (chief Dramaturg) assisted by a number of Dramaturgen, secretaries, and filing clerks.

Here scripts offered by the numerous *Theaterverlage* (theater publishers' agents who distribute scripts in mimeographed or printed form, arrange for translations, and fulfill a number of functions beyond those performed by English or American theatrical and literary agents) are read, reported on, and registered. Here the repertoire is carefully planned to provide a balanced diet for the requirements of the public of the city served by the theater in question.

Since the theater in a German city is regarded as one of the principal cultural amenities, on a par with schools, universities, museums, and public libraries, its function is clearly defined: above all it has to keep the established classics of the culture constantly before the public. Hence, a considerable part of the Dramaturg's function is to see that the major works should be accessible over a period of years, so that no one could grow up in that city without having had an opportunity of completing his education by seeing the main works of Shakespeare, the German classics, Ibsen, Chekhov, Molière, Shaw, supplemented by some classical Greek or Spanish plays. A theater, for example, which would have failed to provide a production of *Hamlet* or

Goethe's *Faust* over a period of, say, ten years, would be regarded as having grossly neglected its duty, and its artistic director would be in dire trouble. The Dramaturg thus has to keep a watchful eye on the past productions so that he can come forward with new presentations of the standard plays at the right moment. Equally important, however, for the Dramaturg in the German theater is the second aspect of his function: to keep an educated and interested public in his city abreast of the new developments in drama. Here too he is judged by his ability to pick up new trends and not to miss major new plays and playwrights, both foreign and domestic. A theater which was the first to present a new author who subsequently rose to fame gains immensely in prestige, hence the Dramaturg will anxiously watch out for opportunities to present world or German premieres. Here again, a theater that cannot boast of at least one important *Urauffuehrung* (world premiere) or at least one *Deutsche Erstauffuehrung* (first production of a foreign play in Germany) per year will lose a good deal of prestige.

Clearly the Dramaturg, charged with all these responsibilities, has to be constantly on the lookout for developments in world drama. But, as he chooses plays for a given group of actors, he is also something like the casting director of the theater and part of his function consists in traveling to other theaters looking for young actors who might be recruited into the ensemble. He has to be aware of the capabilities of the existing acting company, but he must also keep an eye on possible weak points or gaps and try to fill these with new blood. The working out of the very complex casting rosters in companies which may be playing in two different houses at the same time, while often keeping a road company touring in neighboring, smaller cities, demands great ingenuity in adjusting the repertoire, planning the rehearsals for understudies, etc.

But this by no means exhausts the range of duties of the *Dramaturgie*. For most major productions the *Dramaturgie* provides a *Produktionsdramaturg*—a Dramaturg specially assigned to that particular production who goes to the rehearsals and provides background material about the author, the subject matter of the play, and its social or political implications. He is the one whom the director consults about the meaning of difficult or unusual words, whom he asks to make cuts when the play proves too long or unwieldy, or whom he charges with improving the translations of foreign plays.

Being the literary expert in residence in the theater, the Dramaturg has acquired another function: he has become the editor of the specially prepared programme booklet which every German theatre supplies for the audience of its plays. This booklet provides infinitely more than those supplied to English or American theatre audiences. It must contain valuable explanatory and background material, essays on the author and the subject matter of the play, material about previous productions, and all this must be interestingly and strikingly illustrated. The Dramaturg is the compiler, editor, and often writer of this booklet; he must design it, find the photographs or drawings to be reproduced, and do the lay-out of the finished pages.

Being the expert on the repertoire, the Dramaturg has also, quite organically, developed into the public relations man for the theater; he tries to keep critics and newspapers supplied with advance material on each production so that both the general public and the critics will approach it in less than total ignorance.

It should be clear from the above that in an established and highly institutionalized system like the German theater the Dramaturg (or rather the quite heavily staffed departments over which the chief Dramaturgs of the major theatres preside) has very important functions indeed. The German universities, insofar as they have drama departments, are mainly concerned with turning out scholars with the qualifications for this function: men and women who know several languages, possess a vast knowledge of the classical repertoire, can write and translate, and have a strongly developed critical sense which will enable them to discover writing talent.

In most German theaters the chief Dramaturg holds a position of considerable power and often dominates even the top man, the artistic director. Of course, much depends on the personalities involved. Often very sharp conflicts develop between them. The choice of the repertoire and of the company, after

all, determines the character, or artistic personality, of a theater. A successful theater, in the German context (where the
prestige of a city is closely linked with that of its theatre), must
develop a clear-cut personality, a style of its own.

To combine such a house-style with the equally essential task
of providing a well-balanced anthology of past and present
dramatic material is by no means easy. Not many of the
theaters in contemporary Germany have completely succeeded
in this task. The Schillertheater in Berlin is widely respected for
its ability to attract Samuel Beckett to produce his own plays;
the Munich Kammerspiele is widely regarded as the theatre
which is likeliest to produce the best of Germany's younger
playwrights; for a long time the Duesseldorf Schauspielhaus
under Karl Heinz Stroux was famous for its ability to attract
world premieres of writers like Ionesco. However, the
competition is very intense and the fate of artistic directors
(*Intendanten*) is a precarious one. Each fall heads are heard
rolling into the baskets of the artistic guillotines, and there is a
regular changing of the guard in the top positions. The same,
one or two rungs lower down the ladder, is true of the
Dramaturgen. It is a challenging profession, but a very cruel
one too.

The theater of the English-speaking world, if its development
towards the German patterns is to continue, will have to absorb
many of the lessons and methods of the German theater.
Undoubtedly, a function like that of the Dramaturg will become
essential. It will be necessary to develop methods of training
such functionaries. At the moment, there is no recognized
training ground for them. How many graduates of drama
departments of American universities, for example, would be
able to read, let alone translate, plays from the French,
German, or Italian?

On the other hand, much also is to be learned from the
shortcomings of the system as it is operated in Germany. Above
all huge subsidies have led to an institutionalization of the theater which has turned many of these supposedly artistic estab-
lishments into soulless factories and dusty bureaucracies. The
plays coming in must be filed, but the mentality of the filing
clerk must not become the dominant intellectual climate of the

theater. Professionalism and deep knowledge, even scholarship, are needed, but always linked with a readiness to improvise and to avoid pedantry.

Kenneth Tynan, who functioned as literary manager of the British National Theatre under Laurence Olivier for more than ten years, set an example of openness of mind and lack of pedantry which should become a valuable precedent for the future in the English-speaking world.

1978

# Dramaturgy in Stuttgart:
# An Interview with Hermann Beil

Reinhardt Stumm

Hermann Beil is Chief Dramaturg at the Stuttgart State Theater. In 1977 his collaboration with director Claus Peymann on a new version of *Faust* won both men extensive praise in *Theater heute*.

Beil had just read Jhering [the German critic] again and therefore he rejects my first question. No, the interest in dramaturgy is not all that new. As early as the late twenties Jhering had been vehemently calling for it. And at the Berliner Ensemble dramaturgical work was taken for granted from the beginning. We both agree, however, that dramaturgy has had varying significance over the last decades. As long as the theater is only a showcase for whatever plays come to market, then dramaturgy can barely play any role. Yet ten years ago, or thereabouts, it again came into prominence. Why?

Speculations: With the absence of new plays, interest was again directed toward the classics, which of course could no longer be played as the texts were written. So the dramaturg acts as a quasi-author, who develops ideas and reworks plays to make them approachable again, or even puts plays together himself. In all of this Beil sees the dramaturg as one force working in conjunction with several others. And he sees the dramaturg doing much more practical work than before. Well, his literary-theoretical orientation is still used, but only in combination with practical activity.

The dramaturg does everything conceivable. Beil recently has been rehearsing with the actors—of course not as director, he does not have such ambitions, but from his more precise knowledge of the material he becomes one of the forces in the collective working out of proposed staging ideas.

Earlier it was different. Then there was the occasional request: Write me something to add here or there. So Beil would sit down at his desk and stage spiritual wrestling matches with the material, write analyses, develop concepts. Nothing would be more boring for him now, he contends. Everyone (director, scene designer, dramaturg) has to sit down together at one table and plow through the problem together—and therefore the result is clearly a collective achievement.

The specializations begin to break down, the disciplines get mixed up. Anyone can approach *St. Joan of the Stockyards* the way Beil did, when he reread it recently and came running into the theater: You can play that today, if you just scratch away the traditional German method of costuming it—then it's suddenly something very concrete—and then a very naked, very bloody play will emerge.

Nothing is accomplished according to a preconceived program. Plays, inclinations, ideas are all developed in reaction to the environment and one's inner world. The dramaturg sees himself—in Stuttgart—among a group of people all of whom are probing their experiences. They must be encouraged, supported, and sometimes pushed. One is preoccupied with the theme of very strong love problems, another wants to do *The Just* as a play with a theme about the confusion of concepts. Then that has to be set into motion on stage. Simultaneously the theater has to react to the city, its audience, and events in the outside world. Dramaturgy is a sort of switchyard for all of that.

Beil has been in Stuttgart for three years. He came from Basel, where for six years he had been the stable point in a hectic field of theater activity. How does he look at these years in Stuttgart? Beil:

"I came here because I thought: Here is a renovated house with a certain tradition—Palitzsch had a method, things used to be so, there was a responsive audience, and there was an idea: to rejuvenate a stagnant state theater. So the question became, how far can you take it and where will it lead? Here we come to one of the main functions of a dramaturg: if he discovers that a method is becoming a style—and hence a lifeless and deadly one—then he has to ask: What have we done? And what do we have to do so that we don't fall into a rut?"

"It is very straightforward. In everything that we do there is the question: What is important here and why are we doing this? I think that the theater can always justify itself on purely rational grounds, even when projects are being planned that suddenly take on a very wild form—and even on a personal level, just for myself, there always has to be a very rational, justifiable center."

"Everyone expects the dramaturg to furnish the concept of the season and some kind of theme. If he doesn't, the theater is reproached for having a 'pluralistic' repertory, a bits-and-pieces season. And in this context the 'face' of the whole season depends essentially on how the individual production is portrayed. Even the most diverse pieces acquire something in common when they share one director. In the old days I always used to formulate unifying season concepts—but I have become terrified of that, because nowadays I find the current project onstage much more compelling than a search for proof that we are following a unifying concept. I think that the intensive exploration of the current production far more clearly conveys a method of playing, a possibility to see, hear, and comprehend, than the imposition of a unifying concept. Otherwise, the play may often be legitimized only be means of the unifying concept. I've noticed by now that I can't even formulate any general line or connecting 'idea,' certainly not in nice-sounding phrases that could be reprinted neatly in *Theater heute*."

The dramaturg used to sit in a library and do research. The results of his work would then be made available to the director, who could proceed with them as he wished. That's not how it works anymore. The dramaturg has to learn along with everyone else. He has to hear what the director, designers, and actors are thinking, he has to move around within their imaginations. These long-winded early sessions can be wild and exciting. The dramaturg, of course, sets up the preliminary concept: Faust, the intellectual, breaking out of the Middle Ages into the modern era and journeying through time. Or he formulates an emotional, undefined relationship to the play: a girl like Kaethchen, a person who loves boundlessly. Then it gets thrown around and finally you get a tangible approach and a series of situations, what they have to express and how they have to be translated. But nothing is yet accomplished—for it still has to go into rehearsal and there the draft will undergo violent and decisive changes. There is the acid test: how can the actors play these ideas? That's why the dramaturg has to attend rehearsals, to find the errors and the strengths of the concept.

How can any sort of season be developed at all given these principles?

Hermann Beil makes a vague gesture—those kinds of questions are incredibly difficult to answer, because they are asked from positions that his theater abandoned long ago:

"It is discussed continuously, for months. Everyone expresses his wishes and ideas. One person wants to construct a beautiful dream, so for the next season we choose *Iphigenia,* the picture of a completely harmonic and utopian world, an antithesis to our own consciousness full of fear and injustice. A desire arises and becomes attached to a play. Peymann, for example, expresses an inclination, after all this *Faust*-stuff, to do a very forceful, linguistically harsh, concentrated work. Someone else finds that it's time to put it on the line again with some hard social material, and to do away with all this frivolous entertainment. That's how the balls get thrown in and tossed around. The repertory ends up a collection of tendencies and wishes, curiosity about new plays and excitement about the writers. We tie the authors in as directly as possible."

And then comes a central theme, the kind one hears so rarely from Beil, since he normally draws such careful distinctions and mistrusts any glib generalizations.

"I believe that a repertory requires the most massive contrasts and contrary themes. However, if one always asks, 'Is this something to interest me?,' then they have to come together rationally."

Beil would never advocate Claudel, for example, simply for reasons of presenting these extremes. He also finds it unnecessary to use a theater as a vehicle for the conveyance of the latest plays. Nor can the theater be a museum for the preservation of works. It must always be inventing anew, for there really isn't anything to preserve. He always comes back to the point that the work can only be accomplished collectively.

Communication with the public is still left largely to the dramaturg—even if Peymann [the director of *Faust*] repeatedly answers questions for school groups, for example. Conversations in the foyer after performances, often until well past midnight. Invitations to schools. Receiving groups at times other than performance. Occasionally evening calls at the theater itself. Beil persistently maintains that dramaturgy has to answer for its theater and defend it on even the most trivial points. After all, a theater cannot be represented through its program notes alone.

One also has to slow down. But how can that be done without abandoning earlier positions? After all, it is supposed to become more, not less. Beil has a "fixed idea," as he puts it. It should now be time to concentrate very forcefully, in other words to follow up much more precisely, lingeringly, and insistently on the plays, themes, and their contents. How can that be accomplished while maintaining the current number of productions? Reducing the number of productions isn't what we're after. Perhaps, however, a better division of labor and use of resources. That might mean a "larger ensemble" so that the actors too could take a break.

There's something else that irritates Master Dramaturg Beil. The theater is running too well. And because of it he is afraid; there is something like an expectation to fulfill. Therefore he often wants to do a really brash work, a stumbling block, something that won't be accepted without dismay and consternation. Was this one reason for coming up with the plans for *Bambule*?

Beil thinks it over, carefully as ever: "Yes, perhaps it was to generate friction. The proposal by no means came from Peymann alone. It came from Vera Sturm over a year ago. It was discussed with Niels-Peter Rudolph and Valentin Jeker was finally supposed to do it—and he wanted to. Then there was its social theme and of course—you can't deny it—the name entered in too. Frictions and tensions had to arise, for contradictions would be torn wide open—especially the fact that a state theater was staging it would elicit a strong reaction."

"But there was another issue: the piece was written by a woman. Moreover, since she wrote it, her work has developed in a completely different direction, which no one could have anticipated. This became a theme to think about. How did it happen? Were the deeds depicted in the play the cause of it? Was it her declared powerlessness in the face of these deeds? The search for motives was investigation that went way beyond the actual content of the play and yet would be combined with it. That is a point of view which we have distinctly maintained throughout our work on a whole series of political presentations: Peter Schneider's *File Number*, the *Spanish Evening*, or *Actors in Paragraph Forest*, when our company dealt with 88a [a section of the Federal German Criminal Code dealing with acts of sabotage and treason against the State]. This attempt to depict current events by writing the scenes ourselves and infusing the theatrical material with very precise information usually originated among the actors and gained strong support from the staff. Among these works, *Bambule* was by no means such a departure."

"And when I now reread the letters that we received then—even some barely shrouded threats of murder—when I think about this hysteria we caused, then I ask whether we aren't obliged to do it. That has been a principle behind our work to date, and I hope that we will stick to it in the future, although perhaps with different results. Sometimes we succeed in reacting to events right away. And there the dramaturg plays an important part: observing the run of the play—here in Stuttgart—and examining our relations to the audience. Do we have to hit them hard again or counteract certain tendencies? Therefore we never announce a completely scheduled season in advance. I find it so boring when a season plows ahead like a tank, indifferent to the terrain it's covering or to the changing environment. We can plan a couple of plays firmly, but determine the rest anew over the course of the season. Of course, we already have a whole collection of plans—what we will do with them and when, that we try to find out once things have begun. And that's how it should be."

The last point for our interview in Beil's mountainside apartment—which lies well above the notorious Stuttgart smog, from which Beil reemerges on his daily streetcar ride home after those crazy days in his theater—is the theater's programs. Stuttgart is the only theater besides the Schaubühne which assembles such exhaustive program notes. How did that get started? Beil, who had prepared a stockpile of programs first in Frankfurt, then in Basel, found that kind of work boring. Routine work that doesn't really do anyone any good. His first program, for Gerlind Reinshagen's *Heaven & Earth*, took over one hundred pages in a pure literary treatment of the death motif. If the material is useful for work on the play and for its staging, why shouldn't that be given to the audience too? Besides, Beil takes the Stuttgart audience for natural collectors. Wouldn't they like in time to assemble a theater library? They seem to, for Beil's programs have long since become collector's items. Occasionally, such as for *Faust*, they take on monstrous forms, "but it's Goethe's fault for writing so much! And it's become our policy for classics to supply the entire text with all the cuts, so that the curious spectator can review for himself the changes that we made."

New plans for program books are still being formed; the possibilities are far from exhausted. Beil is thinking of including a log of the production or a history of the play's staging from the première to the present. And with immeasurable pride Beil points out that exactly this form allowed Herbert Gamper to write an analysis of *Tales from the Vienna Woods* which still has not been surpassed in precision. The challenge also excites him: compiling a book that demands much more than the usual program, which he "used to throw together in one afternoon."

We had already covered the subject in detail for two hours, wandering back and forth over the different aspects. The tape recorder was already turned off; there was a moment's silence. Then Beil picked up the thread again: "But when I think it over once more, I really don't know anything about dramaturgy, and I have to face that every time I have to explain something about it. I just work in the theater. I go in around nine in the morning and come home around nine or ten at night, and in between we talk a lot and chatter and make a few phone calls . . . The best part for me is the work with actors—when you can see ideas being transposed and becoming visible."

It's that simple.

1977

# Bertolt Brecht as Dramaturg

Russell E. Brown

Bertolt Brecht (1898-1956) is recognized, thirty years after his death, as perhaps the greatest playwright and certainly as the most important theoretician of drama in this century. Without his doctrine of Epic Theatre, theatre in both East and West would be hard to imagine today. After dominating the socialist and capitalist stage in the years following his death, Brecht has now also come to be recognized as a major lyrical poet. Other facets of this enormously creative artist's career include his work as a filmmaker in Weimar Germany (*Die Dreigroschen Oper* and *Kuhle Wampe*) and as a dramaturg.

Like Lessing in the eighteenth century, who revived German theatre as a dramaturg in Hamburg and as a brilliant critic-theoretician, Brecht was not content to write great plays but followed them into the theatre, working as a producer, director, and dramaturg. But whereas Lessing's later life was marred by personal and professional disaster, so that he died embittered and isolated in the ducal libraries of Wolfenbüttel, the Marxist Brecht returned from American exile to preside successfully over a major theatre, the Theater am Schiffbauerdamm in East Berlin, in that part of Germany which was struggling to create socialism.

Already an *enfant terrible* of Weimar Germany, a savage critic of bourgeois society still without a positive ideology, Brecht became the dramaturg at age twenty-five of the Munich Kammerspiele. He dodged the assigned preparation of a Shakespeare play by adapting Shakespeare's contemporary, Christopher Marlowe, whose *Edward the Second* was translated and transformed in collaboration with Lion Feuchtwanger. Brecht directed the play as well as acted as dramaturg. Jan Knopf calls the project Brecht's first "kollektive Produktion" (p. 41). A Berlin production saw Brecht withdraw as co-director, but its

success did aid Brecht's move to Berlin. There, for a single season, he became co-dramaturg (with Carl Zuckmayer) of the
prestigious Deutsches Theater under Max Reinhardt. After
making impossible demands (complete control of programming, changing the theatre's name to Episches-Rauch-Theater),
Brecht vanished from this theatre, appearing only to pick up his
paychecks.

After his conversion to Marxism in 1926, he worked as a dramaturg with Erwin Piscator, the other great leftist innovator of
modern German theatre. In this instance Brecht was part of a
team, for Piscator had organized a dramaturgical collective
(Willett, *Context*, p. 89) of some twelve writers (including Felix
Gasbarra and Leo Lania) in Berlin's Theater am Nollendorf-
platz. Brecht worked on productions of Alexey Tolstoy's
*Rasputin* and Hasek's *Svejk* (*The Good Soldier Schweik*). The great
success of *The Threepenny Opera,* which premiered August 31,
1928, at the Theater am Schiffbauerdamm, enabled Brecht to
move from his secondary dramaturgical role with Piscator to a
more dominant position in the latter theatre. His experiments
in opera and didactic drama and work with Kurt Weill, Hanns
Eisler, and Paul Dessau then followed.

In the exile years (in Scandinavia and California), Brecht was
cut off from the German-speaking theatre (although a few of his
plays were put on in Zurich) but nonetheless created his greatest plays both as a poet and as an enemy of fascism. His few
essays into foreign theatres were generally disastrous, as in the
New York Theatre Union production of *Die Mutter* (*The Mother*)
with which he interfered in 1935.

After his disappointing Hollywood years (he wrote a few
scripts, for example *Hangmen Also Die*), Brecht was called before
the Committee on Un-American Activities of the U.S. Congress,
which was investigating communism in the entertainment
world. One congressman on the committee, which was satisfied
by Brecht's clever testimony on October 30, 1947, was Richard
M. Nixon.

Leaving the U.S. the next day, Brecht lived for a year in
Switzerland before returning to Germany. With an Austrian
passport (obtained through his wife Helene Weigel and Gott-
fried von Einem) he chose the GDR over West Germany, where

on January 11, 1949, he directed *Mutter Courage* with his wife in the title role at the Deutsches Theater. It was a "Modell-Insze-nierung" with detailed plans, analysis, discussions, and many photographs which were published in book form.

Brecht now was allowed to form his own theatre troupe, the Berliner Ensemble. This company performed first as guests in the Deutsches Theater, then in 1954 took up residence in Brecht's old rebuilt theatre of the twenties, the Theater am Schiffbauerdamm. The troupe was generously supported by the state: Brecht had sixty actors and two hundred fifty staff members in all; production and rehearsal time were virtually unlimited. Thus, like Shakespeare and Molière in their time, Brecht had his own private theatre to mount productions of his own work and that of others, to put into practice his theory of Epic Theatre, and to train a whole generation of theatre people, actors, stage designers, composers, and dramaturgs. In addition to veteran actors of the pre-Hitler and exile period, many amateurs were used. Brecht assigned the position of managing director ("Intendantin") to his wife; he himself was nominally only a "Mitglied des Künstlerischen Beirats" (a member of the artistic committee).

As in the Piscator days there were many young dramaturgs, whom Brecht trained, including Heinar Kipphardt (now a successful dramatist) and Käthe Rülicke-Weiler. When the dramaturgy stage of selection, adaptation, and study of the play was completed in team-style, Brecht often directed the play to be performed. The collective studied theoreticians like Stanislavski, Piscator, and Aristotle as well as making field visits to social groups like those to be portrayed (farmers or industrial workers). Plays were also brought out of the theatre into the factories, and opinions of the working class were solicited and integrated into the productions.

The play texts, sacred to traditional theatre, were radically altered and adapted by the dramaturg and others, since the goal of production was the practical change of society rather than the sterile celebration of a remote classic.

The primary principle which he taught his collaborators was that of the *Fabel* or story. The chain of events must be clearly and strongly estab-

lished not just in the production, but beforehand in the actual play.
Where it was not clear it was up to the "Dramaturg" to alter the text, in
order to cut unnecessary entanglements and come to the point.
(Willett, *Theatre,* p. 152)

As in the *Mutter Courage* production and already in a Swiss
production of *Antigone,* model books were created with hundreds of photographs and analysis of stage design and characters. The great productions of this troupe included *Mutter
Courage* and *Der kaukasische Kreidekreis,* both of which were performed at international theatre festivals in Paris and elsewhere
abroad. Shakespeare's *Coriolanus* was prepared for four years by
the troupe.

In addition to individual "Modellbücher," the Berliner
Ensemble published detailed records of six major productions,
*Theaterarbeit,* which discuss and illustrate the plays in detail
(over five hundred photographs, along with essays on directing,
dramaturgy, settings, costumes, music). Documentary films
were made of performances of Brecht's *Die Mutter* and
Strittmatter's *Katzgraben* (Brecht's directorial attempt to present
problems from the agricultural sector of the "Arbeiter-und-
Bauern-Staat"). Many hours of tape-recorded rehearsals also
exist.

Although enormous amounts of theatre production records
exist—along with specific work-oriented essays by Brecht such as
his "Anmerkungen zur Oper 'Aufstieg und Fall der Stadt
Mahagonny'" (1930)—Brecht never produced an exhaustive
description of his theory of Epic Theater. He came closest perhaps in his "Kleines Organon für das Theater" at the beginning
of his last GDR phase in 1948. A major attempt to present his
dramaturgy in a dramatized form, *Der Messingkauf* (1939-1951),
in which philosopher, author, actor, actress, stagehand, and
dramaturg discuss theatre on four successive nights, remained a
fragment. Brecht himself appears as the "Stückeschreiber," but
his ideas are also incorporated in speeches by the philosopher
and the dramaturg. The latter acts as an intermediary between
philosopher and actor; his main essay-speech is "Über Rollenbe-
setzungen" ("On selecting actors"). The dramaturg wants to
avoid actors whose face and body naturally mirror the role they
play; by choosing "inappropriate" types, an actor's evolution

into the character can be shown (Knopf, p. 451). Elsewhere Brecht once said that men playing female roles, as in productions by soldiers at the front, often made an eminently feminine impression.

But no single text of Brecht has emerged as a definitive statement of his Epic Theory. Its evolutionary nature is evidenced by the fact that at the end of his life Brecht envisaged a new kind of theatre, which he called "dialectical theatre" (Hill, p. 209). The dynamic evolution of Brecht's theory, its fragmentary, sometimes ambivalent, work-oriented exposition, has created a plethora of conflicting interpretations and systematizations reminiscent of scholarly attempts through the ages to complete Aristotle's fragmentary analysis of drama in the *Poetics*. But here the problem is an embarrassment of riches. Because of the complexity of Brecht's dramaturgy and the wide dissemination of his concepts of Epic Theatre and "alienation," I will not characterize them; my purpose is to describe Brecht's work as, and concept of, a dramaturg. Unfortunately, Brecht wrote mainly about the actor and the spectator, with little analysis of the managerial functions of producer, director, or dramaturg, and their interrelations.

Nevertheless, some generalizations can be made. Whereas the dramaturg traditionally selects the plays for a theatre's production, sometimes adapting and editing them, and sometimes advising the director or even the actors about historical or aesthetic considerations, Brecht did all of these things at once. He both magnified the role of the dramaturg and submerged it in the collective of the theatrical company. The dramaturg, as he emerged in Brecht's climactic, Berliner-Ensemble phase, was freed from the secondary role of literary advisor and academic liaison to assume an unheard-of degree of involvement in the real-life, day-to-day staging of a play. He performed the functions of an author, director, even producer. Simultaneously, however, in true socialist style, he was reduced to part of a collective, to one of a team as in the ideal socialist workplaces of factory and farm. Characteristic of Brecht's disruption of traditional functions in play production was the ascendency of Caspar Neher, his old set designer, in the Berliner Ensemble. Neher, for example, concerned himself with details of actors' movements on the stage, using dozens of sketches to illustrate them (Willett, *Theatre,* pp. 156-157). As Manfred Wekwerth, a major figure in the Berliner Ensemble, wrote:

> Brecht eliminated the succession of tasks that had developed through occupational specialization in bourgeois theatre. First, through his own person. He was a playwright, dramaturg, and director. Sometimes also a composer and stage designer. The stage designers, composers, and the dramaturgs worked together from the outset on the scenic realization of the story. (p. 148; my translation)

In summary, Brecht's experience as a dramaturg has three phases. At first, in 1923, he played a more-or-less conventional role in Munich, then he joined Piscator's collective dramaturgical structure in Berlin in 1927, and finally he himself sponsored a dramaturgy training group in East Germany from 1949 to the end of his life. There Brecht was, on the one hand, democratic, adaptable, and part of a team, but on the other hand also a dominant, charismatic, famous, and politically favored leader who shaped productions according to his own inclinations and theory, whatever particular role he assigned himself on each occasion. He added the role of the wise theatre veteran, his Chinese-philosopher *persona,* to the flamboyant and spoiled child-genius of the past.

1986

### Works Consulted or Quoted

Gray, Ronald. *Brecht the Dramatist.* Cambridge: Cambridge University Press, 1976.

Grimm, Reinhold. *Bertolt Brecht.* 3rd revised edition. Stuttgart: Metzler, 1971.

Hecht, Werner, Hans-Joachim Bunge, and Käthe Rülicke-Weiler. *Bertolt Brecht. Sein Leben und Werk.* Berlin (East): Volk und Wissen, 1969.

Hill, Claude. *Bertolt Brecht.* Munich: Francke, 1978.

Knopf, Jan. *Brecht-Handbuch: Theater. Eine Ästhetik der Widersprüche*. Stuttgart: Metzler, 1980.

Rülicke-Weiler, Käthe. *Die Dramaturgie Brechts. Theater als Mitte der Veränderung*. Berlin (East): Henschelverlag, 1968.

Wekwerth, Manfred. *Brecht? Berichte, Erfahrungen, Polemik*. Munich: Hanser, 1976.

Willett, John. *The Theatre of Bertolt Brecht. A Study from Eight Aspects*. 3rd revised edition. New York: New Directions, 1968.

Willett, John. *Brecht in Context. Comparative Approaches*. London: Methuen, 1983.

# III

# DRAMATURGY IN
# AMERICA

"A 'pure' critic must be disinterested, impartial, frank, and unfettered; an 'in-house' critic, or dramaturg, must be interested, partial, discreet, and loyally bound to his production."

—Richard Gilman

# American Dramaturgy:
# A Critical Re-Appraisal

Peter Hay

"The question is," said Alice, "whether you can make words mean so many different things."—"The question is," said Humpty Dumpty, "which is to be master—that's all."

Lewis Carroll, *Alice in Wonderland*

## I

Ever since Stanislavski it has been accepted wisdom that an actor needs motivation. But if an actor requires a reason for crossing the stage, audiences want to know even more why they should come into the theatre and watch that actor cross the stage. Surprisingly little thought is expended within or outside our theatre on the chain of interrelated questions that need to be answered before the whole dramatic experience makes sense. Dramaturgy, I believe, is a process of making sense both for the production and the audience. A good dramaturg helps to articulate that sense.

Dramaturgy is a term most frequently employed to describe the structure of drama. As such it tends to be regarded as a mortician's tool, because most structural analysis is done on dead plays in the study or in classrooms. The theatre employs its share of anti-intellectuals who stamp everything they are too lazy to understand as academic. On the other side there are just as many theatre people who get overwhelmed by academic theories and scholarship, because research is a more tangible form of activity—and more easily understood by actors—than thinking. People on both sides often forget that the purpose of dissecting a corpse is to learn what to do with the live body.

There seems to be a problem of finding an adequate definition in the English-language theatre for dramaturgy and the role of the dramaturg. When I was the first "dramaturge" at a

major regional theatre in Canada in the late sixties, I spent a
good deal of my time explaining what the term meant. Ten
years later while working at the O'Neill Playwrights' Conference I was continually ambushed by actors and visitors who
seemed alternately exhilarated and troubled at finding out just
what a dramaturg does. In the brief Bibliography of Dramaturgy
recently published by the American Theatre Association,[1] Günter Skopnik is cited for an article in *World Theatre* (1960) with
the title, "An Unusual Person: Der Dramaturg"; twenty years
later, there is my little piece called "What Is a Dramaturg?", and
a year later Lloyd Richards asks the same question in another
program note at Yale.[2] Also in 1981, James Leverett wrote a
summary of the first TCG conference on "Dramaturgs and Literary Managers: A Major Conference to Define the Role." It
had small attendance compared to the nearly one hundred and
fifty who came to the second TCG conference this summer,
many of whom were artistic directors. The *New York Times* head-
lined the event (23 June 1983) "Stage Conference Asks What Is
a Dramaturge?" After many years of readily supplying etymological explanations from the Greek, I have concluded that this
apparent inability to understand a relatively simple word that
has been in the English language at least since 1859[3] is not due
to an unusual obtuseness in theatre people, who after all can
master the intricacies of a computerized lighting board and
have no difficulty using other Greek words like "telephone."
Nor does the whole answer lie with insecure (artistic) directors
protecting their turf, as Tom Walsh, dramaturg at the Syracuse
Stage, is reported arguing at the TCG conference: "I've sensed
general resistance throughout the world of directors to working
with us. There's the idea that we're going to be meddlesome
and superfluous, and that somehow things could roll on more
strongly without us."[4]

Some believe that the problem is not with directors but stems
from trying to graft some foreign concept onto the English-language stage, which it does not need since it has evolved from a
different historical tradition than the resident theatres of Central Europe. But the presupposition that the American theatre
in its various transformations is doing well enough without
dramaturgs, has not been, in my opinion, critically examined. If

it were true, why has there been such a proliferation of dramaturgs and other literary types in the past few years, especially if many of the people who hire them do not adequately understand their function?

Such questions lead to the core of some of the practical and structural problems of non-profit theatre. André Gregory's fear back in 1965 "that the regional theatre, by the time it is mature, will have bored the shit out of millions of people all over the country,"[5] is a prophecy nearing fulfillment. A great many, perhaps the majority, of the productions in our regional and non-profit theatres have no directorial concept, no reason for being, and no connection with the audience: in dramaturgical terms, they do not make sense. Many of the dramaturgs or literary managers know this and feel powerless to do anything about it. Powerlessness is something dramaturgs share with their two major constituencies: the playwrights and the audience. We have been too busy trying to answer Alice's question, while ignoring Humpty Dumpty who had his finger on it all the while.

## II

All I can hope to do within the confines of this brief article is sketch or summarize the philosophical and historical reasons why dramaturgy should be emerging now as a central issue in the American theatre. I believe that these arguments will in themselves provide a broader understanding of the nature of dramaturgy and its various functions in the theatre. We need to assess also what has been happening during the past quarter century in this field other than continuing indecision whether the final -g in dramaturg should be pronounced hard as in German or soft as in French. (Until the *Times* article I thought German was winning.)

In fact, there has been substantial progress. For a recent study conducted by the American Theatre Association, Felicia Londré, dramaturg of the Missouri Repertory Theatre, sent out a detailed questionnaire to 130 theatres which drew response from 61 people involved in dramaturgical work.[6] To my knowledge it is the first and only survey of the state of dramaturgy in the American theatre. Despite its incompleteness (the fact that the majority of theatres did not respond does not mean that they do not employ dramaturgs), the survey unmistakably shows that working dramaturgs have become much more accepted in both large and small theatres than one might suspect from the debate about what to call them. For example, two of the responding theatres employ three full-time dramaturgs or literary managers, four others have two, and twenty-four theatres have at least one full-time dramaturg.

Dr. Londré's survey does not differentiate by function between literary managers, dramaturgs, and associate and/or assistant artistic directors, but the emerging picture is that many more theatres now admit to a wider range of dramaturgical responsibilities than was the case fifteen or even five years ago. Fifty-one out of 56 respondents stated that they were involved in play selection, 38 in making decisions about casting; 31 directed showcase productions, 19 attended auditions in other cities, 18 worked to raise funds, 15 directed major productions (including four Literary Managers), 16 wrote or translated plays, 11 acted; 7 conducted business management, 4 house management; 2 designed, 2 worked in the shop, and 1 in the costume shop. Additional activities include producing a new-play series, supervising workshops and playreaders, teaching, talent scouting, and editing support materials.

The respondents spend on an average three times as much of their time (35.67%) reading scripts than attending rehearsals. This is not surprising, given the difficulty of establishing the concept of a production dramaturg, but the figures should also correct the popular misconception that the literary department of a theatre exists only to read scripts. In the largest resident theatres there are dramaturgs who do not read scripts unless they are working on their production.

According to the Londré survey, research takes up an average of 11.64% of dramaturgical time, 10.71% is spent on "reflection, analysis, and discussion," and 5.35% on public relations. Under other activities (7.14% of their time) dramaturgs embrace a very large range of responsibilities: writing, conducting seminars and producing literary evenings, being involved in project development as well as educational outreach, and "acting as an ombudsman."

When asked what were the most important attributes in looking for a dramaturg, the respondents ranked background in theatre history and criticism as paramount, experience as a director next, and finally experience as a playwright. Although training in dramaturgy fell outside the scope of Dr. Londré's survey, she mentions five responding theatres using part-time dramaturgs as interns.

There are perhaps half a dozen dramaturgy programs at various universities in the United States. Yale's is the best known and has produced by far the largest number of literary managers and dramaturgical types working in the American theatre. Many of the most successful graduates of the program are the most critical of it, and there is an inevitable process of disillusion between the historical theory of how dramaturgy is supposed to work, and the reality of the Yale Repertory Theatre and the O'Neill Theater Center. The latter has employed largely critics and reviewers as observing rather than working dramaturgs. There are degree programs also at the University of Massachusetts, the University of California at San Diego, and most recently at SUNY-Stony Brook. I am involved in establishing two very different kinds of programs in Los Angeles, one at the University of Southern California and the other at International College. But probably the best formal training in the United States does not mention dramaturgy in the title: the Stanford doctorate in directing, which aims to turn out director-scholars. It has the explicit requirement for directors to be intellectually equipped with strong dramaturgical skills, with an implicit recognition that the most effective dramaturgs in the American theatre function as directors.

An increasing number of theatre departments offer individual courses in dramaturgy, although we are still some way from the professional theatre and film schools of Eastern Europe, where there is a core curriculum in dramaturgy that everybody—actors, directors, designers, technical staff, as well as future dramaturgs and critics—must take. All in all, there are fewer directors who look blank when dramaturgy is mentioned or worried when it is explained. Occasionally I even hear one talking about "my dramaturg."

But in a number of significant ways there has also been too little advance in the past twenty years towards integrating the dramaturgical functions into the organizational structure of non-profit theatres. Most of the working dramaturgs in the country are of such recent vintage that it is too early to tell whether they will last or prove to be a passing fad. Jon Jory, artistic director of the Actors' Theatre of Louisville, of all the regional theatres the one most identified with the development of new plays, only very recently got around to appointing a dramaturg, long after setting up a very large literary department. Russell Vanderbroucke says that he was an elder statesman at the recent TCG conference, having been Literary Manager of the Mark Taper Forum for five years. The most senior literary manager in the country is also a Southern Californian, Jerry Patch of the South Coast Repertory. Patch, as one of the three original founders of the company, is probably also the most tenured.

A great number of dramaturgs (nobody knows how many) are women, especially compared to artistic directors, which arouses at least the suspicion that this reflects the relative ratio of power, as it does in so many other fields. My impression, however, is that male dramaturgs are just as frustrated whether they work under female or male leadership, and that the weakness lies with the job rather than gender. This may mean that there are more women willing to occupy it, while men look to become directors or associate artistic directors. But some of the most prominent companies in Los Angeles are run by women, such as Peg Yorkin's L.A. Public Theatre, Susan Lowenberg's Theatreworks, and the great success story of the past couple of years, the L.A. Stage Company, run by Susan Dietz and Susan LaTempa. None of these are feminist groups, which obviously have a clearer dramaturgical program in terms of ideological content and knowing their audience.

The business of new-play development requires separate and longer treatment. For now I must simply observe how few playwrights are employed on a permanent basis by any of the permanent companies in America. The Guthrie Theatre has perhaps the best record in recent years (Barbara Field, John Olive, and Richard Nelson have worked there), though no playwrights are on the payroll presently. Given the history of many classic dramatists who ran their own companies or were closely associated with one, given that developing plays is futile if their authors do not acquire theatrical experience, I must conclude that American playwrights are either chronically unemployable or that the American theatre does not want them.

Another problem is that there are no well-known let alone routine examples of director-dramaturg relationships in the country. Since dramaturgy depends for a large part of its success on interpersonal chemistry and long-term trust, one must have quite a few working teams of dramaturgs and (artistic) directors before one can talk about dramaturgs as an established profession. (One exception to this situation is the long-time collaboration of Joseph Chaikin and his dramaturg, Mira Rafalowicz, who has worked with the Open Theatre and Winter Project/The Other Theatre.)

Even as dramaturgical tasks multiply, many of the people holding the title of dramaturg do not function fully as such. Often they are excluded, bypassed, and prevented from performing their tasks by people who have a title with the word director in it. Or they withdraw themselves, claiming to be too busy reading scripts to attend rehearsals. The literary office in many theatres has come to resemble the story department of film studios and television networks, which exist not to discover fresh talent but to filter out new material and to bar writers from access to those who can actually make things happen. The real dramaturgical power rests with the artistic director, who sometimes delegates it to an associate or assistant.

By itself there is nothing unusual in this, and ultimately it does not matter by what other title a dramaturg is called. What matters is that the functions exist and that people should perform them with skill. Sometimes a director will also design the production or write music. Or an artistic director directs and acts in a play. We do not generalize from any of these special situations that there is no need for designers or that all artistic directors should act or direct. But many of the problems in our theatres do stem from just such a fallacy: that every artistic director is equipped to deal with complex dramaturgical issues as well as administration, casting, fund-raising, and other political activities. There is contrary evidence that not every director can also be a full-time researcher or Shakespeare scholar, especially if he must travel the country in search of directing jobs every three or four weeks.

## III

Dramaturgy is the discipline of a dramaturg, as directing is that of a director, or acting that of the actor. If there is a paradox in an increasing number of dramaturgs encountering increasing confusion about their role, it is symptomatic of a larger problem that cannot be answered by explanations or examples from a dictionary. There are still theatres which can plead poverty or ignorance as obstacles to adopting dramaturgical practices; but when a company is rich enough, sophisticated enough, cognizant enough of its own problems finally to hire one or more dramaturgs and then proceeds not to employ them properly, the reason usually boils down to one thing: there is no dramaturgy to be practiced. Many of our biggest and best known theatres produce play after play without the benefit of dramaturgy, or—in my definition of the word—without any attempt to make sense. The question is: how and why did this come about?

The reluctance to accept dramaturgy and dramaturg as English words reflects a deeper resistance to thinking about the theatrical process as a whole. As busy practitioners we pretend that we do not have time to question the philosophical basis of what we are doing, or that we can take for granted unspoken agreement on the subject. Even in the atmosphere of university theatres, reputed to provide more time and security for exercising the mind, very little thought goes into choosing a play for reasons other than the number of female parts. It is as if we were afraid to ask "why?" in case the answer might negate the value of asking. A strange paradox given the philosophical bent of characters like Hamlet and Prospero, who remain more popular than ever on our stage.

The main job of a dramaturg is to keep asking why. Why are we doing this play? Why this season? Why here? Why does our theatre exist? Why do we exist? Why has theatre worked elsewhere or in the past? Why do our audiences come? Why does ninety to ninety-five percent of the local population stay away? Why are we, inside the theatre, excited about the plays we are doing and why are we not spreading our excitement to the community?

A sound etymological and working definition of dramaturgy is "making drama work." Everybody in the theatre should be involved in the process of play-making or making drama work. But given the enormous human and technical complexity of preparing even the most straightforward production so that it can open on a certain date (determined long before any of the difficulties that inevitably arise could have been foreseen), it is hardly surprising that everybody in a theatre company concentrates on the mechanics of how to get it done, hoping that the why will take care of itself. Yet, as Dr. Victor Frankl has pointed out, life works exactly the other way around.[7] He observed that only those survived the Nazi concentration camps who knew why they wanted to live; those who could not find meaning in their life died faster than those from whom they stole bread. In order to find the "how," we must first know the "why."

Meaning is central to human existence and art. Every artist must seek meaning for himself. In the performing arts, the quest is more complicated because some kind of consensus has to be reached first within a group of artists and then within the larger tribe represented by the audience. The drama does not work, and it cannot be made to work, if the artists and audiences that are involved in it do not seek the meaning of their own work and of the work itself. I am not suggesting that there are always answers when the questions are asked, only that there can be no meaning to play-making without a conscious quest for that meaning. Every good production is the quest itself.

It would be too simplistic and neat to say that the dramaturg asks the "why" and the director deals with the "how." Clearly, the latter must also ask why, and the former has to be aware of the limitations that every production is heir to. But it is important to distinguish in the theatre between the text which represents the thinking of usually one individual mind, who is often rooted in a different time or place, and the performance which is the result of a collective consciousness. The text is inert but lasting, the performance is evanescent but alive; the two are fused for a few hours to create a unique meaning. This dramaturgical process is exclusively for those people who chose on a particular occasion to come together on stage and in the auditorium. If there is no meaning there, a great many people will have wasted their time. This central fact about the theatre has not changed one jot for two-and-a-half thousand years; it is probably the reason why it survives as an important institution in the face of competition from the commercialized mass media. As Martin Esslin has put it:

> . . . in a world from which spontaneous human experience is more and more disappearing through the cancerous growth of overorganized, overmechanized, and ready-made patterns of work, behavior, thought, and even emotion, the genuine need for theatre is growing apace—for a theatre in which human beings can regain their autonomy of feeling, in which the denizens of a thoroughly secularized, demythologized, emotionally dehydrated society can return to the roots of what need not be called religious experience, but which might be called a contact with the ultimate archetypes of the human condition, the awe and mystery, the grandeur of man's lonely confrontation with himself, the universe, and the great nothingness that surrounds it.[8]

The dramaturg, inasmuch as he is concerned with the text, must have a more lasting perspective both backwards and forwards in time than the director who is in charge of the momentary performance and meaning. The best directors I have worked with have also been the best dramaturgs: their primary motivation and talent lay in carving, creating, and shaping a meaning out of the text, rather than imposing on it some flashy but nonsensical concept which is sometimes mistaken for meaning.

Having pronounced these rather lofty principles about the nature of theatrical meaning, I can think of a great number of glaring exceptions and contradictions. The ones we need to consider are definitions of theatre as entertainment and show business. The significant difference between the theatre in Europe, where dramaturgs have existed for two centuries, and the evolution of the English-language stage, where concepts of dramaturgy have generally failed to take root or adapt, is the gulf that separates a public institution from a private concern. Despite the revolution brought about by the establishment of many hundreds of non-profit theatres in England, Canada, and the United States since the end of World War II, there has been little thought given to the organization and responsibilities of what are supposed to be, after all, public institutions. Yet theatre is our oldest institution in Western civilization, and there are many well-documented examples of what it has been and why it has existed in many different societies.

Organization reflects a power structure: who has it, who should have it, and what responsibilities power entails. The smallest public company owned by private shareholders is more regulated and held accountable by the SEC and other governmental watchdogs than any of our major theatres, which are given millions in public funds or tax-exempt donations each year.

## IV

The profound differences between private and public theatre are understood very imperfectly in most communities. We are made occasionally aware by controversies that seem to erupt from nowhere. For example: in 1980 the Mark Taper Forum was admonished by Dan Sullivan, critic of the *Los Angeles Times,* for producing Neil Simon's *I Ought to Be in Pictures* as an obvious tryout for Broadway. Sullivan argued that the Taper is being funded publicly to take risks on lesser known playwrights and not to underwrite the commercial risks for Broadway producers. Artistic director Gordon Davidson countered that Neil Simon should have the same right of access to the Taper as any other American playwright, and that it is in the public interest for his theatre to make money from commercial productions, so that it could continue to take risks greater than the one involving Neil Simon. Both arguments have merit, but what surprised even the arguers is that a debate could erupt with such bitterness at a time when the regional theatre movement has reached some maturity, and the Mark Taper Forum has proven itself to be one of its paragons.

Money is not the only issue. When the Prospect Theatre in St. Louis was threatened last year with loss of public funds for producing Christopher Durang's *Sister Mary Ignatius Explains It All for You,* the problem was not simply an attempt at censorship by a special group (Catholics), or the separation of church and state. Surely the question in all such debates is to what extent a public theatre can go against the wishes of a large part of its public. The Salt Lake City Acting Company stages a revue every summer called "Saturday's Voyeur," which mercilessly satirizes Mormon religious tenets and every aspect of Mormon life. The show sells out without the benefit of any advertising and subsidizes the company's winter season. The Church of Jesus Christ of Latter Day Saints clearly could exert pressure on the producers to moderate or even close the show. So why is the show still running, and in a building that used to be a Mormon church? Because in a highly regulated society, the theatre serves a number of public functions, whether to legitimize some forms of dissent, or demonstrate the tolerance of a ruling ideology, or to provide laughter and release. The tragic poets of ancient Athens, as well as Aristophanes, constantly made fun of the official state religion in the midst of what was after all a religious festival, and very rarely did any one of them get into hot water for impiety.

How does dramaturgy fit in with such issues? Dramaturgy is much more a function of the public than of the private theatre. It is the rebirth of the public theatre that has created, more than any other factor, the profession of dramaturgs and literary managers in English-language countries. The private commercial theatre has known the dim shadow of the dramaturg for a long time under the restrictive but nevertheless revealing name of "play-doctor," who is called in only when the play is in danger of dying. Having attended a number of such deathbed scenes, I am familiar with the smell of fear and panic on such occasions. But, of course, dramaturgy involves a great deal more than surgery or resuscitation after the vital functions cease (if there were any to begin with); it is not even preventive medicine. A preferable medical analogy, as I have written elsewhere, is that of midwife: the dramaturg routinely assists at the birth of a play or production, without any presumption of complications or miscarriage.

Ideally, there will be a dramaturg present at the birth of the theatre itself. G. E. Lessing, the father of modern dramaturgy, was invited to Hamburg to articulate the purpose of a new kind of theatre.[9] His *Hamburg Dramaturgy* chronicles one particular attempt to create a national theatre in Germany. Lessing's critical essays on plays and productions, which the theatre itself published and disseminated, served the administration's purpose by involving the public in a debate about what it was doing, and how it fitted in with the literary and theatrical trends in other parts of Europe. The famous eighteen-hour discussion that led to the founding of the Moscow Art Theatre took place between a director with the immortal name of Stanislavski and Vladimir Nemirovich-Danchenko, the producer, playwright, and dramaturg, better known in English as What's-his-name.

It took Great Britain more than a hundred years of debate, during which time she grew less and less great, to establish a National Theatre, something no Balkan country would be caught without. Canada, Australia, and the United States are still far from comprehending even the concept. The vitality of the English theatre tradition, largely fed by generations of great actors, has blinded many people to a three-hundred-year aberration in its history. From the Restoration of Charles II in 1660 to the rise of publicly funded, non-profit companies following the Second World War, the theatre of the English-speaking world was largely private. I call this an aberration, because from its primitive and Greek origins Western theatre has been in most countries and for most of its three thousand years of history, very much a public place, vitally concerned with political, social, and religious issues. Shakespeare had lost so much meaning in less than two generations that even Dryden found his masterpieces rude and unpolished. Dr. Johnson did not understand *King Lear* and Hazlitt thought it was unproducible. Until very recently the classics were rarely done, and done even less in order to make dramatic sense of them. And it still causes something of a sensation in our own age when a Peter Brook tries to make sense of Shakespeare with help from a dramaturg like Jan Kott.

What we are seeing is the tentative revival of the idea of a public theatre, after the violent caesura of Cromwell's Protectorate and the subsequent degeneration for three hundred years. Although the theatre was restored, it was not the same as before: the silly *beau monde* of Charles II's court, with a theatre-going audience of two to three hundred fops, cannot be compared with the dozen competing public theatres of Elizabethan and Jacobean London, the biggest of which could accommodate up to three thousand people at a performance, or three percent of the total population. Later, the rise of Drury Lane established a new kind of criterion for theatrical success, which was completely unknown to the Greeks, the medieval guilds, or even the companies dependent on royal and aristocratic favor. It remains predominant today: the box office.

The box office, which is the sole criterion for play selection, casting, and every other decision on the commercial stage, ideally plays no such role in the public theatre. In Athens poor people were paid to go and see plays as part of their civic duty. Wealthy citizens vied for the honor of producing at the great dramatic festivals; their only return was public approbation and honors. In contrast, total commercialization has led to a narrowing of the dramatic scope. Bernard Shaw had to prove himself at the box office before his ideas would be taken seriously; even then he could express himself better in the prefaces to the published plays. Shaw's plays are produced today in English mainly because they are amusing and theatrical despite their seriousness; but in the public theatres of the world they are heard for the same reason that he wrote them: the ideas that they contain. Here, even among theatre people he is considered a bit of a bore, while abroad it is accepted that not every drama has to be a hoot. European dramatists whom he championed, like Ibsen and Brieux, never became huge commercial hits, because in their own countries where there was a public theatre, they did not have to make similar artistic compromises. It is for this reason that many of the best foreign playwrights continue to find very slow and limited acceptance in the English-language theatre.

Despite the proliferation of literally hundreds of non-profit theatres in postwar America, I think it is too early to predict whether the idea of a public theatre will take root in a land which did not have it before, in a country, moreover, founded by the same Puritans who were responsible for killing the public theatre in England. This is not the usual doomsaying about the health of the theatre, but simple acknowledgment that in America theatre is part of the entertainment business, where commercial factors can bring about very rapid and cataclysmic changes in a relatively short period of time. For example, I have not seen the following facts on too many trivia quiz shows: in 1900 there were approximately 5,000 so-called legitimate theatres in the United States, which had declined to 200 by 1946 and to 90 by 1949.[10] Fewer than two percent survived a half century during which the American population doubled, with an even greater shift to urbanization. There are no forces in the public sector that can create cultural institutions at even one-tenth of the rate that commerce can. Lincoln Center's failure, though unique in some particulars, is a reminder that shiny buildings named after wealthy benefactors are no guarantee of permanence even in a city so rich in patrons and talent as the nation's theatrical capital. The Kennedy Center in the political capital is an example of what happens to the concept of public theatre in a society that has no understanding of what it is: instead of presenting the best American plays of the classic or current repertoire, it is used as a dumping ground for bad commercial plays that do not even make it to Broadway.

## V

This historical perspective is necessary if we are to understand that the dramaturg in the English-language theatre is evolving from causes and needs that may be deeper than perceived. I do not believe that dramaturgy is a forgotten eighteenth-century German discovery, which took this long to be dusted off. After all, other ideas in the theatre have spread a greater distance and much faster than Artaud's plague. For example, the director as a separate functionary is about a hundred years old; his rise to absolute power in the theatre has been parallel rather than coincidental with Prussian absolutism and the general love affair we have been having with totalitarianism in the twentieth century. There were many opportunities, notably when Max Reinhardt and Stanislavski came to be known and admired here, or when scores of Americans visited Moscow in the twenties and thirties, to observe how dramaturgs work and note their impact on productions. But the connection was not made, because English-language visitors (even one as acute as Edward Gordon Craig) never had anything to which to relate the dramaturgical function within the structure of the private theatre that they knew.

It was only with the emergence of public theatres, with the box office no longer the sole criterion for producing plays, that certain dramaturgical functions are becoming recognized as essential. The change is evident in the shifts of meaning in theatrical terminology. Company no longer means just a haphazard collection of actors hired for particular parts who stay together only for the run of that play and disband when the show closes. Today the word may denote a collective united by similar aspirations and ideology, or theatre artists brought to work together for a whole season of plays under the aegis of a resident theatre. The word "season" itself until recently referred to all the plays by different producers that were presented within a year on Broadway or London's West End. Now it is as likely to denote a list of plays produced by one theatre company.

It was the need to sell to a stable, definable audience a whole season of plays rather than just one that more than anything else led to having dramaturgs and literary managers in the American theatre. Whereas the commercial stage operated for centuries on the assumption that every new play should be as much like the previous success as possible (which is why it is so hard to tell Restoration comedies or Victorian melodramas or French farces apart), it does not make sense to produce for a subscription audience six or seven plays that are exactly alike or even in the same genre. Whereas a road company that brought to town the latest Broadway hit from New York had no responsibility to a local audience beyond putting on the show for a week or two and spending the rest of the time like tourists, most of the play-makers of the resident theatres are members of the community, have their children in local schools, pay taxes, and enjoy civic benefits as well as responsibilities. Whether a show bombed or triumphed on the road, the road company moved on, whereas a bad season or a controversial play will influence subscriptions for several years to come.

The concept that a season should have diversity—a mixture of classics and contemporary works and a smattering of new plays—is widely accepted. But I do not think that this practice has been examined critically or lately. The standard subscription drive, as popularized by Danny Newman, uses familiar merchandising techniques to sell the idea of going to the theatre itself rather than content, that is, the plays themselves. This assumes that people will want to attend the theatre six or seven times a year regardless of what they see, just as they watch a daily or weekly series on television, or buy the main selections of the book club. Because of the initial success of building audiences from scratch in communities which had been without local theatre for two or three generations, there has been a general blindness to the costs and flaws in the system of establishing and maintaining subscriptions.

Again I only have space to mention some of the drawbacks. After a few years when the subscription audience stabilized at ten or twenty thousand, the success of any play in the season is determined by the average number of non-subscribers who are expected to attend. Non-subscribers are those who by definition do not come regularly to the theatre except when they are interested in seeing a particular production. As anybody who works in the theatre knows (except perhaps Danny Newman), plays are not like other merchandise: that is why some plays run for five years and others close before they open. Some appeal to more people because of subject matter, the name of the author, quality of writing, acting, directing, and other production values. The idea that an unsuccessful play must run the same length of time as a runaway success is illogical, yet almost every major resident theatre gets locked into this absurdity. Maintaining the same subscription level becomes the main agenda for such theatres: letting it fall or rise too rapidly can affect adversely the scheduling for an entire year. The way theatres believe they can best maintain their subscription audience is to provide more of the same, to become as predictable as possible. Plays that do not fit the standard menu either do not get produced or are shunted to a studio, a second or even third stage. Suddenly there is a new category: not a comedy, tragedy, domestic drama, or farce, but a second-stage play, *viz.* one that might rock the boat on the main subscription season. The majority of new plays, and I would add, the most interesting plays, are done on a second stage, which becomes on a miniscule scale what public television is to the networks.

Yet the subscription levels do not necessarily hold. As with any static population, a substantial number each year does not renew, because people get older, turned off, they move and even die. What might appeal to one generation bores another; the differences between movie and television audiences are not simply matters of taste, but also age and geography. But unlike the mass media, the theatre is a local phenomenon, and the various pressures on a non-profit theatre from a board of directors, national and local funding agencies, educators, and even audiences are more akin to those experienced by a school board than by commercial show business.

The greatest impact on a theatre and its policy is exercised by the Board of Directors, even when it is manifested in a single function: the power to hire and fire the artistic director and other senior personnel. This happens with sufficient frequency that some boards may be said to be bored of directors. The boards of major cultural institutions tend to be composed of public-minded, wealthy, and influential citizens or their spouses, and they wield ultimate power usually through a small executive committee. The Board of Directors of a typical non-profit institution in America is designed on a corporate model. It is made up of largely the same types you would find on corporate boards: lawyers, accountants, businessmen, and socialites. The rationale for such a board is twofold: fiscal responsibility for public funds should be in the hands of people who understand money; and they can attract corporate and private donors to supplement public funds which are never adequate. However, the public proportion of financing for the arts has steadily grown during the past twenty-five years while the contribution of the private sector has proportionately declined. Yet the composition of the board has not reflected this shift; a narrow elite in each community has extended its considerable private power over the public arts, with consequences that are directly reflected in the art that is produced.

Boards are self-perpetuating: new members are proposed by old members, as in any social club, which is essentially what they are. It is rare to find a union official, a senior citizen, a teacher, let alone an artist sitting on a board. So when a theatre is in trouble (usually measured by falling subscriptions towards the bottom line), the board fires the artistic director and hires a new one, repeating the process until the balance sheet improves. I have yet to hear of a whole board, or its executive committee, resigning, admitting its own mistake for having hired the wrong artistic directors and thereby run the theatre into the ground. The board remains intact, ostensibly as a guarantee against undue political influence by governments and their funding organizations.

Yet it should be evident by now that the main problem is not one of too much political control, but too little. In the old court theatres of Europe, there was a direct and uncomplicated relationship between the sovereign as patron and the players. Now that constitutional governments have replaced the kings and princes, a direct line of responsibility is being maintained between the elected minister of culture, the mayor or city council, and the appointed heads of major cultural institutions. There has been no attempt to establish an equivalent model of public accountability for the public arts in America. In effect, we do not have public arts in this country, but rather organizations partially funded by the public purse which remain under private control. Boards of directors are not elected and represent a much smaller constituency than they sometimes claim: ninety percent of the population that does not attend plays and concerts, subsidizes the ten percent that does. The ninety percent is not just unrepresented on the board: with some notable exceptions, there is no conscious attempt to expand the repertory to attract new audiences. As I have argued, once the subscription roster has stabilized, there is very little room for newcomers, except to take the place of someone who cancelled or died.

This goes a long way to explain why so few theatres have worked out a philosophy, or public policy, which might guide the selection of plays as well as their interpretation. The political process, which is what makes public theatre important and even essential, has been deliberately removed. The sanitized and private tastes of a well-meaning but unrepresentative social class have replaced the public agenda that many of the plays discuss. Shakespeare, Shaw, and Ibsen are played for entertainment, not for what they have to say: that is why most productions of the classics are unintelligible. Foreign and native playwrights who have something important to say often languish in obscurity because they have been rejected by the commercial theatre. The box office, whether in maintaining subscriptions or developing a property for Broadway, dictates the season, just as it does in the commercial theatre, not the concerns of the community. That is why our theatre, in British director Michael Kustow's telling phrase, has no audience, only customers.

There can be no public theatre without dramaturgical functions, whether these are performed by dramaturgs, directors (artistic or otherwise), or, after opening night, by the local critics. Non-profit theatre is not necessarily public theatre, especially if its ultimate aspirations are only validated by the box office or Broadway success. I would like to believe that issues of dramaturgy are surfacing now because there is a faint but growing recognition that something is missing from the seasons and productions of non-profit theatres, that the frantic activity of maintaining subscription levels, of selling seven plays for the price of six, of producing always the same few classics, of putting on one play after another—all this is extremely tiring if there is no meaning to the production and no *raison d'être* for the company. There are as many different meanings as there are localities, and each company must find the connections between its activities and the community, between the text and the human condition.

I would suggest that the dramaturg is a trained professional who, ideally and if permitted, can identify such meanings and bring forward public issues both for the company and its audience (including those who do not but might attend), one who can translate those issues from or into a dramatic text. One of the most obvious ways is given the least space by respondents to Dr. Londré's survey: preparing adequate program notes to place the production in a meaningful context. This is performed in almost every European theatre by dramaturgs, but hardly ever in America even by those companies that employ dramaturgs.

Much of the intellectual debate recently about theatre in the United States has been trying to reconcile the *Hamburg Dramaturgy* with what I would call a Hamburger Dramaturgy: the fast-food, mish-mash metaphor for the American quick-fix. If the rather fragile public theatre is to survive, however, American dramaturgy will evolve in the long term not on the European or any other model, but for the same reasons as elsewhere. It will be defined not by a list of tasks, whether so much time is taken up by reading scripts and so much by working on production, but rather by an agenda for making plays within a community that is consistent with the public agenda. The real debate, which is still to come, will not be about whether dramaturgs are essential or a luxury, whether they help or complicate the artistic process. The battle still to be fought is between those who have established corporate replicas of the private court theatres and those who are working towards creating a genuinely public theatre; between those who have evolved new forms of non-profit hucksterism, where the public is made to take the risks and the baths instead of private investors and producers, and those theatre artists and eventually audiences who need, nay demand, to see a wider meaning in the art and practice of theatre.

1983

# Notes

1 Rosemarie Bank, "Commission Produces a Bibliography of Dramaturgy," *Theatre News* (American Theatre Association), 15, No. 1 (Jan./Feb. 1983), p. 6.

2 Peter Hay, "What Is a Dramaturg?", a C.A.S.T. (Los Angeles) program note reprinted in a 1980 Theatre Communications Group (TCG) newsletter. Lloyd Richards, "What Is a Dramaturg?", a Yale Repertory Theatre program note to the November 1981 production of *Mrs. Warren's Profession*.

3 The *Oxford English Dictionary*, under "dramaturgy," gives the following example from the *Times* of London: ". . . Schiller was starving on a salary of $200 per annum which he received for his services as dramaturg or literary manager."

4 *New York Times*, 23 June 1983.

5 André Gregory, in a speech delivered at the *Tulane Drama Review* Theatre Conference in November, 1965, and quoted by Julius Novick in *Beyond Broadway: The Quest for Permanent Theatres* (Hill & Wang, 1968), still the best book on the problems of regional theatres.

6 Dr. Felicia Londré, "Results of ATA Commission on Theatre Research's Survey of Current Practice in Dramaturgy" (1983, based on the 1981-1982 season); unpublished at the time of writing, this important and illuminating survey may be obtained directly from Dr. Londré, who is dramaturg of the Missouri Repertory Theatre, 5100 Rockhill Road, Kansas City, MO 64110-2499.

7 Dr. Victor Frankl, *Man's Search for Meaning: An Introduction to Logotherapy* (Beacon Press, 1959).

8 Martin Esslin, "The Role of the Theatre" (in *Reflections*, Doubleday, 1969).

9 See F. J. Lamport, *Lessing and the Drama* (Oxford, 1981), chapter V, and J. G. Robertson, *Lessing's Dramatic Theory* (Cambridge, 1939).

10 See, for example, Hubert Hefner's "Decline of the Professional Theatre in America," *Quarterly Journal of Speech* (April 1949).

# The American View: The Future for Dramaturgs on U.S. Campuses

C. J. Gianakaris

The collaborative nature of the stage has been argued for and won handily by theorists and practitioners alike. The long list of credits found on any play program gives concrete testament to the multitude who contribute their skills to realizing a stage production. In theatres on college campuses across North America, however, there is one position only rarely listed on the roster of those bringing theatre to life. The generic term in question is *dramaturg*—a strange, foreign-sounding title only vaguely understood outside the most inner sancta of university theatres. Small wonder that a possibly apocryphal story tells of a suspicious student-actor who, upon admitting he does not know the meaning of the term "dramaturg," then adds, "but I think it's German for 'smart-ass.'"[1]

The truth is that the function, if not the actual profession, of the dramaturg has probably been with us from the beginning of the theatrical enterprise. Precision in defining and tracing the development of dramaturgy is nearly impossible, though, because of the variable tasks falling under its rubric. With respect to definition, the semantic heritage of the word is fuzzy at best. Indeed, the title "dramaturg" often is used interchangeably with "dramaturge" and "dramaturgist." The original Greek root for the term—*dramatourgos*—is of limited help, since it literally means "contriver." Nor is the German word much clearer, its literal meaning being "producer." All the same, there is an accepted definition that derives from the authority of custom, that is, the predominant usage for the term. In Europe's professional theatre over the past century, in particular, the title of dramaturg has come to mean "literary manager." Of course, "literary manager" covers a wide territory. But in as compact a definition as we can comfortably make, the dramaturg can be identified as that person with the responsibility for editing old scripts and developing new ones, for assembling appropriate background material, and for overseeing all literary aspects of a theatre's operation.[2]

Professional theatres apparently see cost-benefit advantages for their total program in the wide range of functions associated with the dramaturg. Many consequently employ dramaturgs on their staffs permanently. In a recent survey conducted by Rosemarie Bank, for instance, it was discovered that over a hundred dramaturgs currently are serving professional theatres in the United States alone.[3]

But mounting plays on a college stage involves different circumstances and logistics compared to mounting them in the professional theatre. Are there sufficient parallels between the two differing operations to persuade us that dramaturgs can also be used profitably in university productions? What about the hiring of a dramaturg, for example, when university theatre programs cannot budget for the post? This last concern is an honest one frequently voiced but one also easily resolved. I herein propose that many common tasks exist for dramaturgs both in professional and academic theatre settings. Moreover, the similarities in duties suggest that academic theatres can benefit significantly from the work of a dramaturg, as has been proven in the crucible of professional houses. Even more relevant to an academic theatre are the contributions a dramaturg can make to expand the educational richness of a university's theatre program. Nor, finally, does my proposed dramaturg place any extra financial burden on the budget of a university theatre department. The key to these magical benefits awaiting college theatres is quite simple and should be self-evident: the inviting, for different productions, of different *faculty dramaturgs* drawn from related academic departments—i.e., communications, foreign languages, and especially English.

We are getting ahead of ourselves, however. Using my personal experiences as dramaturg as index, I want to expand on each of these points. First, we need to elaborate briefly on those functions of the dramaturg which pertain both to the professional and academic theatre worlds. Next, we should detail ways in which a director's colleague—say, from an English department—represents a potentially valuable resource as faculty dramaturg. Last, we will pinpoint those qualities in a dramaturg that contribute importantly to the educational mission underlying most college theatre programs.

Beginning at the beginning, consider the plays which comprise a company's season. Somehow, the managing or artistic director is responsible for the selections that will serve as his theatre's forthcoming season. Unless dedicated to a particular author or period, professional and academic theatres alike feel mandated to offer balanced seasons each year. At universities, moreover, there is an added expectation that theatre will provide the students with long-term educational benefits. The classics and modern masterpieces consequently dominate the main stages of most college theatres. A school drama program ordinarily cannot overextend itself on behalf of new plays, lest the educational function of the theatre become diluted. Some professional companies, by contrast, consider the development of new plays and playwrights one of their specific aims. Such troupes, therefore, endorse a regular process for evaluating new scripts, even mounting (occasionally) new plays thus "discovered" and thought worthy of being staged. It is the regularly employed dramaturg in these instances who typically heads up the play-reading duties of the company. Because the artistic director of a professional theatre rarely has time for the careful perusal of submitted original-play manuscripts, the dramaturg becomes invaluable and almost irreplaceable. The literary background of the dramaturg in these cases can be ideally harnessed to such projects.

Although not so aggressively, college theatres also search out original scripts and undertake some experimental pieces on a lesser scale. Nearly all solid theatre programs in colleges, for instance, provide for the staging of one-acters, original works, and other unusual shows unlikely to draw a large audience. But rather than present these plays as part of their general fare, colleges oftentimes mount them in smaller lab settings. As in the professional theatre, the judgment of a reader well-versed in all types of drama can prove critical for designing a winning season. A selectively chosen professor-as-dramaturg usually will possess the key qualifications for the consulting role in play selection, since he has been trained in the close reading and analysis of play texts from different epochs and countries. The philosophical ramifications of a script's theme are standard considerations, too, for someone steeped in "drama as litera-ture." Thus the presence of that literary perspective—particu-larly when choosing a season—increases the likelihood of meaty, thought-provoking shows on the playbill for a college theatre. At the same time, as for assessing original playscripts, experienced dramaturgs reassure us that the professor-drama-turg can quickly "catch on" as to which attributes of a solid *liter-ary* text translate into an effective *stage* production.[4]

Whether new or old, a playscript requires careful choosing where different editions or versions or translations are con-cerned. And, of course, plays seem invariably to need cutting or editing to suit the circumstances of any given playhouse and its audiences. Again, a dramaturg's literary expertise can prove of high value for the director. Shakespeare's dramas are a case in point; they bristle with textual and literary choices to be made, probably best by someone intimately familiar with the problems of variant versions, dubious authorships of certain scenes, Eliz-abethan orthography, and the like. Cutting scripts, as is the norm with Shakespeare's works, is best carried out by a dra-maturg. His training allows him quick judgment of which pas-sages or scenes are expendable from the point of view of plot. In the script-editing process, though, as with others impinging on the final production, the dramaturg's choices always are dependent on the director's approval. The relationship between director and dramaturg is a crucial one, requiring prearranged guidelines concerning final authority in a production—a topic to be touched on later.

A more typical sequence of events, however, has a dramaturg being brought into a college production after the play selec-tions have been made and when preparations are being initi-ated to mount a specific show. The dramaturg in that case—whether a professional or an academic on loan—offers enor-mous potential assistance on two related fronts: first, as experi-enced researcher for the play (i.e., of its stage and cultural his-tory, the author's overall intentions, and the piece's thematic objectives); and, second, as sounding board for the director while the production's total concept is being developed. Coming to the task, as he does, with wide reading knowledge of so much of the background material needed for evolving a concept, the dramaturg again can be of limitless help to a director who elects to bring him into the essential preliminary deliberations. A surprising number of English professors who teach dramatic literature also possess some knowledge of theatre history, as well. All such information, such enlightened perspective, is put at the disposal of the director by a dramaturg.

Another advantage accrues that too often is overlooked. Because the dramaturg is part of the formulating strategy for a production, he is an obvious choice to assist with auditions and casting. Just how vital is it to make the right decisions with casting cannot be emphasized too much. As a *New York Times* stage critic insists, "It's long been axiomatic that casting is the single most important decision that a director . . . must make."[5] Finally, in yet another related connection, thanks to his ecumenical knowledge of the drama and its historical-intellectual background, a dramaturg can further relieve the harried director by providing program notes, news releases, and general promotional squibs. A dramaturg may even have a unique "pipeline" to the playwright whose work is being performed. Such was the case during my terms as dramaturg for *Equus* and *Amadeus* because of my personal connections with Peter Shaffer. I suspect that my firsthand dealing with the dramatist in those instances resulted in program notes and news releases that offered more memorable comments than, say, those scratched together from theatre annuals and handbooks by a time-pressed director racing to meet a printing deadline. It is worth the director's remembering that English professors write most of the books published about dramatists and dramas; their special "savvy" therefore constitutes a rich resource for any director to tap.

The dramaturg's regular attendance at rehearsals can reap other rewards for the director. Though a dramaturg might not be present at every rehearsal, he probably should attend early ones to answer questions about word-meaning and pronunciation, the significance of certain scenes and puzzling dialogue, and the dramatist's overall thematic intent. For inexperienced student-actors, the dramaturg's talks on the play's background can be highly informative as well as useful in creating their own stage portrayals. In an academic institution, after all, the educational factor dare not be overlooked. To take part in a theatre performance at a university becomes an autonomous learning episode for a student. Not only are the performers and crew gaining knowledge of theatrical technique; they are also expanding their knowledge about the aesthetics of dramatic literature, the historical and cultural roots behind a playtext, and most important of all the situation of mortal mankind in a universe riddled with conflict.

All these matters, it will be recognized, share much in common with the close literary study of a piece of writing. Certain directors realize the implicit learning-aspect of stage production and amplify it. In those cases when I served as a dramaturg (for a university production and for a community-theatre staging), the learning dimension was in fact highlighted. The director in each instance assembled relevant essays I had been asked to find and provide regarding the play and its times; he then copied and distributed them to his cast as a catalyst for the performers' initial consideration of the work to be mounted. The director did not hestiate to divert some of the actors' questions directly to me, as dramaturg, for full response. All evidence points to certain conclusions: the general illumination of the text gained in the joint efforts of director and dramaturg contributed markedly to the formation of the actors' characterizations and to the speed with which those characterizations were arrived at.

A blatant "teaching" component may not be prominent in preliminary rehearsals in the professional theatre, where the basic assumption is that the performers are experienced and well-read. Character-building thus ordinarily belongs to the performer's solitary process. All the same, a director desirous of creating a unified approach to a script often needs to modify his actors' individual characterizations. In such "fine-tuning" endeavors, the dramaturg, through his detailed observations, is invaluable as the director's ally.

Beyond his function as the literary-cultural "expert" in residence, the dramaturg serves as a second pair of eyes at daily rehearsals. Not every director, it is true, wants a second opinion on a scene's progress. Michal Schonberg, Literary Manager at the Stratford Shakespearean Festival in Ontario, has noted that maybe half of the visiting directors brought in to Stratford (from 1981 to 1985) elected *not* to use a dramaturg. Reasons for a director's reluctance to utilize a dramaturg are uncertain. Obviously, variables enter into a production, with any of a number of factors convincing the director to go it alone (i.e., the professionalism of the actors on hand, time limitations for mounting a production, the unique personality of the director—and of the resident dramaturg). Schonberg insists, however, that it usually is a personal matter bordering on instinct that determines whether the director chooses to employ a professional dramaturg. Schonberg's point has been reiterated by a visiting director at Stratford, Ronald Eyre, as well as by Michael Lupu, one of three full-time dramaturgs at the Tyrone Guthrie Theatre.[6]

But once a director agrees to take on a dramaturg, he gains a reliable "sounding board" for his own responses to the daily rehearsals. Typically, the dramaturg sits near the director during rehearsals, taking notes as do most directors. Once the actors have left the rehearsal area, the dramaturg outlines his notes to the director, point by point. Rather often, both director and dramaturg in the run-throughs will spot the same sections they consider problematic or which they deem sound. In those cases, the director's views are confirmed by another expert auditor. In instances where the dramaturg sees some feature unnoticed by the director, the dramaturg's value again is shown, since he ends up magnifying the observing capabilities of the director. On those occasions when the director and dramaturg disagree over an element in the rehearsal, the dramaturg's main value lies in airing the issues openly and promptly. However, once the director takes into account the dramaturg's points and then makes a decision on the matter, the dramaturg automatically must give way. If a prospective dramaturg cannot accept such an absolute arrangement, he should not be considered for the part. The involvement of a dramaturg in no way alters the fact that the director *alone*

remains responsible for final decisions in staging a drama. And
with that responsibility comes ultimate authority.[7]

But one other perspective needs attention. Until now we
have concentrated on ways a dramaturg from an academic
department can assist the university theatre. We need to flip the
coin to its other side and ask, what's in it for the academic-dra-
maturg? No monetary reward is forthcoming in most instances.
Nor do many department chairmen put much weight on one's
dramaturgical work when tenure and promotion decisions are
to be made. So, why should a professor, already accepted as a
teacher of dramatic literature, volunteer his services as a subor-
dinate to a colleague in another field?

Several convincing arguments can be made. For one, English
professors who know dramatic literature nearly always recognize that they deal with half the dramatic experience in a classroom. The other, perhaps larger part of the theatrical process—performance—takes place elsewhere, on the stage inhab-
ited by actors who breathe life into the printed dialogue of the
text. Astute classroom instructors realize they need to teach
more about a play than its use of verbal imagery or the economic status of the dramatist at the time he wrote the piece.
What better way to inform oneself about the production aspects
of a printed playtext than to contribute one's expertise to actually mounting a drama? By taking an active part in the produc-
tion/performance dimension of play-making, the literature professor is investing time and energy to expand his knowledge of
the phenomenon called drama or theatre. He learns about the
mechanisms for bringing the printed word to life for audiences,
not only readers. He is, in short, training himself to become a
better classroom teacher and a shrewder scholar in his field.
His published research subsequent to his work as dramaturg
cannot help but be better informed.

Ultimately it is the student in the classroom who gains from
the academic's expanding understanding of staging procedures,
just as it is the student-actor on the rehearsal stage who learns
something about dramatic literature from a participating professor-dramaturg in the theatre. My experiences in the theatre—shared with other literature teachers who have also been
dramaturgs—have led me to increasing use of the small-scale

staging of scenes within the classroom itself. The performance values inherent in dramatic dialogue seem far clearer to students asked to transform printed words into give-and-take speech during a staged scene. Philosophical conflicts which a professor may insist exist in the printed text leap forward on their own energy, becoming confrontations between opposing characters when a passage is blocked in even the most rudimentary fashion. The result is a more comprehensively educated student of dramatic letters—and of the theatre.

Earlier in my discussion, I mentioned that university theatres enjoy an enviable position in having easy access to learned academics who could serve as dramaturgs at little or no cost. Does this mean that *any* professor of dramatic literature can be tapped? Obviously not. Two critical criteria stand out: one, the interests and background of the person, and, two, his attitudes and personality.

At a recent conference taking up the relationship between faculty directors and faculty dramaturgs, Professor D. Terry Williams explained his thinking when choosing a colleague from another department to act as dramaturg in a production he was to direct.[8] Williams has noticed that certain academics are never seen at university stage productions or at local theatre events, even though they teach drama courses in literature departments. If these colleagues display no interest in "live" theatre, Williams never considers using them as dramaturgs. On the other hand, if a literature instructor often attends stage performances and maintains regular communication with the theatre staff, thereby reflecting clear interest in production matters, then that teacher holds promise as a dramaturg, in Williams' estimation. Further, if the faculty member has published often and intelligently about drama, the odds get even better that he will have pertinent insights to share about a production in preparation.

Once a faculty peer is invited to join the production team as dramaturg, the director has a top-priority task to complete immediately: he must establish guidelines with the colleague, laying out what kind of assistance he seeks from him and how much.[9] Conceivably the director already has in mind a firm vision of the overall staging and wants no second perspectives on his concept. Such a stance, naturally, is the director's prerogative. The professor-dramaturg then would concentrate on matters of, say, textual authority, cultural and historical background for the use of actors as well as designers, and program notes.

If the director has fewer preconceived notions of the production's concept and if he has full confidence in his chosen dramaturg, he might well involve his colleague in far more activities, including an influential say in daily rehearsals. The essential point is that the director of a university-theatre show has little to lose and much to gain by bringing in a fellow academic as dramaturg. The director, after all, always holds the upper hand in any director-dramaturg collaboration. Should a faculty-dramaturg unfortunately end up having little to offer an evolving production, the director can subtly reduce the dramaturg's activities to a minimum—i.e., specified background research and perhaps a rough draft of program notes. If the dramaturg's insights and suggestions are found to be moderately helpful, the director can blend into his production the worthwhile ideas while discreetly ignoring the rest. Since he controls how much—and how little—use to make of the dramaturg, the director remains in the driver's seat.

The role of dramaturg as I use it in this discussion extends beyond that of a simple literary advisor—though that function, too, may be part of the total job description. At the very least, the literary and intellectual strengths of a peer in the English department can be put to good use in preparing the best acting text and providing essential background information to assist the performers. Colleague-dramaturgs on campus, however, can and do perform on a more ambitious scale when they enjoy the director's confidence in their abilities. The academically trained expert can offer invaluable guidance to the soundman of a production, for instance, in choosing appropriate songs and music for a period play (Shakespeare's works leap to mind, of course). Similarly, the authenticity of costume and set design can be verified through a scholar's careful research—research for which the set designer usually does not have the time. My own background as dramaturg has included taking aside a student-actor to work with him one-on-one, using my own taped interviews with the playwright (Peter Shaffer, the author of *Equus* and *Amadeus,* to be specific) to clarify acting problems facing the student. (The nude scene of Alan Strang and Jill Mason in *Equus* is an obvious case in point.) Here the dramaturg becomes a vital extension of the director, taking on a duty that will save the director time that he does not always have to spare for individual performers.

To this point I have commented generally on tasks best handled by a dramaturg and on the relative ease with which a university director can obtain the services of a professor-dramaturg. Finally I would like to consider what qualities produce the best dramaturgs on a college campus or in the professional theatre.

We can take our first cue from the standard definition of the dramaturg as a theatre's literary manager. Clearly, the foremost of his attributes should be very wide reading in world drama of all eras, in dramatic and performance theory and criticism, and in theatre history. There is no viable substitute for an intimate acquaintance with those stage pieces that constitute the world's greatest dramatic achievements. Each new mounting of a play requires a cultural-philosophical context, which, in turn, means weighing previous interpretations and stagings of the same script. Without knowledge of what has preceded it, each new production becomes just another stray shot, aimed blindly into an aesthetic void.

Extensive play-going is a second necessity for the dramaturg. Just as vital as his intellectual perspective on plays is the dramaturg's visceral knowledge of live performance. How does a particular audience respond to a given scene in a masterpiece? How can a dramaturg hope to advise a director on creating a memorable effect if he has not himself been caught up in the magical energy of the stage? One of the best ways to train oneself to isolate effects in order to analyze what produces them is to write theatre reviews. A person experienced in writing critical reviews of productions for the press would probably have the edge on a simple theatre-goer for the job of dramaturg. In my own case, reviewing has been a basic learning tool; skills polished while reviewing dramatic and musical performances for both print and broadcast media were put to immediate use when I functioned as a dramaturg.

Nor is scholarly writing about the drama out of place in the education of an effective dramaturg. Academic writing necessitates more extensive probing of a play's thematic considerations than does periodical reviewing, and each "consideration" can translate into a theatrical payoff as a production is being prepared. Moreover, it is axiomatic that any kind of writing—academic or popular—can improve one's powers of oral communication as well. Is it possible for someone who does not express himself well to assist a student-actor in discovering clues to word inflection and blocking strategy? It would be tempting, in fact, to mandate an internship as a theatre reviewer for any graduate student seeking to become a professional dramaturg.

Some of the finest professional dramaturgs working today are or have been directors or playwrights first. Although it seems unreasonable to expect all dramaturgs to possess such specialized background, many academics from literary fields have nonetheless at least served as *judges* of playwriting contests, or of the tenure cases of university directors whose productions they then had to critique. Such experiences can help ease the literature professor into the role of faculty dramaturg. One additional experience proved enormously helpful in preparing me for the duties of dramaturg. And it is an obvious one: actual performance on stage. Intellectually, one might perceive that a rehearsed scene is not working, but sometimes it takes performance experience of one's own to know how to solve the problem, how in fact to make the scene work.

When one considers everything that goes into the making of a good dramaturg, it is fair to wonder if any academic training program can compress such training and experience into a reasonable curricular package. Several prestigious academic theatre programs in the United States evidently believe such a regimen is possible, since they offer degrees in dramaturgy.[10] Although most dramaturgs functioning in the United States up to now have been self-trained, there is no reason why graduates from dramaturgy programs cannot succeed as well. The final, and perhaps most critical, element of successful dramaturgy cannot be much influenced by any academic curriculum, however. I speak of the person-to-person relationship between director and dramaturg. Professional dramaturgs and university directors alike insist that "all bets are off" concerning the usefulness of a dramaturg if the director and dramaturg have personalities and expectations that do not mesh. Earlier I noted that good "chemistry" was essential between two such artists if they were to work together productively. Some professional directors declare that instinct tells them at once if the chemistry is right, or not right, with a given dramaturg. And in those instances where the chemistry is bad, the director feels he must refuse to take on the prospective dramaturg. If his instincts inform him otherwise, a director then might invite the collaborator aboard. I say "might" because even when the chemistry is deemed right, some directors choose to work alone. The respected British director Ronald Eyre, for example, is adamant that there exists no "profession" of dramaturgy but only the functions, which theoretically can be managed by almost anyone close—sympathetically as well as intellectually—to the director.[11]

In view of the above discussion, I would venture to say that the future for the "function" if not for the "profession" of dramaturgy is bright in the United States. Professional companies already exhibit confidence in the dramaturg, both here and in Europe. Dramaturgs on our university campuses, however, remain for now a rarer species. All the same, I cannot imagine university theatres' resisting much longer the advantages so readily available to them in the form of the faculty dramaturg. College theatre directors and college teachers of dramatic literature cannot ignore indefinitely the benefits entailed in artistic collaboration. Eventually, I suspect, aesthetic self-interest, if not outright altruism, will prove a determinant. Both professionals have too much to gain to allow such an enriching collaboration to go unexploited.

1986

# Notes

1 The anecdote is told in an informative essay on the subject of English professors in the theatre. See Ken Davis and William Hutchings, "Playing a New Role: The English Professor as Dramaturg," *College English,* 46, No. 6 (October 1984), p. 561.

2 Peter Arnott, *The Theater in Its Time* (Boston: Little, Brown and Co., 1981), p. 364.

3 Rosemarie Bank, "Shaping the Script: Commission Produces a Bibliography of Dramaturgy," *Theatre News,* 15, No. 1 (1983), p. 6.

4 Richard Trousdell, "New Writers, New Plays: A Dramaturg Measures What's Wrong (and Right) With Them," *Theatre News,* 17, No. 4 (1985), p. 2. My background adjudicating playwriting competitions tends to confirm Trousdell's findings.

5 Frank Rich, "Casting Can Make or Break a Show," *New York Times* (August 11, 1985), Sec. 2, p. 3.

6 At the 1985 annual convention of the American Theatre Association (ATA) in Toronto, one of the most successful sessions was called "Staging the Classics at the Stratford Shakespearean Festival: The Literary Manager-Dramaturg-Director Relationship" (August 5, 1985). Speaking on the panel were dramaturg Michal Schonberg and visiting director Ronald Eyre, both from the Stratford (Ontario) Festival. In the audience and commenting eloquently was Michael Lupu, dramaturg at the Tyrone Guthrie Theatre in Minneapolis. I had the pleasure of attending the session, and the points made about it in this essay derive from notes taken during the session.

7 Dramaturg Michael Lupu (Guthrie Theatre) expanded on this notion while speaking from the audience during another informative panel at the 1985 ATA convention. This other session, where your author gave a paper on "*Equus*: As Seen by the Dramaturg," was called "The Director-Dramaturg Relationship in University Theatre Productions." Originating and leading the panel was Professor D. Terry Williams, chairman of theatre at Western Michigan University (Kalamazoo).

8 D. Terry Williams, "*Equus*: As Seen by the Director," a paper given during the session "The Director-Dramaturg Relationship in University Theatre Productions" (ATA Convention, 6 August 1985, Toronto).

9 Directors and dramaturgs alike in professional theatre insist on clearly stipulated guidelines to define the director's expectations of his dramaturg—a point emphasized by dramaturgs Michal Schonberg and

Michael Lupu, and by director Ronald Eyre, as noted in footnotes 6 and 7 above.

10 Among the better known schools giving degrees in dramaturgy are Yale, Stanford, and Stony Brook in New York.

11 See footnote 6.

# Dramaturgs in America:
# Two Interviews and Six Statements


## Dramaturgy at The Guthrie:
## An Interview with Mark Bly                 By David Moore, Jr.

Mark Bly is Dramaturg/Literary Manager of The Guthrie Theater, where he has been employed since 1981. Previously Bly worked in literary departments at the Arena Stage in Washington, D.C., and the Yale Repertory Theater.

**MOORE: How is the dramaturgy department at the Guthrie set up? What does the theater define as the responsibilities of your department?**

**BLY:** Our normal complement is two full-time dramaturgs; a part-time literary associate who can function as a production dramaturg when needed; a part-time librarian; and a part-time dramaturgy intern who is usually a graduate student from a university theater program. Michael Lupu and I are the two full-time dramaturgs and we report directly to the artistic director of the theater. The other members of the department report to me. About a year ago, for the first time, all of the heads of departments at the Guthrie were asked to write a job description for each member of their departments. The dramaturgs' job descriptions alone ran to nine pages typed single-spaced. As in any dramaturgy or literary department, we serve the usual functions of receiving and reading scripts. At the Guthrie my department is also generally responsible for approving all written copy concerning our productions. Printed material such as press releases, which are put together by another department, must be approved by us to help insure factual accuracy; and in our public pronouncements we adopt a uniform and appropriate aesthetic approach to individual productions.

Beyond such routine matters, the Guthrie's dramaturgs also serve the theater as production dramaturgs and as planners who generate ideas and artistic projects for the theater. The two functions are interrelated: as planners we come up with ideas for future projects and seasons; as production dramaturgs we follow through and help to bring the individual projects to their fullest possible realization on the stage. Of course we generate ideas for projects and productions all year round, but the season-planning process in which we specifically fit all of our ideas into a workable schedule for the following season lasts about four to six months. The artistic director makes the final decision, but the dramaturgs provide many of the initial ideas. During this process we may contact directors whose work we find exciting, and ask them what plays they might be interested in directing. We try very hard to develop ideas that excite the artists who will be involved with the production and that will galvanize them into action.

I think that at the Guthrie we tend to worry less than some other theaters about creating a so-called "balanced season," with its deadening, soporific smorgasbord effect. We do try to choose seasons that will stimulate and offer opportunities for growth for our resident acting company. When we come up with a possible season that looks challenging on the surface, I draw up a chart that indicates part-lines for each actor or actress in our company, so that we know whether we will have appropriate roles for most of the company. The charts also give us a sense of how many additional actors or actresses must be hired for what amount of time, so that we can determine a budget and casting requirements for the acting company for the proposed season. People who think that season-planning is just a matter of picking eight plays that will sell well at the box office have no conception of the aesthetic process and artistic judgment involved. At least at this theater, season-planning requires intimate knowledge of the plays and characters, individual actors and actresses, the proposed directors and designers, as well as the artistic vision and goals of the artistic director and the organization as a whole.

**How do you function as a production dramaturg?**

Once the season is planned and finally opens, Michael Lupu and I continue to be involved with the season through our work as production dramaturgs. Usually Michael and I each dramaturg three mainstage shows per year. Our literary associate may also dramaturg one mainstage show per season. At the moment, the Guthrie doesn't have a second stage, but that situation is expected to change during the next year and we will have to re-think our work assignments. Generally, with the consent of the artistic director, Michael and I decide between us who will work on which show, taking into account our schedules, individual areas of expertise, the wishes of the director, and our own aesthetic longings. We have evolved an informal system between us that has been very successful in my opinion: one of us serves as the principal production dramaturg who is named in the program, and the other serves as a secondary dramaturgical "consultant."

The primary production dramaturg works intimately with the director, attends nearly all rehearsals, and produces the elaborate Guthrie program/magazine for that particular show. The secondary "consultant" dramaturg attends rehearsal only at certain critical points to see how things are progressing: early run-throughs, early previews, etc. The principal production dramaturg provides the day-to-day dialogue with the director and has insight into the evolution of specific moments in the production. The secondary "consultant" production dramaturg provides a check or reminder system, validating some artistic choices and debating others. Frequently the most important function of the second production dramaturg is to stimulate the first to push for specific changes he has been contemplating for some time. At a smaller theater, the function of this second production dramaturg could really be performed by an artistic director or anybody else on the staff who has sound critical abilities. In my experience, these duties that our secondary production dramaturg performs are the full extent of the production dramaturgy performed at most theaters. Mind you, I do think that there is value in even this much dramaturgical assistance, but this kind of dramaturgy barely scratches the surface of what we call production dramaturgy here at the Guthrie.

One of the first things that a principal production dramaturg assigned to a particular show does is sit down with the director and discuss the play. Some directors already have very firm notions about what they intend to do, but others really want this discussion period. We might discuss the text or possible cuts, or the director's vision for the play. Some directors are not yet ready to discuss their approach at this stage. Most production dramaturgs compile for the director, designers, and actors basic background material on the playwright and the historical context of the play. I like to take my research one step further by constructing a production history in addition to the basic research. The kind of thing I put together is very production-oriented and not just mere academic detail. For example, when I dramaturged Liviu Ciulei's production of *Twelfth Night,* I wrote an essay/letter that discussed some of the major stylistic and imagistic approaches, character interpretations, and thematic explorations of past productions. I also included descriptions of those productions; photos or drawings (when available) of actors, sets, and costumes; observations by the artists involved in the productions; and relevant or useful audience and critical responses. The production history is a document that can give the director something to which he can react. It makes clear that the production at hand is part of an ongoing discussion with artists past and present. Finally, and for me, most important, the production history can help to establish a "theatrical" ground for discussion with the director, rather than a "literary" one: we shift from talking about literary aspects to talking about theater.

**In providing this material to Liviu, as you did on *Twelfth Night,* did you choose to provide a diverse array of contradictory ideas or did you make interpretative decisions according to bents of your own? Was your goal to open Liviu up in a direction he might not have been inclined toward initially?**
My job is to support and complement the director, so I provide him with a wide variety of ideas to get him thinking. Sooner or later I do generally voice an opinion about which choices I would make, but the director has the right to make the final decision. I do have a prejudice about the types of material I will

put under Liviu's eyes. Having worked with him for five years, I know what he considers useful. I don't waste his time on other things. We wouldn't still be working together after all this time if we didn't share some of the same vision, if we weren't headed toward the same objectives. I know, for example, that Liviu wants to stay away from "cosmetic conceptualizations," interpretations that are simply appliquéd on top of a play. I agree wholeheartedly, so I wouldn't waste Liviu's time or my own by bringing this type of past production of *Twelfth Night* to his attention. On the other hand, I know that the work of painters like Rauschenberg, Dix, Tooker, Lindner, Magritte, Schwarzer, Ernst, Delvaux, and Grosz inspires him and helps shape his productions. For his *Twelfth Night,* the carnival images from Fellini's film *The Clowns* were important inspiration. So I like to bring Liviu lots of visual material, especially when he is in the very early stages of developing a design or a "look" for the show. When I interviewed Richard Nelson, he said that a critical moment for a production dramaturg to be around Liviu occurs when Liviu is creating his set design. I agree completely. Nearly everything else flows from those moments of inspiration.

**Liviu Ciulei has referred to certain interpretations of the classics as having an "archaeological approach." What does that mean to you? Could you define with reference to your productions at the Guthrie?**
I would define an "archaeological production" as some naive attempt to recreate the way a play was originally staged. This leads to "museum productions." We do not encourage such work at the Guthrie. Let me tell you a story. Lucian Pintilie directed Molière's *Tartuffe* for us in a setting that looked like a cross between an insane asylum and a slaughterhouse. It was a radical, fascinating production. Michael Lupu dramaturged the show. I kept pinching myself and saying, "I'm watching *Tartuffe!*" Pintilie was delving into the text in a way that one rarely sees, and it was not a cosmetic interpretation. He was scraping away all of the accumulated debris that generations of "faithful productions" had created. As the performance began, the setting was 17th-century France. Gradually, history and time seeped into that setting, so that somewhere in the second act

you noticed that one of the actors had on a shoe that was from another era. At the end of the play, Tartuffe arrived in a 1936 Cord vehicle crashing through the back wall of the stage. The seeping time had suddenly become an explosion—historical artifacts exploded onto the stage. In one of the after-play symposia, a woman in the audience said, "Now really, do you believe that this is the way Molière performed this play?" Gerry Bamman, the actor who played Orgon, is wonderfully witty and perverse, so he replied, "Well, it is very difficult to say how it was originally performed, since the photographs and tapes of performances from that era are not very reliable." That remark says everything there is to be said about the value of "archaeo-logical" or "faithful" productions.

**How do you and other production dramaturgs at the Guthrie participate in rehearsals and previews?**
Very actively. A lot of people believe that once the dramaturg has helped the director in the initial stages of planning, and distributed background material, that he does little more than sit in rehearsals and give etymological clinics. I think Des McAnuff said it best in a recent speech at the Hunter College dramaturgy conference: "Any dramaturg who feels that his role on a classic is limited to doing research is brick ignorant about what a meaningful production of a classic entails." I agree, and I would extend the same sentiment to dramaturgs and contemporary plays as well. If I had to reduce, in a theoretical way, what I do in rehearsals to two words, I would say, "I question." Dieter Stürm, in *Utopia as the Past Conserved,* said that the "doubting process" is a central maxim of all rehearsal work, indeed all work, at the Schaubühne. For them, this doubting entails a "destruction of illusionary knowledge (*Scheinwissen*) and the questioning of precipitous analyses." I think this questioning spirit informs the work of the best dramaturgs. Most dramaturgs, however, don't phrase what they do in quite that way. They say, "I'm the objective voice in the rehearsal hall." To me, "questioning spirit" and "objective voice" aren't necessarily the same thing. Whenever dramaturgs discuss their "objectivity" on a production, they invariably refer to how much time they spend in rehearsal. There is a very widespread atti-

tude among dramaturgs that one's Objectivity Quotient is inversely proportional to the amount of time one spends in rehearsal. It seems to me that in trading involvement in rehearsals for a theoretical objectivity, these dramaturgs have given away far more than they have gained. I think a dramaturg can have a "questioning spirit" even if he attends every single minute of rehearsals. I don't believe that a dramaturg appearing intermittently for only an hour or two a day can have a profound impact on a production. In my experience, I have consistently accomplished more for the production by spending time in the artistic trenches. In a recent interview I asked Garland Wright what he as a director thought of "objectivity" in dramaturgs. I'd like to quote him because what he says is diametrically opposed to a prevalent (and, I think, wrongheaded) attitude in production dramaturgy today:

> I do not think you can be truly objective if you haven't been subjective first, or at least exposed to the subjectivity of others. I do not believe a production dramaturg can give *do-able, useful* notes if he does not know the source of that work. By that I do not mean the theoretical or dramaturgical source of the work. I mean in rehearsal, what happened one magical day when the actor improvised that moment, and it worked brilliantly—and it has never worked brilliantly again. If a dramaturg does not know that, the source of the moment, he cannot retrace its roots to decipher what has gone wrong.

Another aspect of the whole "objectivity" question is whether a production dramaturg, no matter how much or how little time he spends in rehearsal, should get involved in the psychological relationships between actors and director or the problems of an actor unable to find the essence of his character. At the Guthrie we have new outside directors coming in regularly. It is to the benefit of everyone involved if the director and the actors learn to talk to each other and deal with each other in both psychological and practical ways as quickly as possible. The dramaturgs at the Guthrie tend to act as facilitators in this process, so we are frequently involved in the psychological relationships between director and actor; and actor and character. We never, never supplant the director or get involved if the director doesn't want us involved or if we'd do more harm than good. But because we have been through so

many productions with some of our actors and know their
strengths and weaknesses (as they know ours!), sometimes we
can make a real difference.

Perhaps this is the place to add that I do believe that a good
production dramaturg who really gets involved in rehearsals
can make a very positive difference in a show. However, no
dramaturg can insure a great show every time—no director can
do that either. I think the best evidence for the value of a good
production dramaturg is simply that once a director has worked
with one, that director thereafter tends to be our best adver-
tisement.

### How do you give notes in rehearsal?

The first thing is, I try never to suggest that a director is wrong.
This is a *faux pas* not because directors believe they are infalli-
ble, but because really, in theater, there are simply "choices": no
"right" or "wrong" in a traditional sense. Also, I believe a common mistake that we make as dramaturgs is to think that a
director does not realize that he has a problem with a particular
scene. Therefore a note given during a preview that reads,
"Note No. 142: the Pyramus-and-Thisbe scene is dull. Can't it be
funnier?" is not only outrageously annoying but not particularly
helpful. Directors of any real merit know what isn't "working."
What they are usually desperate for is a solution and not some
general observation that any audience member could make. I
have no set method of giving notes. It depends largely on the
director, how well I know him, if it is a run-through or preview,
and how volatile the situation is. However, I generally prefer to
give notes personally to avoid any confusion that might arise.

I also tend more to ask or raise questions in my notes than
make direct pronouncements on the scene or performance. I
do this for two reasons. First, even if I have made a legitimate
observation, I don't want the director to feel he has "failed" or
that I am trying to "score a point." Secondly, I frequently do
not know why a beat is not working, and so I prefer to open a
discussion with the director by raising a question about the
problem. In my experience, sometimes merely bringing up the
question is enough, even if all you are saying is: "I saw this.
What was your intention?" The best directors will reflect on

your question for a day or so, and then generally clarify their intention during the next rehearsal. Finally, sometimes I feel there is more to be achieved in a scene and that the director and actors have arrived at a fixed solution too early in the rehearsal process. I like to make general, often seemingly oblique comments through my notes, such as: "It's odd, but today I heard something else in that line that I never heard before. I wonder if there isn't another color also inhabiting that line." Directors do not take such remarks as frontal assaults, and they frequently result in the director and actors making discoveries—usually larger than the one you had envisioned.

**What is your approach to editing the Guthrie program book?**
I consider the creation of a program that magnifies and supplements the audience's experience to be a critical part of the production dramaturg's responsibilities. Our program has two parts. There is an "outer wrap" section which contains basic organization and staff information as well as a schedule and articles and interviews about upcoming shows at the theater. In addition, I always include one feature article that deals with some aspect of theater not related to the specific production at hand. I've printed pieces ranging from an article on Georgio Strehler's latest work to Peter Sellars' speech at the National Press Club to Des McAnuff's speech before the Literary Managers and Dramaturgs of America conference last fall. Audience members who faithfully read this part of the program get a pretty good overview of the issues being discussed in professional theater circles today. This "outer wrap" carries the advertising that pays for the program and allows us to distribute it free to our audiences. Inside the "outer wrap" is the "center section," which is generally sixteen to twenty 8½ x 11½ pages devoted to the production on stage. I have overall editorial responsibility for the program, and I always edit the outer wrap, but the production dramaturg for that particular production is the creative impulse and has primary responsibility for the theme, content, and overall look of the center section. We always discuss the program with the show's director, but in my experience, the director is generally concentrating on the production itself and leaves the production dramaturg to his own

devices in putting together the program material. Our publisher supplies us with staff designers to help the production dramaturgs create and lay out the graphic elements of the program. The right designer, working hand-in-hand with an inspired dramaturg, can create magic. The wrong designer can wreak havoc with bad advice and sloppy attention to detail. But no matter who is the designer, it is the production dramaturg who must find a way of distilling the essence of a production into sixteen pages of words and graphics. Only he and the director know the show intimately enough to do this at this stage. The style and theme and content of this center section are almost totally variable, but are always connected somehow to the production at hand. Sometimes a series of images in the program can help the audience to grasp the thoughts and ideas behind a production much more quickly than textual material.

For example, for our production of *Cyrano de Bergerac* I created a series of images connected to the moon and flight. The cover of the program displayed a distant image of the moon. It was a modern photograph treating the moon as Cyrano did: as an idealized, 17th-century romantic symbol of love, purity, and intellect. The program then moved both textually and graphically from "Cyrano's World" of the 17th century to "Rostand's World" of the 19th century, complete with iconography from the period—a large vertical photo of the Eiffel Tower with its Promethean thrust and a tiny horizontal photo of the Wright Brothers' Kitty Hawk flight. Then you turned the page and leaped forward into the 20th century and images of John Glenn and moon rockets surrounded by T. S. Eliot quotations and Tom Wolfe's description from *The Right Stuff* of Chuck Yeager breaking the sound barrier. At last you turned to the final page and the moon up close. It was no longer a mythical, idealized version of the moon, but the thing itself, cratered and pockmarked—the image of the 20th century. So I used two distinctive images of the moon to frame the center section of the program. These contrasting views of the moon reflected director Eddie Gilbert's belief that Cyrano was the last of a dying breed, a heroic romantic, who nevertheless was faced with choices that were modern. Also, that the play is poised at the edge of the 20th century, full of existential questions of choice.

I used these two perspectives of the moon to convey the tension the director felt between the romantic and the modern aspects of the play. For Emily Mann's *Execution of Justice* I used fragmented photos of the historical figures and events surrounding the Dan White murders to reflect visually the chaos that enveloped and fractured that San Francisco community. These descriptions oversimplify the thought behind the programs, but this may give you some idea of how the production dramaturg tries to relate the program to the production.

**I'd like to move on to another topic. You work for a very large theater whose fiscal survival is always an issue, as uncomfortable as that is to contemplate. I wonder what your relationship is as a dramaturg to the theater's financial situation, and to fundraising efforts.**
I think a dramaturg would be irresponsible if he were not aware of the economics of any given situation. Those charts that I do every season to aid in casting are also the basis for formulating a budget for actors' salaries—"actor work-weeks" in budgetary parlance. I also make it my business to know details of the budgets for individual productions. Then when the need arises, I can make suggestions about how to rearrange the budget or how we might augment the budget with in-kind donations. I also make it my business to talk frequently with the Guthrie's Development Department. We exchange information on upcoming projects and potential sources of funding. They have been very supportive of our special artistic projects and I try to assist in any way I can that department's fundraising and grant-writing activities. I think dramaturgs can and should be actively involved in fiscal discussions at a theater. The achievement of artistic goals and the achievement of financial goals are not mutually exclusive, but may in fact be enhanced by mutual cooperation.

**What do you fear most about the profession of dramaturgy, in its present state or for its future evolution and development?**
In his work *The Book of Laughter and Forgetting,* Milan Kundera wrote, "The struggle of men against power is the struggle of

memory against forgetting." I guess I fear that in this country we seem to be showing not only a tendency, but almost an eagerness to "forget." I think dramaturgs are in a position to influence the kind of social, political, and moral questions that are presented on our stages. But I fear that we too often abdicate our responsibility to push for productions that ask meaningful questions and that challenge this tendency to "forget." When I worked on *Execution of Justice,* I was attracted to the script because it is one of the few contemporary plays that raise meaningful questions about justice, our value systems, and our sense of communal responsibility. The play contains testimony from the transcript of the Dan White murder trial and interviews with key community leaders in San Francisco. What struck me was that a major activity or "motor" in the play is the act of remembering. The play is in part "about" memory and how we choose to remember only certain events in a certain way and choose to forget others. This act of choosing what we will remember and therefore what we will allow to influence our world view is very pervasive in this society at all levels. I remember last year when Ronald Reagan first decided not to visit the Dachau concentration camp. His rationale was, "I feel very strongly [about not] reawakening the memories . . ." What he meant was, "These memories don't fit my current interests and agenda." I believe that it is sometimes necessary for our society to face unpleasant memories of the past in order to get at some important truths about ourselves and make wise decisions for the future. When we start "blocking out" portions of our culture's history, we limit ourselves as creative individuals and as people able to control our own destiny. Dieter Stürm, in *Utopia as the Past Conserved,* described the condition of Western culture rather accurately when he said, "Not only is there curtailment of creativity, of subjective conditioning for all forms of rich imaginative creation, but also a complete *amnesia* regarding vast areas of human relations. In other words, a forgetting of human possibilities for action and development." If our society and its leaders ignore and forget the major social issues of our time and the deep divisions within our culture (not to mention the smaller but very telling *faux pas* of our "Teflon President"), then we must *remind* them. We must encourage new plays that address these issues, and stage classics so they're not mere museum pieces, but have meaning and immediacy for our audiences here and now. As dramaturgs we must help directors to probe and penetrate beyond the *Scheinwissen,* the "illusory knowledge" that leads us to predictable, surface analyses of the classics. Our starting point must be a questioning and doubting process that will help us uncover those innate contradictions, conflicts, and tensions in a script that have an immediacy, that still vibrate for our culture. To put it simply, our goal as dramaturgs must be to help create theaters so anchored in our culture and so attuned to the conflicts and tensions of our society that cultural amnesia for our audiences will no longer be possible. How can we demand anything less of our theater and ourselves?

1986

## The Literary Manager As "Resident Highbrow": An Interview with Russell Vandenbroucke at the Mark Taper Forum          By Carol Rosen

On June 12, 1980, Russell Vandenbroucke, then a two-year veteran in his position as Literary Manager of the Center Theater Company at Los Angeles' Mark Taper Forum, discussed both the daily routine and the revelations of his job. Along the literary management grapevine, the Mark Taper appointment was considered to be—a plum. Vandenbroucke's boss was the Taper's passionate and socially aware Artistic Director, Gordon Davidson, whose theater was (and still is) located in an unglamorous downtown section of the city of Los Angeles, and whose vision of theatre is inclusive rather than exclusive.

From its inception in 1967, Gordon Davidson has dedicated the Taper to "the feeling that a creative theater makes its mark with new material—especially as it relates to the community and the society around it." Here, production policy stressed a commitment to developing "indigenous" works, so here, conventionally marginalized playwrights, actors, and audiences were positioned center stage. Most notably, major productions of both Luis Valdez' *Zoot Suit* and Mark Medoff's *Children of a Lesser God* emerged at the Mark Taper Forum. When Vanden-broucke joined the Taper production team, that theater was also widely known for its willingness to foster the transfer of productions among loosely affiliated companies, both in New York and elsewhere, to better champion and promote socially relevant plays, such as Daniel Berrigan's *The Trial of the Catons-ville Nine* and Michael Cristofer's *Shadow Box.*

A flow chart of the 1980 Taper would appear to be a dra-maturg's monopoly board. It was the Mark Taper Forum The-ater, after all, whose physical plant then included a 742 seat mainstage thrust space primarily devoted to new plays, prefer-ably American, and three second tier spaces, each with a particular mission and constituency: (1) the New Theater for Now (a site to polish potential mainstage plays), (2) the Forum/Lab (a 99-seat workshop space for experimental pieces devel-oped for the "Playworks" festival), and (3) the Improvisational Theatre Program (a young ensemble touring company). All these stages were covered by the umbrella term Mark Taper Forum, and although each fiefdom had its own literary man-agement head, all were part of the team led by Vandenbroucke, in service to the expressed mission of the Taper to nurture new playwrights and to serve as an artistic home to the local commu-nity.

The literary manager's "schizophrenia," to which Vanden-broucke ironically referred several times in the course of our conversation, seems to come with the territory. Apparently pos-sessing a natural instinct for backstage diplomacy, enabling him to be alternately invisible and ubiquitous at the Taper, Vanden-broucke fit the American definition of the dramaturg as hybrid: unassumingly adept at both theory and practice, he was regu-larly required to juggle his isolating identity as resident ideo-logue (or as he slyly phrased it, "resident highbrow") with his team-player identity as savvy production planner and "public articulation" person. This theater historian and critic, then—whose scholarly book, *Truths the Hand Can Touch: The Theater of Athol Fugard,* would soon be published by Theatre Communica-tions Group—was also a potential artistic director. In fact, Vandenbroucke later went on to head up Chicago's Northlight Theatre.

Yet even in 1980, one can hear the disappointment felt as a learned and pragmatic literary manager at one of America's premier, well-intentioned and focused regional theaters describes the limits placed on his creative input and power. Folding himself into his chair for our interview, the soft-spoken Vandenbroucke projected self-possession, subtle, self-deprecating wit, and a gentlemanly loyalty to his boss and to his theatre. Hesitant to complain, he did, nevertheless, express a guarded hope for more clout, that is, for a chance to make a real contribution to a playwright's artistic growth, to an audience's world view.

Throughout the interview with Vandenbroucke, we can hear two major resounding concerns: his wish to steer clear of the "faddish" chase after new American plays; and his hope that American theater artists might more frequently get to encounter and to re-invent the "classics."

**CAROL ROSEN:** *What is the job description for a literary manager in America?*

*RUSSELL VANDENBROUCKE:* Most people ask, "What does a literary manager *do*?" And the first thing a literary manager does is to explain what a literary manager does. I mean, I presume you're not asking because you don't know but because you want . . .

. . . *your definition, your observations* . . .

Right, you want a concrete answer to how it works here. At the Taper, we're mostly new-play oriented. So there's a kind of dramaturgy—dramaturging—that I *have* done, but tend not to do here. We did *The Tempest* two years ago, but in terms of a lot of poking around the library, that side of classic interest is not so pronounced here.

Although for this season, we've announced that instead of doing plays en suite, we are going to do a rep in the spring, this time next year. So I have been doing a little more work in that area.

Since the job is defined by the personality of the place and since we mostly do new plays and since we mostly don't do things in rep, it's a slightly different set up than, say, the Guthrie.

*You're not doing many translations, for example.*

No. I—no.

*Is your time mainly spent reading new plays that come in?*

Yes, I obviously read lots of plays. [He gestures at script-laden bookcase and laughs.] I have an associate, and other people read here in this office.

These plays [points to a shelf] are the ones that we've done. And that's just a library. In fact, there are *none* waiting to be read. There's no play, I think, in the office that hasn't been read as of this second. But that's only a fluke, because they're somewhere else. They're with my associate who does the first read.

*What are your other responsibilities as literary manager?*

I do program notes; I have a sort of PR-slash-public articulation function in the sense that I write . . . in the context of the program or Gordon articulating the season, that kind of thing. I handle that: how we talk about what we do.

I mean, I don't write ad copy, I'm not saying that, but there's a certain amount of—just—articulation that comes out of here besides what gets done in brochures or in ads and so on.

*How much input do you have into what's done?*

Not enough.

*Is this lack of input a negative aspect of this kind of job?*

I'm probably as negative as most [of my colleagues quoted in the Fall 1978 issue of *Theater* devoted to American dramaturgy], more than most. That issue was initiated before I started the job here, and my predecessor forgot to answer or didn't or whatever. It just happened at the transition.

You know, there's no one . . . I think there is *one* person, Beth King [working with Artistic Director, Jon Jory, at the Actors' Theater of Louisville] comes to mind, as someone who *only* is a literary manager. And I don't mean that critically or sarcastically or anything else, but among all the other people holding this job, there are people translating, people writing plays, people teaching, or people publishing—a magazine in one case, or they're actors, or people writing criticism, and so on, blah, blah, blah.

Partly I think that's for a variety of reasons, among them that they're people with various talents, not all of which get used fully, just in the job. Plus, related to that, there are a lot of areas involved in the running of a division or program like this that aren't terribly fulfilling or interesting perhaps. And it's for financial reasons in some cases, too, obviously that people do other things. But it's also another outlet for an interest or a curiosity you're pursuing.

It's just something that a person [in this job] does. And I write criticism. I've had a thing in *The Times* in January. I'm writing another thing now. I have a contract for my book on Athol Fugard. I've written a lot on him for *Theatre Quarterly*. And there's a long piece, sort of 18,000 words, on regional theatre in the next issue of *Theatre Quarterly*.

*But you're surely not suggesting that this is not a full-time job, right?*

Oh yes, this is.

*It sure looks like a full-time job to me.*

Oh, yes, this is, you know, seven days a week.

*Leaving little time for the other stuff you mentioned.*

Not enough of it. I have a big problem handling it, so it's very frustrating. If you talk to other people, you find that there's a high level of frustration in this job, even for the most powerful literary manager, say, a literary manager whose taste and thinking are most similar to those of the artistic director he's working for, even in that case, wherever it is.

So the person is obviously hired for his opinions and his taste on the one hand, and although you're not reading solely for yourself, when you like things, you like to see that reflected in the work you do.

*So in defining what a literary manager does, we find discontent in what he does not get to do today.*

Maybe I'm not speaking for others, but I think there is probably a bit in all of us that would like to be dictators and have the power of veto, and say, "These are the five plays, the *two* plays, the *whatever*." Assuming it's a person who has certain convictions and aesthetics and ideas, I presume many of us would like to see them implemented.

I'm probably sounding a little egotistical, because at the same time there's a recognition that in my own case, at least, I am *not* a producer. I don't have a certain kind of understanding of audiences and so on.

I'm the resident highbrow, or the resident devil's advocate, which I see as part of my job, too. It's part of what I *should* be doing, I think.

So to the extent that we have strong convictions that we want to see implemented, when and if they are not implemented, that is a common frustration. That's common. It's endemic: no literary manager has, I think, as much say as he wants.

*Are you thinking of specific instances here at the Taper when you felt that your aesthetic principles were undermined?*

No, I don't want to sound like I'm complaining. Sure, as they say, there's no accounting for taste. And a single play read by five people will never have a unanimous opinion about it. And about the next play, we'll agree. In a sense, we are talking fairy tales, because it obviously is not mathematics with the right answers and wrong ones.

I would say there are plays I feel passionately about doing that haven't yet gotten on. But I wouldn't say that I've given up. If there's something I care about enough, I just don't give up on that.

As you know, I also worked for the Yale Rep for awhile. And one of the things I like about working for Gordon [Davidson at the Taper] is that he listens. He's not surrounded by sycophants. He cares about other people's ideas and passion and so on. So I don't by any means want to suggest that I'm not listened to. Theaters aren't democratic institutions and shouldn't be. And Gordon Davidson is probably the best person in the country doing what he does.

This past season we did six plays [as mainstage productions]. We did *I Ought to Be in Pictures, Says I, Says He, Children of a Lesser God*, and the two Lanford Wilson plays, which had been done previously. *Talley's Folly* was performed almost to the word the same as it had been previously, and with the original cast. But *Fifth of July* was done here in a fairly radically different version. I think Lanford [Wilson] said it was something like 60% rewritten, even though it had already been published. In a sense, it was a new play. But we also brought in the new play, *Division Street*. And of all six plays we did this past season, *Division Street* [Steven Tesich's new play, set in a pluralistic contemporary America] was the play that I most wanted to do.

It's something that we will continue to do and that I am in favor of. I think there's a kind of faddishness about new plays in this country that I am wary of. There was a time when regional theaters did not do new plays, either at all or certainly not to the extent that they do now. They waited for a play to be tested, probably in New York where selection of plays, I think, was a little less adventuresome than it is now. Although I think it can be more adventuresome yet.

I'm certainly applauding the willingness of theaters everywhere to stick out their necks. But the production of new plays has exactly doubled between 1966 and 1970, something like that. . . . I've talked about this for a long time. See just the numbers, how many new plays are being done now versus a few years ago.

*Are you suggesting that this sudden and dramatic rise in the number of new plays produced by regional theatres is part of a fad?*

I think there's a bit of faddishness in it, yes.

*How many new plays do you get a year?*

Here? 1,200, 1,300, something like that.

*Yet you think there's a dearth of good American playwrights.*

Oh God, yes.

But [on this topic] I'm schizophrenic. On the one hand, there aren't enough; on the other hand, there are more plays worth doing than any theater, this theater among them, can do. Even last year, say, when we did the Playworks Festival, we did—I don't know what the numbers were overall—maybe 19 plays in a year. And that is a large number of plays to be able to do. Still, there were other plays worth doing in some manner, maybe not main season, not in the lab, but *some* way, that we didn't do.

So the schizophrenia is, yes, there *aren't* enough good ones, but there are still ones that have certain merit, certain value, that you'd like to see done in some manner. But I'm not at all optimistic about the [talent out there]. I don't think we're overwhelmed with terrific writers.

*Are you suggesting that the Taper reconsider its focus on new American plays?*

[Vandenbroucke sighs.]

*This season at the Taper is dominated by contemporary American plays.*

Yes. And it has been historically. If you look at all the plays we've done, we obviously don't do the classics as much as the Guthrie or Arena or A.C.T. Since I've been here, we've only done *The Tempest.* John Hirsch directed and Anthony Hopkins played Prospero.

I don't want to sound like I have special access to the truth or "what this theater should be." I mean, my God, Gordon [Davidson] has done pretty damn well without my advice. I just want it clear that there's a difference in taste and personality between us, but I don't think this means lack of respect or appreciation one for the other. Certainly not in my direction.

I just want you to understand the tone of this: that at the same time in my own sense of myself, again, that self is schizophrenic. I mean, I am a critic. [But] I work for the Taper, and it's weird trying to write from another point of view, because in a sense to a reader I'm always perceived as a spokesman.

But in the *I Ought to Be in Pictures* program I wrote something called "Theater for the Eighties." It's almost like New Year's resolutions that will probably *not* be 100% something that Gordon would write.

*Now, to return to your sense of the "fad" of new American plays sweeping regional theatres . . .*

Yes, I would say I don't know about [it being faddish at] the Taper, but I would answer it generally as yes, there is a self-fulfilling prophecy that Americans don't have the classical tradition. We don't do the classics very well. Therefore, we don't try them very often. Therefore we don't do them very well. You know what I'm saying?

It's just an old idea. I think the interaction between the new and the old is very healthy for actors and audiences. And that's my sense of what theater should be.

I think as far as the faddishness thing, the Taper has been doing mostly new plays since 1964, before I would say it [doing mostly new plays] had become what I would now call faddish. When the American Place Theater was started, I think in '64 or '63, there was a need for a theater that said, "We will only do new American plays." I don't think there's a need for such theaters now, and there are now *many* that are primarily devoted to new work.

But there is another point about doing plays [at the Taper] that have already been done elsewhere: part of this [questioning of such a policy] is our American culture: "if it's new, it's better." We want "new, improved" soap suds and Tide . . . and everything. It's the old thing, which I call "the virgin-play syndrome": if it's been touched by one theater, it's verboten.

That's obviously absurd. But there was a time—and I think it's changing now—when the asterisk in the program and the summary at the end of the year that said, "We have presented these premieres," was the be-all and end-all. Well, it's pretty insane to think that a play is only worth doing if you can have your stamp on it.

And so back to the Lanford Wilson plays [*Talley's Folly* and *The Fifth of July*]. I very much approve, applaud, and encourage doing plays that have been done elsewhere. And I don't see that as refuting or going against the interest in the plays.

*The Taper is sometimes described as a "playwrights' theater." Is there a "family" of playwrights, maybe Susan Miller, Ted Tally, Michael Cristofer, Luis Valdez—as there are, say, playwrights at the N.Y. Shakespeare Festival—whose plays are assured a home here?*

Is a family defined by more than one offspring? No? If we do the second play does that make the person a part of the family? I don't know. There are people we commission. We haven't done an Oliver Hailey play in several years. We've only done one by Ted Tally [*Terra Nova*]. We've commissioned him to do another. Michael Cristofer's play [*Black Angel*] will be the fourth of his that we will do. I'm sure we'll do another Luis Valdez play in the future. So sure.

I don't know how much to make of that. Every theater does it and it's expected. You begin relationships with actors or directors or designers. You like their work. They like working with you. And bonds get created. It doesn't mean that they're exclusive, that they're monogamous or whatever, but yes, there is a sense of appreciation for a person's work and vice versa.

*Does the Taper get very involved in developing plays by resident playwrights, with Gordon Davidson, like, say, Joseph Papp at the N.Y. Shakespeare Festival, getting actively engaged in helping shape the work-in-progress into a mainstage play?*

I can't imagine plays being produced any other way. In other words, playwrights are always in residence here. Usually from the point of casting on. Usually throughout the entire rehearsal period and the entire preview period. Sometimes someone has other commitments and other projects going and it's a split focus.

There is a statement that I end up making in every single colloquy and I'm sure that people are tired of hearing it, but: We unfortunately still tend to think of playwrights primarily as writers rather than as wrights. You know: shipwrights and all of that.

*Yes, so "wrighting" can continue throughout the rehearsal process here. Richard Schechner subtitled his essay on Megan Terry "The Playwright as Wrighter."*

Oh really? No, I don't know that essay. Well, it's the same thing. And you know, from Thespis on up, most playwrights have been involved in the nitty gritty. They're not up in a garret somewhere. The garret playwrights are the exception. I always feel like I have to explain this to the public, because they want to know what changes happened [during the rehearsal process].

Changes are *de rigueur*. Some plays go through more radical changes than others. Some plays are transformed more than others. I can't conceive of this not happening unless it's not a very good theater. And it has nothing to do with respect for writers—pampering, as it were. If you respect them so much that you can't broach the problem with the last scene or whatever, that's ridiculous.

So it should often be the case that the text might undergo some unknown transition. It should be the rule rather than the exception. I suppose I should do a production casebook for a show here some time.

*While the Taper is widely considered a "playwrights' theater," even more specifically, it is known for its focus on "indigenous" playwrights. That is, it aims to be a regional theater in the purest—most literal—sense of the word: an L.A. theater.*

Yes, with Luis [Valdez, author of *Zoot Suit*], that was the most clear instance of a repeated desire by Gordon to be what you stated about regional theater. We're housed in L.A.

And the reputation that I haven't exactly heard voiced or seen in print, but that *will* happen after this season—given that four or six shows will be done in New York and one has already been there—is "Ah, that Taper, it's producing things with its eye over the shoulder." In fact, *not*. It's nice when that happens, but this is our home; this is where we work. And with the bicentennial of L.A. coming up season after next, it's probable that we'll see another play or several plays that are very indigenous.

There's no ongoing group of [local] writers working here, but there are a number of writers with whom we have had past relationships whose scripts we would probably want to hear. In other words, we do readings of plays sometimes without any thought or concern over whether or not we're ever going to do them ourselves. We do them to let the writer hear his play. We do that frequently.

We did *Jazz Set* in Playworks last year, a Ron Milner play. We've done two of his plays. He also had a commission this year. We've been on the brink of doing something with the Negro Ensemble for a couple of seasons . . . we were going to do *Home* [by Samm Art Williams], but that was picked up for the New York production so that fell through.

We're always reading plays, so we're more accessible to unknown playwrights than many theaters now in the country. A lot of places have kind of shut down their operations for logistical reasons: the "risks-and-reward ratio" or whatever.

*Earlier you said you receive 1,200 scripts a year. Who reads them all?*

My associate, Marion Barnett, is the first reader for 90% of them.

*What percentage does she pass along to you?*

I would say I probably read about a third or a quarter of the plays.

*And they're mostly wretched?*

(Pause. He laughs.) Yes.

*What's wrong with most of them? What makes them not worth producing?*

This will sound like a glib answer, but: they're not original and they're not imaginative. American theater always has been—and, God forbid, maybe always will be—dominated by a certain kind of family realism that I personally find mostly very boring.

Plays go in cycles. Death and dying has been killing us for the last four or five years. And plays about the handicapped: disability plays.

And there are certain constants. There are barroom plays, which are plays that throw together a group of people. It doesn't necessarily have to be a bar. There was one just today, people stuck in an elevator. Anyway strangers thrown together.

You can take it to a certain level. Who was it who did the analysis of the twelve plots that exist, or was it 22? I mean, take it far enough, and how many different plays did Shakespeare write? Four?

But still, it's easier for all artists to imitate rather than to do something on their own. I think one of the bad legacies of the 1960s has been a lack of concern for craft, which is partly [the basis for] my feeling about "the new-play fad business," and for my desire or wish that there was more attention paid to the classics. It's not just for their own sake, but I think it would have a good effect on writers to see models other than the current ones because they [the current models] haven't been particularly instructive.

Now, Richard Nelson is one of the more interesting writers in the country. And he's done three translations that I know of now and is working on a fourth. There may be some others that I don't know about. And aside from his personal interest in that, it's had a terrific consequence on his own writing. I think that would serve a lot of writers.

*There is a third characteristic usually attributed to the Taper. We've been talking about how it is widely identified as a playwrights' theater, and as a center committed to promoting indigenous artists. Ever since its production of* **The Trial of the Catonsville Nine** *in 1971, the Taper has also been widely per-*

*ceived as a theater with a social conscience, interested in produc-*
*ing plays that focus on social issues.*

Yes, there have been a series of those plays . . . Hampton's
*Savages* . . . Sure, Gordon has that reputation.

The question is: how valid is it? It is, and it isn't. We just did
*Division Street,* which some people have called jingoistic. It's sort
of a quandary. On the one hand, you don't want to be a "mish-
mash theater" that doesn't stand for anything, where you do a
little bit of this and a little bit of that, a couple of classics, two
serious ones: middlebrow programming.

On the other hand, most theaters—most directors, most
actors, most writers—don't want to be so limited, so typecast,
that they do only one kind of play. The interesting thing about
Michael Cristofer, and the new play of *his* that we've been doing
[*Black Angel*], is that he never repeats himself. "Never" is an
exaggeration, but he's a writer with considerable range. At least
as wide as the four plays he's done.

*Would you characterize Tesich's* Division Street *with the adjec-*
*tive you just quoted, "jingoistic"? Or do you just see it as a very*
*pro-American play? Or is it related to the traditional emphasis on*
*drama as social commentary at the Taper?*

Yes, it is very pro-American. Sure it is. It's hopeful. . . . That's
what Steve [Tesich] thinks about America.

Now you ask the question, "Does the Taper agree with it; is
that the way we saw the play?" The question is: does that [the
play's point of view or "message"] reflect the Taper?

To consider it theoretically, you choose a play and then you
want to see it realized on its own terms. For the sake of argument, let's say that whatever its statement about America, it was
not the same as mine or Gordon's. When a play makes a
particular statement of whatever kind, I think you still want the
play to be on its own terms.

There might be cases where you wouldn't choose a play
because it didn't coincide with your own preconceptions and so
on, but once you do [choose to produce the play], then you
want to see it realized artistically, not socially or politically or
anything else.

*Walter Kerr once likened a regional theater to a "cultural Howard Johnson's." Do you define regional theater differently? Do you consider the Taper a regional theater?*

The term regional theater is oftentimes used synonymously with nonprofit theater. And a third of the nonprofit theaters in this country are in New York City. Probably none of them consider themselves regional theaters.

There are many differences between the Public Theater and the Circle Rep, and there are many differences between the Long Wharf and Yale Rep. But basically in many ways they're similar, and their physical location has nothing to do with much of anything.

I don't consider regional to be a pejorative term. I don't consider regional theater equivalent to parochial theater. There's plenty of bad theater in New York as we all know. And if you made a list of the designers and the writers who work here, and if you gave it to someone who's on the moon, saying, "These are the people that work here. How is the Taper different from another theater?", they would find differences, but I don't think the differences would be related in any way to geography.

*One would think that geography could play a part in casting at the Taper. With Los Angeles as your location, you might expect American film actors to work onstage here, much as British film actors like, say, Albert Finney, still perform at the National Theatre.*

Yes, in a sense, but none of them is the equivalent of Albert Finney. The conclusions to be drawn from that have to do with the state of acting in American culture: namely, that until, you know, Marlon Brando! . . .

There's a great difference in the American tradition versus the British. Most actors learn their craft in the theater still, but until very recently, American actors did not have a tradition or an inclination or a willingness to return to their roots once they made it. Whereas for a long time Olivier and those folks would go anywhere [at low pay] to play [onstage] in London.

Geography plays a part because the centers of the three [entertainment] industries in England are all in the same place. Whereas here [in America], the centers are 3,000 miles apart.

. . . And theater is probably more important in British society than it is here. Until recently, the number of actors—of whatever the equivalent of Albert Finney is in this country—who continue to work for theater were very few: Meryl Streep and Michael Moriarty and Al Pacino—

The point is that Marlon Brando's generation did not [stay active as stage actors]. There are exceptions: George Scott has stayed active. Helen Hayes prefers the theater. [But] there was a generation that was much more interested in getting out of the theater and staying out forever.

And obviously, regional theaters don't pay very good salaries to actors. So they have to supplement that.

I don't have any argument with people doing both or all three [film, theater, and television] simultaneously. . . .

*I'm sure you're aware that some New York stage actors, transplanted to Los Angeles for T.V. or film jobs in the last decade [1970-1980], have tried to stay active onstage out here, establishing small theater groups of their own in L. A. William Devane was involved at the Matrix; Ralph Waite started the Los Angeles Actors' Theater; and one company was even called Actors for Themselves.*

Sure, there are a number of cases like that. . . . The Group Repertory Company [is another].

I do hope it [the abandonment of stagework by American film actors] is changing a little bit. Meryl Streep has done a lot of work for Joseph Papp [at the New York Shakespeare Festival]. Michael Moriarty did at least one show that I know of at Playwrights' Horizons. Kenneth Haigh spends seasons at Yale Rep. And Keene Curtis [appearing at the Taper in *Division Street*] is probably as good an actor as there is in this country. He's not a star; I mean, the public doesn't know him. But I can't imagine anyone playing that part better.

*Would you consider the Taper part of a "network" of regional theaters? What kinds of connections have you fostered with other regional theaters, especially in light of your interest in prolonging the life of exciting new plays and productions, regardless of which theater gets credit for the "world premiere"?*

Peter Nichols' *Forget Me Not* was done here after it had been done at the Long Wharf. They also did *Shadow Box* [by Michael

Cristofer]. This ties back to what I was saying before about sharing, and about the diminution of this [notion of] exclusivity and
of the virgin-play syndrome.

And yes, it is not exactly a regional network, but [there is] a
sense of sharing work, and the desire to extend the life of a
production. Theater is ephemeral but you certainly never can
accept that or live with it. We'd like it to live a little longer.

*Most regional theatres have a "second stage" for workshop pro-
ductions of unpolished plays-in-progress. The Taper seems to have
three second stages: The New Theater for Now, the Forum/Lab,
and the Improvisational Theater Program. What are the different
functions served by each?*

What we would like to have is a 350-seat flexible space where
we could do plays for runs of varying lengths. Right now we're
caught between 64 performances in the 750-seat house [the
main performance space at the Taper] and the Lab, our second
space—and we don't even call it our second stage—an 80-seat
theater. There are obviously a number of plays that aren't ready
for the Taper, or that are of a particular nature so that they just
are not right for it, and so on. So the Taper's "second stage" is
a myth.

[But] it's not quite a myth. I mean, we own the Aquarius
Theater in Hollywood [a 1,000-seat proscenium theater], and
there are plans to have this second theater there and have been
for a number of years. I think Gordon would say the most
pressing need of the theater is to have that other space.

ITP [the Improvisational Theater Program] doesn't really
have a home here per se. It tours schools. The *Christmas Carol*
we do at Christmas time is their production. They did a double
bill called *Bugs and Guns* in the Taper.

And New Theater for Now is a program rather than a theater. It's sort of the attempt to meet the need of that second
space as I just described it. That is, larger budgets, say, than Lab
productions, longer runs than Lab productions, not as long as
the Taper. A chance to serve a particular play at a particular
stage of readiness, and to expose it to a larger audience.

So for the Festival last year we used three theaters. We used
the Taper for four plays; we rented a theater in Hollywood for
four plays; and we used the Lab for four plays: two sets of one-

acts on a double bill. So we happened to rent a theater for those ten weeks.

But the physical theaters are just here and the Lab is in Hollywood . . . sort of near the Hollywood Bowl. . . . There's no money to build one [a lab], and I don't know where we'd put it [here, in this complex]. This idea of setting up a second theater has been fairly in the front of Gordon's mind for a number of years, and so a lot of different possibilities were looked into around town.

It would be nice to have a sense that we're all together. And it's one of the problems . . . that we're over here and the Lab is over there. . . . But that's our life.

*It sounds as if L.A. is just like New York, only wider.*

Gordon said when he moved out here, "Yeah, L.A.'s just like New York—without Manhattan."

*You've been here for about two years now. How has the Taper changed? What changes would you like to see? Where is the Taper headed?*

I think we will move a little more into the area of repertory in the next years as part of this interest in the classics. It's not that this [interest] has never existed. Probably in the thirteen seasons, we've done 10 or 15 classics or something like that.

I know Gordon has—in fact, I heard him repeat it again on Monday—long hoped for a permanent company of actors. There's a loose company here in the same way that the Long Wharf or the Public has a group of actors, many of whom have worked here more than once. But that's still not a company. I know that's a hope, a dream that Gordon has.

How has it changed? The other night after the play, a man came up to me and said he'd been a subscriber here since the very beginning. . . . And he just thought everything was so wonderful, especially the last two seasons. It was just "incomparable!"

So maybe I say that as a way of saying that instead of change, I think [we have achieved] more consistency. I think on the production side, you will seldom come to the Taper and see a play badly directed, badly designed, not ready. There's a certain professional consistency of a very high level, below which we don't sink. At least, we haven't in two years.

I don't mean this to be a whitewash or anything. There are plays I haven't liked, performances and directing jobs that have not been perfect. But I'm saying that—on a scale of one to 100—there's a fairly high level below which we never sink.

And I think that's an enormous accomplishment, given what I see when I go around from theater to theater. I inevitably return depressed about the paucity of good work that I see in general. I think of it as an interconnected organism: if the rest of the theater isn't healthy, the Taper can't be all that much healthier and vice versa. We're all kind of feeding off the same culture, off the same people, and so on. So I very much see it interconnecting. I suppose that's a "Trilling-ian" look at the relation between the society and its culture.

Generally, I have a pessimistic view. I look at the theater around me, and I'm not thrilled by the writing, by anything, *including literary management,* whatever that is. (laughter) I don't want to sound haughty but I have a fairly dark view, and maybe it's my being devil's advocate again, but generally I want more, I want better, I want—I'm relentlessly unsatisfied.

This is a bit of rationalization, yet I truly feel that, with the exception of opera, theater is the toughest thing to pull off because there are so many things that can go wrong and it's so difficult to get it all working together. So I guess the compliment I've just paid [about the consistently high level of production values at the Taper] is to Gordon, who got all of these different fingers and arms and limbs working reasonably well. This is not a mean accomplishment.

*Having listed some of the changes—both actual and potential—that have occurred at the Taper in the two years since your arrival here, would you mind shifting gears a bit?*

*What are some of the changes that you have undergone during your past two years as literary manager here, as the Mark Taper's critic-in-residence, or as you put it earlier, as the Taper's "resident highbrow"? And what are your hopes and expectations regarding the future of American dramaturgy in general?*

You know Eric Bentley's line specifically applying to critics: "None should persist at it for more than five years." Speaking just personally [about the state of theater in America], I don't really know how you can persist in taking something seriously that isn't very good. I think either you stop taking it seriously, or you don't persist for very long. (laughs)

But, it's sort of like Gandhi's comments about politics in India: no matter how much you oppose the government, as long as you are a citizen, you are responsible, you are part of the situation. And so—who was it that said that a critic has "the double impertinence of telling his betters what to write and of telling his equals what to like?" It's very easy for all critics to shoot from the hip, and it's just as easy to denigrate everything as it is to puff everything, which, in a sense, is the same sin.

I know that I tend to take a fairly disparaging view of what I see around me, and that that's fairly easy to do. It doesn't prove integrity.

*Are you suggesting that critics and dramaturgs have a limited productive life-expectancy before they burn out?*

Do I look burned out?

*No, you may still have a few good years left. . . .*

I think Michael Feingold has done it longer than anyone [in contemporary American theater], off and on. And while translating, directing, and writing his criticism at the same time. . . .

*. . . John Lahr was literary advisor at the Vivian Beaumont Theater when it was headed by Blau and Irving. . . .*

. . . And I think Ann Cattaneo's been at the Phoenix maybe three years. . . . [Awhile ago] Joel Schechter read plays for the American Place Theater. . . . Circle Rep has had a fairly rapid turnover. . . . And Steve Lawson was at Circle in the Square for less than a year. You could do a kind of statistical [analysis of a dramaturg's life-expectancy in the job], but first of all, it [this job title, literary manager in American theater] hasn't been around that long. Maybe it's [just] a problem of the people that are still doing it, because no one knows how long they're going to last.

So the answer is yes, I think we have a short life-span. I don't think anyone grows up wanting to be a literary manager.

1980

**Dramaturgs in America: Six Statements**

### Jonathan Alper
Literary Manager at the Folger Theatre Group,
Washington, D.C.

The Folger Theatre Group devotes itself exclusively to Shakespeare and new plays, in equal measure. In my several seasons as literary manager/advisor at the Folger, I have found that my attention has been focused, in different ways, on both kinds of theater.

If, as I believe, literary managers are primarily either playwrights, critics, or directors, I fall into the third category, bringing to the work the strengths and limitations of a director's point of view. Reading through the mountain of manuscripts submitted to the Folger each season has been one of my chief duties. (This work has now largely been entrusted to Bob Stevens, my co-literary advisor.) Because of the volume and widely variable quality of the scripts submitted, I read quickly, for sheer "producibility." My criterion has to be, "Does the Folger want to produce this play *now?*" The play reports which went into the theater's files offered a brief appraisal of the quality and stageworthiness of the writing, but direct responses to playwrights had to be limited to expressions of interest in further work, or simple rejection. The limitations of this situation have been frustrating for all of us at the Folger, restricted as we are on the subscription series to two or three new scripts a season. (The Folger's catalogue of new plays includes Tom Cole's *Medal of Honor Rag,* Jack Gilhooley's *Mummer's End,* Chris Sergel's *Black Elk Speaks,* and Israel Horowitz's *Mackerel.*) We hope to be able to start an active studio for work on new scripts as soon as space availability permits. The theater normally has a fairly sizable *ad hoc* company of actors on call for the classical work; and if, as seems likely, approximately twenty percent of the scripts submitted are worth further work in an unpressured, exploratory atmosphere, both the playwright and the theater could benefit. Working with playwrights, outside of a production situation, is the logical extension of the literary manager's job in a theater devoted to producing new work, and the studio work we have already done on a limited basis has been very rewarding.

As a director, I have strong feelings about the kind of new script I would want to work on, and undoubtedly this has colored my response to the scripts I have read for the Folger. I am drawn to playwrights with a sharp sense of verbal rhythm, and a spare, resonant theatricality—qualities found to some extent in four plays given their American premieres at the Folger: Storey's *The Farm*, Bond's *The Fool*, Canadian poet Michael Ondaatje's *The Collected Works of Billy the Kid*, and David Hare's *Teeth 'n' Smiles*, the first three directed by Theatre Group Producer Louis Scheeder, the last co-directed by Louis and me. I respond strongly to the direct, clean, concentrated theatricality in these scripts (although, as a matter of interest, Hare describes his work as "florid" in comparison with Bond's); and it is with these plays that I have probably been at my most useful as a sounding-board for the director.

Shakespeare production at the Folger presents wonderful opportunities to anyone doing preparatory work on the text, since the theater itself is an adjunct of the Folger Shakespeare Library, one of the world's leading Renaissance research institutions. The Library has centuries' worth of prompt scripts of all the plays, along with acres of collateral source material and criticism. I have worked on the texts of two of the Shakespeare offerings of the past seasons, which I didn't direct myself—*Henry V* and *Midsummer Night's Dream*—actually preparing a working text for the former, with cuts, revisions, and transpositions. Recently, however, I have begun to have reservations about the value of this kind of preliminary work on another director's text. I am coming more and more to believe in the value of working from an uncut text, in rehearsal at any rate, shaping the final text through direct work with the actors. But beyond this, I have found that any cutting or revision one does on a classical text presupposes a particular point of view and production concept: one is in essence choosing a particular line to take, narrowing the possible meaning to be communicated. This is ultimately a director's work. I know that on the four Shakespeares I have directed at the Folger over the past three seasons, this text work has been an essential part of my own preparation. The more one works on Shakespeare, of course, the more one develops the specific verbal sensitivity demanded for a full understanding of the plays. I can easily imagine a co-directing situation, where a literary manager/director would conceive a production with another director, preparing the text alongside preliminary design work and casting, the two then staging the production in tandem. This is, after all, a fairly common practice in Europe—it has been accepted as standard procedure at Britain's National Theatre—though perhaps it is not quite as common here. It seems to me that such a mutual shouldering of responsibility is inherent in the dramaturg's preparation of the text.

A special kind of public relations work has also been part of my job at the Folger. This would perhaps not be quite as important at a theater which specializes in what might be called the standard modern texts, as does our neighbor Arena Stage—their season started off this fall, for example, with *The National Health* and *The Caucasian Chalk Circle*. I have felt that our combination of classical work and often unfamiliar and difficult new work called for some direct attempt at explication, through program notes and the subscriber newsletter, as a way of clarifying our intentions in the choice of material we produce. We find that the responses of our subscription audience, exposed to a some-times rigorous and highly verbal diet, have developed along with the theater itself. In effect, we are working towards a cross-fertilization between the classical work and the new scripts, striving to enrich our response to one kind of theater with the sensibility we develop in working on the other. This has really been the major theme of my work as literary manager at the Folger.

1978

## André Bishop
Former Literary Manager at Playwrights' Horizons,
New York

I'm grateful for the opportunity to be forced to define a job that, at the moment, I intuit more than I understand. My academic background for the job is only respectable: I rely on my instincts and emotions more than on whatever I have inside my head. One thing I know: I don't see my work as being *passive*. Reading plays, writing recommendations, and passing them on to an artistic director is only the beginning. I'm an *activist*—part of this is my personality, my early training as an actor—part of this is the highly-charged atmosphere of Playwrights' Horizons.

Most people who have some brains and a definite feel for theater can read a new play and respond to it. I don't see reading and evaluating plays as a big deal. The next step—what to do with that play and, more importantly, that playwright—is harder, and varies from play to play and author to author.

I've been given the opportunity at Playwrights' Horizons to function both as a dramaturg *and* a producer, and I see the role as one. I can't imagine it any other way. To produce Off-Off Broadway in a working atmosphere is a different sort of producing. We are concerned with the process and the experience for the playwright—though we are aiming for a result, we're not overly concerned with "results." Still, I involve myself as much with the public airing of a play as I do with the text. I work closely and personally with every playwright whose work I like, but I find that if a play is actually to be performed I spend more and more time with the director. I get angry when directors misinterpret or, worse, uninterpret a playwright's world, contenting themselves by just throwing everything up on the stage and hoping it comes out all right. If the play fails, it's usually the playwright who gets blamed, and often playwrights, especially young ones who have limited experience seeing their work produced, don't know that the play is being ruined or are afraid to speak up if they do.

I'm happy if the director has found the play's basic meaning, and if the style and rhythm and all the other production elements evolve organically from that base. This sounds simpleminded, but how many times have we sat through plays in all kinds of theaters where we weren't even given that! I'm of the school that believes in having the playwright around all the time, and I tell young directors that if they would only get to *know* the playwright they are working with, chances are they will find a lot of clues right there to give them the meaning and style of the play.

I try to bring the text of a new play up to a certain point—and then it has to take off in the open with actors and an audience. And *then* we go back to work. I try to give the playwright an overview of the full (and hopefully limitless) potential of his script, and I try to impress young playwrights with the importance and excitement of writing for the stage, of work that is uniquely of and for the theater. I'm always on the play's side and usually on the playwright's—the two don't always go together—and I find that I act as a nurse, father, confidant, teacher, dictator, diplomat, pushing and pulling in order to realize onstage what used to be just text. Curiously enough, I find that I use more of every part of myself than I ever did as an actor.

I never force my opinion down playwrights' throats. Bob Moss [Director of Playwrights' Horizons] and I think we know what we're doing, but we don't believe we have all the answers. In the theater, there are no answers, really, and in a way, knowing that makes it easier and gives you a certain calm. Bob often talks about the times when playwrights have rewritten their plays for him and come up with something far worse than what they started out with! I can say, however, that most every play I take on I treat as if *I* had written it, and my involvement is emotional and intense. Of course, there are plays and writers I can't hook into, and there are some playwrights I've worked with who are miles ahead of me and I can't keep up. But, because Playwrights' Horizons is a workshop theater, a way station and a breeding ground for new writers, I'm open to everything. I have to be.

Everyone today is talking about being "developmental." Some theaters are and some are not. Sometimes I feel people use this theme as an excuse when the work isn't good. "Developmental" to Playwrights' Horizons means focusing in on a writer and a play and "developing" by stretching and refining a particular talent as a voice for the stage.

Certainly interest in new plays and playwrights is enormous at the moment—theaters all over the country are clamoring for and, though few of us admit it, competing for the brilliant new American play. Some theaters are interested because they see future funding as a result; others because they want a Broadway hit; others because presenting new plays and working with writers is their only interest and what they do best. But everyone is "looking." This frantic atmosphere, while a wonderful thing for the playwright, creates a problem for producers and artistic directors *and* dramaturgs in terms of defining the identity of their theaters. What the hell are we all really up to? Does simply producing new plays mean we are developing writers?

One of my readers told me the other day that he felt like a scavenger—constantly stewing about, looking for good plays to devour. The image is unattractive, and I told him that I refused to think that way. I feel that if Playwrights' Horizons ever comes to the point where we need playwrights more than they need us, it will be time to close. I don't mean that the theater doesn't desperately need writers in order to survive and grow—obviously. And obviously, playwrights need productions. But if the need for the developmental process is ignored, and my only function as a dramaturg is to quite literally hunt for plays, well forget it. The dependency must be mutual.

I don't think of my work at Playwrights' Horizons as one of give and take—the playwright gives and I take. No. The playwright gives and I give. God knows there are days when I feel exhausted and drained from reading play after play and gearing myself up for yet another supposedly fresh, insightful meeting to discuss a playwright's work. I lose my sense of self. I occasionally get defensive and think dark thoughts about pushy playwrights having to have only one or two scripts in their heads whereas I have at least a hundred. But this martyrdom is idiotic and fleeting. These are the givens of my job and I love them.

1978

## Oscar Brownstein
### Director of the Iowa Playwrights' Workshop,
### Iowa City

When I was asked to take over the playwriting program at the University of Iowa in the fall of 1971, I had two vague notions to guide me: that the absurd separation between the playwriting program and the Iowa Writers' Workshop should be ended and that I should create a program that would provide what I had wanted when I was a playwright at the Yale Drama School (class of 1960). I cite this unmatched pair of goals because they had a great deal to do with why the dramaturgical function was conceived as essential to this program, why that function was defined uniquely here (I gather), and why it branched out into several distinct forms.

In truth, there was another relevant element in my thinking, of which I was fully conscious only in retrospect: that in the decade between my M.F.A. in playwriting and my initiation of the Playwrights' Workshop I had become an historian of the Elizabethan theater. It was to the conditions of the Elizabethan theater that I automatically looked for clues to a fertile environment for playwrights; as dangerous as that is, intellectually (because it is necessarily speculative and therefore admits the possibility of circularity), one must operate from models of some kind, take premises from somewhere, and the world offers no proofs except the doubtful ones of the pudding. If playwriting cannot be taught it is apparent nevertheless that it can be learned by someone with the requisite talents—whatever they are. I wanted to create, so far as I could, the conditions which would foster that development.

The dramaturgical concept here grew from considerations that were at once "political," pedagogical, and idealistic. Joining with the Writers' Workshop created a need to establish immediately a clear distinction between literature and drama and (especially in light of my experience at Yale) to remove any possibility that playwriting would be perceived as essentially a classroom exercise; moreover, there was a need to reassure the Theater Division faculty that the new joint program was not the beginning of a drift by the playwriting program away from the theater as a university establishment or as an art form. I thought it necessary to provide continuous opportunity for relevant experience in the theater for the playwright; but at the time the playwriting program had no independent production capability (as at Yale in the fifties and early sixties, production of original plays at Iowa was largely at the pleasure of student directors in the M.F.A. program), and it was neither likely nor desirable that a playwright would put on a series of playscripts one promptly following the other. Finally, with a mixture of bitter memory and optimism that something more functional could be devised, I was determined to avoid the time-consuming and essentially irrelevant use of playwrights as gophers, clumsy stagehands, and inadequate technicians that was practiced at Yale and Iowa—rationalized as basic training that would make a theater man of the effete playwright.

It was to the role of the dramaturg that I looked for a truly relevant extension of the playwright's experience in the theater. Even the ways that the dramaturgical and playwriting roles differ seem to be instructive, because in his role as a dramaturg the playwright achieves a degree of objectivity toward the work in rehearsal and performance that he could not have toward his own work. The playwright-as-dramaturg can see the play more as an expressive form and less as self-expression.

At Iowa the dramaturg is used as a surrogate for an absent playwright, except that he has no power to veto; he advises the director in everything regarding the script and he is responsible to the director for executing all matters related to the script. It is usually the director and dramaturg, or those two with the designer, who first begin hammering out a production concept. The goal is to give the production the immediacy of an original script (need I say that goals are not always achieved?) and to make everything from concept through script, casting, costume, etc., a seamless whole. Aside from editing the script (cuts, finding the best translation or making one), the dramaturg may provide bridges (including the writing of an ending for an Elizabethan play that no longer has one), work as a play doctor (providing a frame for a play, a new scene, or, more often, trimming as well as pointing lines), and give the director recommendations for a strategy or an analysis of the play, a scene, a speech. The dramaturg attends rehearsals at regular intervals to afford the director the benefit of an inside/outside perspective. When it is an original or new play, the dramaturg's area of concern remains the same, but, of course, his work becomes almost entirely advisory and mediative.

In my experience it is the student directors who accept the notion of the staff dramaturg most easily; and in general the stronger the director (more confident, more creative) the better and more fully he makes use of his dramaturg. However, with faculty directors and with professional directors no such clear pattern has emerged. Not surprisingly, there are problems of established habits and attitudes, and sometimes, despite clear definitions of roles, the dramaturg is perceived as a threat to the director's authority.

Usually the playwrights work as dramaturgs, first with student directors, then with directors from the faculty (or first with student-directed one-acts, then with student-directed full-length productions); in their third year in the Workshop there is usually an "internship" as a dramaturg with a professional company. Not all playwrights are given such internships; not all playwrights, even good ones, are effective dramaturgs, and not all effective playwright/dramaturgs are temperamentally capable of going off to a strange theater and fitting into that organization. And, of course, not all professional companies are suitable places for such internships—how often I have heard professional literary managers complain that *they* are not permitted to function as dramaturgs in their theaters; much less would an intern be permitted to do so.

Back in 1973 I began to try to push for a national dramaturgy program in which promising young playwrights would be subsidized for half of their salaries to work at professional theaters for up to three years. I saw this as having several educational values (to educate theaters to employ dramaturgs, *real* dramaturgs, and not just script-readers or resident intellectuals; and, of course, to provide playwrights with experience in the theater, a professional connection, and the income needed to keep them in the theater and accelerate their development), and I saw it as something potentially capable of transforming the American theater, because I have seen how the general quality of productions is improved by the participation of a dramaturg, and I have also seen playwrights' skill and sophistication grow as a result of dramaturgical employment. A grandiose ambition. Despite some interest here and there in various theaters and an occasional foundation, the project never flew. It is somewhat easier to perform social engineering in an Iowa cornfield than in the boardrooms of major foundations. In general, and correctly, the notion of the playwright-in-residence is seen as a costly failure, and the staff dramaturg is erroneously seen as a mere variant on that.

I'd like to think that some day no theater company will be considered complete unless it has a playwright/dramaturg, but, meanwhile, I'll cultivate my cornfield.

1978

### John Lahr
Former Literary Advisor at the
Guthrie and Vivian Beaumont Theaters

I have been Literary Adviser to two theaters, the Tyrone Guthrie Theater in Minneapolis and the Vivian Beaumont Theater at Lincoln Center. Both jobs differed as a result of differing personnel. At the Guthrie, my job was primarily to bring plays to the theater and do the program notes. I split my time between New York and Minneapolis for about six months. It was a schizophrenic experience, made worse by a truly destructive and obtuse business manager turned artistic director, Peter Zeisler, who effectively blocked the good work of Mel Shapiro and Ed Call as well as whatever play-acquiring I did. And I did bring a lot of new work to Minneapolis—although the playhouse for "experimental plays" didn't have the facilities or management-enthusiasm to really develop in that area. I brought Arthur Kopit's *Indians* to the theater, for example. They were scheduled to do it, but Zeisler finally refused to do the play because Arena Stage was going to mount an earlier production, thereby ruining the Guthrie's chance of getting a review from Clive Barnes and *The Times*. So much for the responsibility of the theater to the community! (And so much for the whole idea of regional theater.) In Minneapolis, there was still "an Indian problem." I learned a lot from Mel Shapiro and Ed Call. And some of the plays I brought to the attention of Zeisler were finally done, most especially S.J. Perelman's *The Beauty Part*. But Zeisler was not really interested in an adventurous repertoire. He was uncomfortable with ideas. And the company's morale, as well as my own, grew low.

At Lincoln Center things were different. Jules Irving was a much friendlier, theater-wise, and receptive director. Jules is a survivor; a father of four; a poker player—it was fun and often difficult to work for him. I'm sure he also found it difficult to work with me. But in New York, where I was writing criticism and starting to write movies and novels, I had more independence from the theater and also more involvement. Jules let you make the job what you wanted. I wanted involvement but not absorption into the Lincoln Center Team. That's what I got. I worked on the productions with various directors, the most rewarding work being with John Hirsch in *Beggar on Horseback* and *The Time of Your Life*. At Lincoln Center, I wrote lyrics for *Beggar*; did an adaptation of Molière's *The Misanthrope*; brought new work to the theater including John Ford Noonan's *The Year Boston Won the Pennant,* Pinter's *Landscape* and *Silence,* Shepard's *Operation Sidewinder.* I got Jules to take options on plays by Joe Orton (*The Good and Faithful Servant* and *Funeral Games*), Robert Coover, Ed Bullins. I also wrote program notes and did general advisory work. It was a much more satisfactory involvement in theater, although, in the end, being Mr. In-Between was profoundly unsatisfactory.

Obviously, the artistic director has the final say about what gets done. He is team captain; and if he is good, he lets everybody get a time at bat. If they fail to produce, they don't play as often . . . Sometimes there was a plan. I would bring Jules plays—like Heathcote Williams' *AC/DC*—that he just could not get with; sometimes he would do a play to give one of the handful of actors from the San Francisco Workshop a meaty part downstairs that they weren't getting upstairs; sometimes it was the availability of a Big Name which got a production cooking, and sometimes—as with *Scenes from American Life,* which was an embarrassment to me and what we'd been trying to do downstairs at our little theater—the production was chosen by the Business Manager, Alan Mandel, who thought it was commercial. He was right. It was nominated for a Pulitzer Prize and got the best set of notices of all the new work we mounted. In Jules's case, the decision to do a play was the result of a long, continuing dialogue among the director; Bob Symonds; his wife, Priscilla Pointer; Mandel; and myself. The former had all been with him in San Francisco and I had joined the family. Jules chose his plays like a poker hand, trying to get the strongest suit and only occasionally drawing to an inside straight. While I was there, *Sidewinder* was the gamble that failed. I think the subscribers were scandalized and many of them withdrew their subscriptions . . . Sometimes, as with *Narrow Road to the Deep North,* Jules thought he had a winner because Barnes had liked it out of town, only to find that his high card was misplayed. Bond's play bombed.

Lincoln Center gave more than lip service to new work—a fact often overlooked by its critics. To Jules Irving's credit, he did do Bullins, Havel, Handke, Pinter, Shepard, Bond. He may not have served the plays well, but somehow, in the curious chemistry of the theater, some new avant-garde work and some new American writers (Dizenzo, Noonan, Cowan, Shepard, Bullins) did get performed in front of an audience suspicious of anything that wasn't certified KULTUR. Upstairs in the main theater, the formula was certain: three classics and one "new" play. This formula could be altered when a star wanted to play in something special (Anne Bancroft and Frank Langella in William Gibson's silly camp about Shakespeare . . .)

Cost defeated most productions at Lincoln Center. A three-week run downstairs was about $60,000 and upstairs, although I have no hard facts, I would guess between $150,000-200,000. Rotating repertory, therefore, was patently uneconomical. And even the new work reflected the economic pressure, becoming increasingly more reduced in setting and performers. There was no permanent acting company at Lincoln Center, although there were a handful of actors whom Jules had brought with him from San Francisco and whom he loyally cast in plays for which some felt they were perhaps ill-equipped. But this is how he and Blau had run the Actors' Workshop and the paternalistic posture lasted at Lincoln Center.

I left Lincoln Center to write novels and books. By the time I left, the "experimental theater" was running into such heavy debt that there were fewer new plays that could be chosen, and the cost made the upstairs choice of plays merely a game of

Drama 101. I mean the classics are all interesting, provocative plays. Anybody can stick their hand in the bowl and pull out a winner. There wasn't much use for me. We just kind of drafted apart, an affectionate divorce, rather than a real venomous bust-up, which the Guthrie was for me.

I think it's very important that theaters have a dramaturg, preferably someone who can combine his critical intelligence with practical theater work. In this way, he can contribute creatively to the stage as well as intellectually to the practitioners. The most fun I had was working on projects I helped create, with directors with whom I could have a dialogue. Critics have something to give to the theater. They need not be enemies. I found that because the managers and workers were forever locked in rehearsal on a ten-month treadmill of production they had no time to think, read, or see new work. They tried. But, obviously, they couldn't cover the necessary range. This is where a dramaturg can be of crucial importance: keeping the theater *au courant*; bringing in new work; offering a dialogue with the directors and management about what the play actually means; and also contributing his own literary efforts—whether songs, adaptations, or plays—to the theater. I don't think I've ever felt more pleasure than hearing an audience laugh at something I'd written. Somehow, being part of a production as well as support for a production eliminated the inevitable alienation of forever being in a position of no risk. I also found—and I think this is crucial for the development of dramatic criticism—that once inside the theater in the role of dramaturg, one's language for the discussion of theater becomes more concrete, more vivid and devoid of the litcrit sludge which sinks most critical writing. Dramaturgical work sharpens your perception and your language. If theaters want better critics, they must open their doors to them. And find a way of making work for them inside the theater as well as outside it. It's the only way for both to grow. I think that critics must get their hands dirty; must learn about the craft from the inside so they can serve the art they purport to love.

1978

## Jonathan Marks
### Literary Manager at the Yale Repertory Theatre, New Haven

My case is different. At Yale we have what must be the highest per capita density of dramaturgs in the country.

First we have an artistic director, Robert Brustein, whose orientation is as much dramaturgical as directorial. Though before coming to Yale he had considerable experience both as actor and director, Brustein's expertise and reputation lay in the fields of dramatic literature and criticism. I would venture to say that in matters of repertory and aesthetic vision, the artistic director here has a greater stock of information, firmer ideas, and better-grounded or more thoroughly developed principles than any other artistic director I know of. They have been elevated, most of them, from the ranks of the nation's directors, so their expertise is in fields other than dramaturgy. I'm not saying simply that my boss is better than everybody else's boss; I'm just saying that he's a dramaturg by nature (though he might not admit it) and that this fact affects the scope of my work.

On the next level we have the Literary Management: not one manager but three; Joel Schechter and Steve Lawson work with me as Associate Literary Managers. (Our attention, I should note, is not unremittingly riveted to dramaturgy at the Yale Repertory Theatre; we all wear several hats. Steve is the artistic director of our cabaret, Joel whiles away his spare half-hours editing *Theater* magazine, and we all teach at the School of Drama.)

This tribe of chiefs, however, does not lack for Indians; we also work with fourteen students in the School's new program in Dramaturgy, the successor to its old program in Dramatic Literature and Criticism. One of these students is assigned to each production at the Rep and each major production at the School. I oversee their work and participate in it to a certain extent—the responsibility is ultimately mine as (if you will pardon the expression) *Chefdramaturg*—but I am keenly aware that I run the risk of limiting the scope and value of the students' experience if my participation is too active.

Another risk in this setup is that an artificial distinction may be created between the functions of literary manager and dramaturg: the literary manager seems to be the one who does whatever it is that I do, and the dramaturg seems to be the one who is attached to a single production at a time, working only with the director, playwright, and cast—the *Produktionsdramaturg*, if you will. In reality (and I assume that the creature we are examining here can be said to exist in the reality of the American theater) these functions are usually discharged by the same individual. The new program in Dramaturgy is being designed in order to train the students in the entire range of dramaturgical functions, but as of now they seem to be rather separate.

As Literary Manager of the Yale Rep, then, I am in a strange sort of squeeze—between, on the one hand, an artistic director who is, to say the least, competent in dramaturgy; and, on the other hand, a covey of dramaturgs-in-training who are developing their competency under my supervision.

Where does that leave me? First of all, it leaves me free to function in a wide variety of activities throughout the School/Theater complex. It leaves me in the curious—unique, I would think—position of being not only a theater functionary (or "office drone," as my friends would have it), and not only a full-time faculty member, but also a part-time or utility actor at the Yale Repertory Theatre. This tends to keep me from worrying about what to do with all my spare time. I do not see my acting, however, as entirely divorced from my functioning as dramaturg. The dramaturg, in my view, is not simply a remote literary figure who descends to bring the weight of his erudition to bear upon working professionals; he too is a professional, and one who must have some organic feeling for the processes of the stage to supplement and inform his intellectual understanding of the theater. Some dramaturgs are playwrights, some direct; I dabble in those activities, but more frequently I act. For a couple of years, as chance and the vagaries of casting would have it, I did not act, but I took up the tattered sock last season for Andrei Serban's production of *Sganarelle: An Evening of Molière Farces,* and realized anew the extent to which my work onstage is integral to my work as literary manager.

I believe that my renewed status as dramaturg-cum-actor—aside from being a personal thrill and an exercise in rediscovering the actor's process through work with an innovative, demanding director—has helped further to establish the *bona fides* of the dramaturg's profession, at least in our theater. A remote and powerful dramaturg, issuing *ex cathedra* bulls on the aesthetics of the stage, will not soon gain credence among theater workers in America, steeped as they are in the tradition of anti-intellectualism. As much as I oppose this native know-nothingism, I approach it as a given that must be rooted out gradually, painstakingly. The intellect of the theater must be championed, but not from on high; the dramaturg must be, in some sense, a fellow practitioner, respected by and respectful of those who put their art, their craft, and even their bodies at the service of the stage. He too must be willing to risk; only then will he be heeded.

1978

## Richard Pettengill
### Dramaturg at the Court Theater, Chicago

The way I've come to see my dramaturgical role at the Court Theater (a classical Equity theater at the University of Chicago) is as one who gathers information and ideas, then shares them with any and all who can benefit. My first step on a production is to do a body of research at the same time that I'm attending the early concept meetings. The research is often inspired or stimulated by these meetings, while the facts, images, and points of view I bring to them can affect the director's and designers' vision in turn. The most fruitful collaborations usually begin with a dialogue on the play with the director, which ideally continues throughout the production process. For example, during preliminary discussions on *Hedda Gabler* with director Susan Osborne-Mott, I raised the possibility that Ibsen broke off his correspondence with the young Emilie Bardach as a result of her naively stated fascination with "lur[ing] other women's husbands away from them." This heightened Susan's sense, she said at last spring's Chicago dramaturgy conference, of Hedda's line "I want—for once in my life—to have power over another human being. To change his destiny," and ultimately her sense that Ibsen could "deliver" women but did not understand them.

My set objective is to underscore and illuminate the production with the materials I present to the artistic team, and ultimately to the audience through program notes, discussions, and lectures. The program notes for British director Maria Aitken's production of *The Rivals* included a spread of eighteenth-century caricaturist Thomas Rowlandson's scenes of Bath social life, laid out in an off-kilter, topsy-turvy fashion to reflect both Maria's sense of the play as a "cartoonish" thing and set designer Ron Green's advent or calendar-like representation of Bath's Royal Crescent. The eight-page program also included an essay on the social milieu of Bath (by Maria herself), a compilation of references to Bath in the literature of the time, and an essay on the correspondences between Sheridan's life and the events of the play, capped by a list of recommended readings.

When I'm not putting the program together, I run the theater's outreach programs, which include preview discussions to get audience feedback, post-performance discussions led by special guests, lectures in the community, a high-school matinee program (for which I make school visits to prepare the students), and extension courses on the theater's repertoire. These leave me time to serve as production dramaturg primarily in the first and final weeks of rehearsal. In the early stages I often work on script matters, helping to clear up obscurities and ambiguities in difficult texts (What might "Ebenezer's bell" refer to in *Under Milkwood*?), or consulting alternate translations to aid the cast and director in exploring verbal options in a new version (Is there any precedent for using the word "vertigo" in translations of *The Master Builder*?). Lots of research requests come in the first week, when the director realizes gaps in his knowledge and needs information, or when the cast members request information to aid their preparation. I've sat down with directors and actors to discuss everything from the Platonic and Shelleyan roots of Edmund's fourth-act speech in *Long Day's Journey*, to the origins of Puck and the

fairies in English folklore, to the possible source of Shaw's
Mazzini in the Italian patriot who is his namesake. I've been
sent running for everything from an 1890s Bulgarian telegram
(*Arms and the Man*), to a 1920s recording of "Keep the Home
Fires Burning" (*Heartbreak House*), to pictures of Victorian
men's hairstyles (*You Never Can Tell*), to the melody of "Come
Back Paddy Reilly" (*The Birthday Party*), the last bit of field
research having been done at a local Irish pub over a pint of
Harp.

Returning to rehearsal in the final week, I can often be of
help as a more objective eye, making observations and suggestions to the director ("Sir Lucius' character reads differently to
me from the way I've heard you direct him"). I also moderate
the preview discussions, encouraging the audience to give us
any and all observations they have, no matter how miniscule,
since their thoughts are often incorporated into the show at this
stage. One previewer pointed out that the metal golf clubs on
our set for Shaw's *Misalliance* were anachronistic: they would
have been wooden in 1910. (A search was made for wooden
golf clubs, though in the end the ones we had were painted
brown.) At *Rivals* previews, Maria Aitken found out that American audiences need a slower beginning pace in order to get
acclimated to such a linguistically difficult piece, though she
decided to stick to her breakneck pace, citing the analogous
exhilaration of being kept at the edge of comprehension by a
modern British wit like Tom Stoppard. The audience's probing
led, too, to a thorough talking-through of what I ended up calling a descending order of reality in Maria's view of the play:
from the "cartoonish" set, to the "candy-shoppe" colors of the
period costumes, to the realistic quality of the acting. At a preview of *Endgame*, a gentleman in the front row exclaimed,
"Who is this Mr. Beckett, and why does he think this is a play?,"
at which point the director and I launched into passionate
accounts of the play's power and beauty. The same gentleman
brought a group of friends back the following week.

Throughout the run I bring in special-guest discussion leaders, such as professors from the University of Chicago and
other local institutions, and directors from the theatre community. Some plays suggest a specialized group of discussion lead-

ers. For *The Master Builder,* I invited a group of prominent Chicago architects to offer responses from the perspective of their profession. For *Long Day's Journey,* Artistic Director Michael Maggio of Northlight Theater came in to offer his thoughts on the play. We're finding that the most interesting responses to these plays often come from people who have a personal rather than an academic connection with the subject matter.

For each production we hold four weekday high-school matinees; we charge very little and we foot the bill for the buses. What with my advance visits and the study guides I prepare, the students are pretty well prepared by the time they arrive. Still, they often astound us with their insights. Following a matinee of *The Birthday Party,* we were trying to explain why it doesn't really matter that Pinter doesn't specify what organization Goldberg and McCann are from. One girl said, "Yes, it's better that way; you can fill in your own fear." After a performance of *Endgame,* we were saying that if there's any hope in the play, it's generational: Clov is still alive, and maybe the little boy will come in and serve him. At which point a little girl in the front row said, "Well, the people might change, but the pain's going to be the same." For us this was a distillation of what we'd arrived at after weeks of hashing through the script.

My own training for this job was not specifically theatrical: actually I'd never heard of such a thing as a dramaturg. I went to the Commonwealth School, Boston, then became an English major at Bates College with a special interest in drama, and wrote theater reviews for the school paper. During a year abroad at Oxford, I surprised my tutors with my study methods. I planned my Shakespeare tutorials around upcoming productions in Oxford, Stratford, and London, and analyzed the plays in terms of the productions. It seemed perfectly natural to me early on to reject the notion that classroom analysis of drama is at all adequate without reference to production.

Having finished my doctoral coursework and exams in English at the University of Chicago, I was offered the position of dramaturg at Court, which I duly accepted as soon as Artistic Director Nicholas Rudall told me what that was. Now in my fourth year, I feel positive about the profession's future, so long as the process of educating not only the public but also the theatrical community continues. My only misgiving is that some theater artists, be it out of ego or ignorance, will never open themselves to the benefits of the dramaturg's skills. Receptivity and collaboration are all. Of the twenty productions I've done at Court, my work has been the most vital, creative, and compelling (judging from feedback) on those whose creative teams have welcomed my efforts and made good use of my abilities. I'm not here to usurp, only to enhance. At best I can go well beyond the cynical notion that the dramaturg does the work the director is too lazy to do, to the magical point where the dramaturgically engaged mind, with easy access to mines of information, can contribute markedly to a director's vision and thus to the ultimate impact of a production.

1986

# Dramaturgy in Two Senses: Towards a Theory and Some Working Principles of New-Play Dramaturgy

## Towards a Theory of New-Play Dramaturgy

To work as a dramaturg on new plays, it helps to be a little of each of the following: theatre artist, critic, scholar of modern drama, therapist, conflict mediator, organizational consultant. Traditional definitions of dramaturgy take one of these roles and qualify it, calling the dramaturg, for instance, a "critic inside the process" or a "director behind the firing lines." While such designations are insufficient for the dramaturg who works on classical productions, they may nonetheless capture the nature of his main function on a project. For example, the dramaturg might serve primarily as a scholarly expert or resource, as an observer and critic of the rehearsal process, or as a textual or translation consultant. In contrast, while the new-play dramaturg might primarily give feedback on the rehearsal process, or consult with the playwright while he is writing, this sort of dramaturg tends to serve at least two or more functions—artistic, critical, organizational, therapeutic, and others.

This is so because the dramatic text and its maker—as well as the performance of the work—demand equal attention from the new-play dramaturg. If the writer is involved at all in the "workshopping" or production of his play, rehearsals will tend to structure themselves around not only the development of the play but also the creative and psychological processes that the writer is going through. These processes may not be the *focus* of rehearsals, but a writer's process can set their general tone and structure. Moreover, many new-play programs, at both the professional and university levels, are committed (or so many of them say) to developing writers as much as plays; in these situations the writer's process becomes primary.

Yet such programs merely emphasize the distinguishing characteristic of new-play development: the presence of the playwright in the collaborative process. In 1978 Arthur Ballet, one of the deans of American new-play dramaturgy, wrote: ". . . [Collaborators] do not adjust well to the playwright as a living organism and part of the process of making theatre; they prefer he show up at preliminary meetings and then on opening night."[1] Although the American theatre may have improved since 1978 in its treatment of playwrights, it frequently falls to the dramaturg to pay special attention to the playwright's involvement in the theatre-making process. The functions that the new-play dramaturg serves are defined by the nature of the writer, his writing process, and his involvement in the workshop or production process.

There are no generally accepted working principles of new-play dramaturgy; such principles are necessarily limited by the experience from which they are drawn. And yet, they are no more limited than, say, anthropological research is by the structure and nature of field work. The "field work" for the working principles that follow include new-play dramaturgy in a variety of professional contexts but mainly at the Iowa Playwrights' Workshop. The latter is a university context, and as such encourages experimentation with new work, as well as some probing of the dramaturg's role in the processes of writers who are either at the beginning of their career or who have taken time out from their professional lives to explore the nature of their work.

Behind the principles of any kind of dramaturgy lurks the question, How useful is it to theorize at all about dramaturgical practice? Historically, the same sorts of questions have besieged performance theory and its relations to acting, directing, design, and other elements of performance. The traditional answers to these questions have been, first, that theory by its nature does not *have* to be useful (or usable) to anyone or anything other than to theorists and *their* practices; second, that there is one kind of performance theory that *is* useful: the systematic approaches for actors and directors developed by such theorist-artists as Stanislavski and Brecht. Much theoretical writing falls along a continuum that runs from practical handbooks for actors and directors at one end to the virtually solipsistic mental pyrotechnics of post-structuralist theory at the other. (Stanislavski and Brecht fall somewhere in between.) But in the talk one hears from theatre professionals and theatre educators, the two ends of the continuum are repeatedly emphasized, as if there were a "natural" dichotomy between theory and practice, between "thinking" and "doing."

It's tempting for dramaturgs to subscribe to this dichotomy by asserting practical and non-theoretical principles, so that they will win the approval of practitioners. But if one purpose of dramaturgy is to "bridge" theory and practice; or, to put it in a less dichotomous fashion, to reassert the linkage between the theatre as a "seeing place" and theory as thoughtful observation, the dramaturg may be a facilitator of the processes by which the theatrical event comes to *embody* thought—and perhaps, in some productions, even theory itself.[2] In this view, the new-play dramaturg is, to borrow John Lutterbie's term, an "interventionist" in the theatrical process and whatever linear or non-linear paths it takes from the conception of dramatic ideas, to rehearsal, to on-stage embodiment.[3]

Few dramaturgs are aware that dramaturgy has a theoretical cousin in the social sciences, known generally as "dramaturgism," less frequently as "dramaturgy," and more broadly as "symbolic interactionism." Developed mainly by sociologists building on the "dramatism" of Kenneth Burke and the role theory and "frame analysis" of Erving Goffman, "dramaturgism" argues that social reality is constantly in the process of being constructed by and through human interactions, in terms of the symbolic values that human beings place on elements of those interactions. Moreover, the dynamics of these interactions are essentially dramatic and theatrical.[4]

The relation of this mode of thinking to the practice of dramaturgy is more than one of terminological coincidence. "Dramaturgism" has ramifications for the dramaturg's role in the process of developing theatre works from first conception through production. The kinds of questions that dramaturgs

regularly ask about their work—*How* should I intervene? In what
ways? *When* and *where*? And, above all, *why*, at this time?—naturally take the form of what Kenneth Burke called a
"dramatistic" analysis, which is one way of examining the
human construction of social reality. (Burke argued that a fully
conceived interpretation of human action is typically formu-
lated in terms of the questions "who," "what," "when," "where,"
"how," and "why"—the same questions that critics apply to dramatic characters.[5]) Dramaturgs think in this way partly because
the dramaturgical function is relatively new, historically speaking, and they tend to be self-conscious about how they interact
with other collaborators. But such self-consciousness can be the
basis for a dramaturg's work as a theatrical collaborator.

New plays arise out of the relations—psychological, emotional, creative, and otherwise—between writer and writing process,
writer and project, writer and director, director and play, etc.,
etc. (I use the word "project" here and throughout to refer to a
play that exists only as an idea, an outline, a treatment, or a
small fragment.) By regularly posing "dramatistic" questions not
only of himself but also of these relations, the dramaturg can
watch how they are affecting the making of the work, and can
intervene in them at crucial points in the creative process. Relations between playwright and writing process, director and play,
etc. inevitably force the project or play in a particular direction;
the dramaturg can observe and comment helpfully on both the
process and the work, at an intentional but not uninvolved distance from them. In short, the dramaturg can function as a
"symbolic interactionist."

The "symbolic interactionist" perspective is not the same as
so-called dramaturgical "objectivity"; rather, it's a usable awareness of the creative process. The dramaturg keeps one eye on
the work and the other eye on the process that makes the work,
neither interrupting nor making an incursion into the creative
process, but gently and persistently posing questions and making observations, with the intent of heightening everyone's
(including the dramaturg's own) sense of where the work
appears to be heading, what it is becoming and might become,
and the various ways in which it might be perceived by an audience. For example, usually the playwright cannot stand to be

too self-conscious about his writing; but the dramaturg can pose strategic questions or give feedback that stimulates just enough *active* self-consciousness to move the process (and the writer) in a particular direction. Similarly, a director might worry about thinking so conceptually that he will become paralyzed in exploring his concepts on stage. The dramaturg can try to stimulate the kind of thinking about the process and about the play that helps the director move from conceptual thinking to stage reality.

In one view, a "symbolic interactionist" perspective is Brechtian. Brecht said of epic theatre that emotion could not be excluded from it, anymore than it could be excluded from modern science.[6] As a "symbolic interactionist," the dramaturg strives for a rational and estranged perspective that doesn't subscribe to a belief of (false) objectivity, of non-subjective analysis. Armed with this kind of perspective, he can be true to "dramaturgy" in the original meaning of the word. He can "work the action," both of the play and of the collaboration; he can help the playwright to create the dramatic and aesthetic actions of the play, and can also "work the action" of the playwright's collaboration with the director and other artists.[7]

## Dramaturgy and the Writing Process: Working Principles

The history of dramaturgy in the United States has been partly that of dramaturgs justifying their work—and sometimes, it seems, their very right to be dramaturgs—in the face of skeptical theatre practitioners who treat dramaturgs as unnecessary appendages or, only slightly more benevolently, as library liaisons. This situation has improved as directors have become educated about dramaturgy and its uses. At the same time, in arguing for their profession, too many dramaturgs assume that all plays need a dramaturg, overlooking the first step in examining the relations among playwright, process, and project: determining whether or not a project needs a dramaturg, especially during the writing process.

This step doesn't exist in dramaturgy on classical plays, at least not in the same way. When the new-play dramaturg intervenes in the writing process, he comes into contact with the delicate and defensive measures inherent in a writer's intuition of what's "right" about his play's language, imagery, action, structure, and other elements. Theoretically, any developing play can benefit from dramaturgy, much in the same way that all human beings can benefit from therapy. But just as the effectiveness of therapy depends heavily on an openness towards behavioral change on the part of the patient, so the effectiveness of dramaturgy varies according to the degree of openness that exists in the writer, the structure of his process, and the nature of his project. Not all playwrights and plays can benefit from a dramaturg.

The question of whether or not a particular writer's process can benefit from dramaturgy needs to be answered in terms of his process and *his sense of that process*. This is not to say that the writer knows whether his writing will benefit from dramaturgy, but that directors, dramaturgs, and anyone else involved in initiating dramaturg/writer collaborations need to be sensitive to the relation between the writer's process and his project. There are three issues that need to be addressed here. First, in what ways might the project, considered alone, benefit from a dramaturg? (Research into and conversations about the world of the play? Conversations about ways in which the material might be dramatized?) Second, how has the writer worked on comparable projects in the past? (Slowly, producing one draft? Quickly, producing fragments that are constantly re-arranged? Slowly, but producing several drafts? Quickly, doing the same?) Third, in what ways does the writer want to use a dramaturg?

The answers to these questions are interdependent. It can be damaging to a writer's process for a dramaturg to proceed on the basis of answers to only one or two of the questions. Any project can benefit from a dramaturg, in ways outlined by the answers to the first question, but no amount of dramaturgical work founded on these answers will do any good if the dramaturg has no sense of how that work might affect the writer's process. Similarly, knowledge of the writer's process alone (i.e., answers to the second question) is insufficient, unless the dramaturg anticipates how the writer's process might affect the project at hand and its peculiar dramatic problems.

The question of whether or not and in what ways the writer's process is open to dramaturgical intervention differs from the question of whether or not the playwright wants a dramaturg (the third question above). Some playwrights think that they want a dramaturg when all they want is daily affirmation. Although such affirmation has its place, many playwrights who want it while they are writing are better off not having a dramaturg until the play goes into rehearsals (for a workshop or production), if at all.[8] In contrast, some playwrights write and rewrite in a manner that is predisposed to dramaturgy. They might do a great deal of reading or research, either before starting to write or while writing, and they might like having someone to help them "process" that research and its significance for the project. Other playwrights work in stages of intense self-reflection and rewriting, which alternate with each other. Although such processes are "open" to dramaturgy, the writer himself may be distrustful of dramaturgy or rigid about whom he will listen to. Further, he may simply be hostile to dramaturgs or to the very idea of dramaturgy. Nevertheless, such tension between an "open" process and a "closed" playwright can make for a creatively fertile tension, through which a dramaturg may be able to "open" the person by concentrating on the dynamics of his process.

Although it would be going too far to say that the relations among playwright, process, and project *determine* whether or not a project is "open" to dramaturgy, these relations can reveal the ways in which dramaturgy might be useful. Furthermore, these relations may also indicate whether or not a particular dramaturg's training, background, interests, and experience might serve a project (and process) well. There doesn't need to be a perfect marriage between dramaturg and project. Instead there might be healthy tensions—areas where dramaturgical background and training might bring new ways of thinking to a writer's process.

All the "dramatistic" questions that follow from whether or not dramaturgy might be good for a project—i.e., What? How? When? Where? Why?—are questions about the relations among that process, the playwright, and the project. Take, for example, the questions of how and when the dramaturg might intervene.

As we've seen, it's best to begin dramaturgical work with some knowledge of what the play might need (e.g., research, feedback on characters or structure, etc.), and with a sense of the playwright's view of his writing process and of what he might want dramaturgically. Of course, the most obvious time for the dramaturg to intervene occurs when the playwright's needs become clear and are acknowledged by the playwright. But if the dramaturg is in a position of having to judge when to intervene, he does best to wait for those times when his sense of what the play needs converges with intimations of how the work is progressing with respect to the playwright's typical ways of working.

For example, if the dramaturg knows that in the past the playwright wrote and rewrote and rewrote one scene or act or segment before proceeding to the next, and that he prefers such a linear way of working; and if the dramaturg anticipates that the play needs feedback on structure, then he ought to give feedback at a time in the process when several possible structures suggest themselves, as well as when talk of structure might make a difference in exactly how the writer proceeds. (Of course, all plays need to be viewed structurally. Whether or not the playwright wants to talk about structure, the dramaturg must become expert at anticipating those "openings" in their dialogue when structural feedback might nudge the writer nearer to his vision of the work and ways of accomplishing it.)

To take a contrasting example, if the dramaturg knows that in the past the playwright has written rough drafts quickly, and has a capacity to rewrite entire drafts in a short period of time; and if the dramaturg anticipates that the play will need feedback on structure, he might wait for a least two drafts to be completed, then read both of them and comment on the structure he sees emerging in or "between" them. He might also encourage the playwright to discuss how he envisions his play in relation to what's currently on paper—that is, in terms of how the drafts compare to the structure and effects the playwright is seeking.

Such examples could be multiplied endlessly, in terms of writing processes that proceed according to different rhythms and that employ diverse strategies (e.g., "treatments," outlines, scene exercises, as well as drafts), and in terms of various dramaturgical concerns. However, there is a principle that comes close to embracing almost all instances: the writing process tends to involve, first, thinking, dreaming, and imagining without writing; second, writing in some form (whether "exercises," outlines, or drafts); and, third, self-criticism. These occur rarely as consecutive stages; indeed, they seem to be more cyclical than linear in their occurrence. The psychic energy associated with one of them might be prevalent at any time in the process, and all three kinds of energy might be present all the time. (However, at certain points in the process one form of energy might be present in a peculiarly intense way.) By focusing on how these energies are at play in the writer's process, on the writer's sense of how his ideas for the play are or are not being expressed, and on the play *as it comes into being,* the dramaturg can seek out the times when thinking/dreaming and self-criticism may be turned meaningfully towards writing.

In this context, the basic principle of "how" to intervene in a writer's process is that the dramaturg should never confuse a critical diagnosis of what the play needs with an informed perception of the writer's vision and process, of the play in its current form, and of the energies that are influencing where the play is heading. For instance, there's an important difference between making comments to a playwright such as, "This character's through-line might be strengthened," and having a conversation about how the playwright envisions the character, and what he feels might still be done to express that vision. In this conversation, the dramaturg can try to determine how the particular energies at play in the writing process might be affecting the form and substance of the playwright's vision *as it is expressed currently* in the text. The "through-line" comment fails to take into account the writer, whereas a conversation about process focuses on the dynamic relations between writer and project, and process and evolving text. No matter how brilliant a dramaturg's textual comments are in critical terms, they can be paralyzing to a writer, leaving him with a set of notes that pokes holes in his work before it is even done. In contrast, comments that focus on process and evolving text can be energizing to a writer, putting him in touch with what he wants to do—with his options.

The basic principle of "when" to intervene is inseparable from "how": usually it's best to intervene when it seems as if the intervention might be energizing to the writer. The dramaturg who senses that it's the right time to intervene will do so with some options about *how* to do so in mind, based on his sense of what might best help the writer to channel his energies in creative ways, and to move the play closer to what he expects from it.

One practical effect of this approach is that it leaves the playwright, at the end of a dramaturgical conference, with a set of options, rather than with a list of critical notes on the text, as if it were finished. There will be times when such notes are unavoidable, but the dramaturg using a "symbolic interactionist" approach makes sure that there are forward-looking options on the list, as opposed to problems to deal with. Moreover, he is careful not to tell the playwright what to do—even what he thinks it would be best to do (at most, he suggests that Option X might be the best option). The dramaturg helps the playwright discover possible paths. The playwright must choose one and go down it, while the dramaturg may wait safely behind, awaiting some word of where the path has led.

How exactly does one arrive at options rather than critical comments? In general, options are arrived at by questions, questions, questions, tentative answers, and more questions—that is, by an essentially Socratic method designed to help the playwright develop a better sense of what he is after, and how he might achieve it. The substance of the questions will vary according to how the dramaturg's sense of what the play needs compares with what the writer thinks, as well as according to the energies at play in the writer's process. But by concentrating on questions and tentative conclusions about text *and* process rather than on textual comments alone, dramaturg and playwright can arrive at a variety of perspectives on the evolving play, and imagine how it might be perceived by an audience if it were being performed today. Comparison among such perspectives helps a playwright see more clearly what he is trying to do.

In the spirit of Ionesco's notion that all plays are detective stories, a Socratic approach restores mystery to the process of play-making, uniting dramaturg and playwright in a common pursuit of solutions to creative problems, and preventing preconceived solutions from forming and becoming "set" too early in the process. More important, the approach deflates the received idea of the dramaturg as someone who holds—or, even more damagingly to the process, *should* hold—the answers to all questions. It releases the dramaturg from the Olympian conceptions with which American dramaturgy has become burdened, such as that of the dramaturg as "conscience" of the process. It turns the dramaturg into a collaborator, with a function as necessary to the writing process as that of the director in the production of the play.

That function is, simply, to help the playwright maintain access to creative thinking, keep writing, and get more and more in touch with his vision. Towards that end, the Socratic approach is particularly responsive to the energies of thinking/dreaming, writing, and self-criticism. The approach *by its nature* forces both playwright and dramaturg to focus on the thinking and writing processes informing the play. It tends to move organically towards a sense of what might come next, either in the process or even in the play itself. And it tends to arrive at specific ideas about how to rethink scenes, characters, actions, structure, and language, or at writing approaches that might stimulate such rethinking.

Because it questions and investigates rather than judges, the Socratic approach helps the playwright suppress as much as possible his self-critical voice and make his thinking and writing less susceptible to that voice's tyranny. However, the Socratic approach doesn't disallow or deny self-criticism. Rather, the approach postpones self-criticism to times in the process when it might be more usefully heard: for example, between full drafts or at points of "rest" between intense periods of writing.[9]

## Dramaturgy and the Workshop or Production Process

These "symbolic interactionist" and Socratic approaches can be applied to workshop or rehearsal processes geared towards "play development." In these situations, the dramaturg's work with the playwright becomes complicated because it has to deal with the director's process and the director's relation to the play, as well as with the playwright and *his* process. Furthermore, the dramaturg must take into account a new aesthetic aim: the staging and performance of either the workshop or the production. (A less complicated situation is that in which a director provides the playwright with feedback while he is still writing a draft of the play. In this situation, the dramaturg's function is to help the playwright translate the director's feedback on the play into writing options, and to "square" it with his own instincts about the play.)

In the workshop or production process the dramaturg is situated uniquely to insure the play—and to some extent the creative (if not the psychological) health of the playwright—against that process. Bearing in mind the relations among playwright, process, and project that have gone into the making of the play so far, the dramaturg can keep himself focused on how the playwright is working, on where the play is going, and on what the play might still become; as well as on how each of these things is affected by the director's feedback on the play, the director's *way* of giving feedback, and the playwright's responses to the director's rehearsal process.

This is not to suggest that workshops and productions are inherently damaging to plays and playwrights, but rather that the rehearsal process is by its nature different from the writing process in important ways. Rehearsals can aid the writing process. In "new-play development" programs they are meant to do so: many such programs are predicated on the idea that theatre-making processes ought to be geared towards play-making (or even, as noted earlier, towards the making of playwrights). Still, anytime actors and directors are gathered together to create something to be read or performed, their creative processes will inevitably be propelled by energies, choices, and actions that anticipate the performed event, no matter how limited the production values of that event.

If theatre purists want to take nothing else from what is known as "performance studies," they should take the understanding that staged readings and workshops are *performances,* guided by performance-driven energies. Sometimes these energies force a play to become more focused dramatically and more articulate theatrically; sometimes they present dramatic and theatrical possibilities that the playwright hadn't previously imagined. (As dramaturg David Copelin has pointed out, there are discoveries that can be made only in extended rehearsals and dramatic values that can be communicated only in performance.[10]) But sometimes performance-making energies, not to mention the social energies in collaborations, run contrary to a play's dynamics, such that the results of a workshop or reading are at best a lesson in what to avoid in the future and at worst damaging to the play and to the playwright's (and other collaborators') morale.

These possibilities represent two ends of a spectrum. More typically, play-making and theatre-making processes affect each other in ways that are productive for both, while the playwright's and director's ways of relating to each other influence just *how* productive. Whatever the relationship among playwright, director, playwriting, and theatre-making in a given situation, the dramaturg can rely on the principle that writing and theatre-making are *fundamentally* different from each other, and that he might intervene helpfully in the points of contact and "gaps" between these processes. In workshops and productions, the questions What?, How?, When?, etc. point the dramaturg towards those points and gaps.

For example, consider a one-week "developmental" workshop designed to culminate in a script-in-hand staged reading. From the start the dramaturg in this situation ought to know that, first, the director imagines what this staged reading—or aspects of it—might look and sound like; second, that the playwright does as well. (One cannot assume that agreement at early meetings means that these imagined readings are alike.) Let's say that in rehearsals the director chooses to suggest certain critical movements and gestures, and that the playwright supports this approach. And then let's say that, as these gestures and movements take on their own theatrical life in rehearsals, expressing as they will tend to do the actors' early emotional and psychological impressions of their characters, they come to differ in physical reality from what the playwright had imagined. The playwright might then feel that certain aspects of the action, as he imagines it, are being misrepresented.

When and how should the dramaturg intervene? The answer depends on how the writer's and director's processes (not to mention the writer and director themselves) are affecting each other. One way to determine these effects is to focus on whether or not the writer's process has anything to do with how he is responding to what's going on in rehearsals. (This is a different matter from whether or not the playwright's response seems valid to the dramaturg.) For example, does the playwright's response reflect his uncertainty—or perhaps too much self-defensive certainty—about the nature of particular actions in the play? If so, do the director's choices ultimately matter, in terms of the play's development beyond the current workshop? The playwright might think of the director's approach as an alternate and valid method of staging, yet choose to rewrite parts of the play to strengthen his own sense of its "gests," to use Brecht's term. On the other hand, the playwright might feel that it's important for him to see the play the way he imagined it. Whatever the playwright's inclination, the dramaturg can help him see what his perceptions of the staging process have to do with the play and its development, and can assist playwright and director in arriving at an agreement (or an agreement that disagrees) about how the play will be represented in its current theatrical manifestation.

As with examples drawn from the writing process, these sorts of examples might be multiplied infinitely. While the dramaturg's goal during the writing process is to be sensitive to the thinking, writing, and self-critical energies at play in that process, his goal during the rehearsal process (for either a workshop or a production) is to remain aware of how those energies are being affected by and affecting the theatre-making process. The dramaturg is well-situated to help the playwright channel the theatre-making experience towards writing, to help him focus on how the play might be reworked after the workshop (or production) at hand.

Despite the fact that workshops and staged readings usually have a declared intention to serve the playwright and the play, the basic principles of new-play dramaturgy are more or less the same for both productions and workshops. Both involve the making of a performance event, the process for which can either help or hurt a play—or not affect it at all. Workshops and staged readings are supposedly designed to suppress production demands and values in favor of attention to the dramatic text; however, as we've seen, they possess the dynamics of performance events. They do not by their nature serve the play; they have to be made to do so.

In relation to a director, the dramaturg's chief task can be to point out when the workshop or production process seems to be failing that purpose. Usually the best way of doing this, however, is not to point out problems and failures as such, but rather to support those aspects of staging that seem to reveal the play; and only *then* to question, in an open-ended way, choices that seem less helpful, less revealing. If the dramaturg's work with a playwright is to intervene in his process, the dramaturg's task with the director is to help him see when and how his process seems to be illuminating or obscuring the play. In workshops and productions there is no such thing as *the* play, on which playwright and director can absolutely agree; there are only interconnected visions and processes, and the evolving representation of the play on stage. The dramaturg can reinforce the ways in which the director's vision seems to serve the play, discourage those which do not, and help the playwright see how the director's work, although it might contradict the production in the playwright's mind, sheds light on what the play is or might still become.

The main difference between workshop and production dramaturgy is that, in the former, the dramaturg can focus on the playwright and the play, whereas in the latter the dramaturg might have to divide his attention between writing and production concerns. Still, in the production process the dramaturg also does well to help the playwright focus on the play, and moreover to help him work through the ramifications of non-verbal production elements—physical staging, design, etc.—for the play's further development. Such elements tend to take on a life of their own in rehearsals and in production, and may open several prospects on the play. The dramaturg can help the playwright sort out those meanings and what they signify for both the play and his writing process. For instance, does the staging present the playwright with images that lead to new lines or speeches or scenes—or images—that ought to be written into the text?

Such concerns are sometimes best relegated to discussions following the first performances, when the concerns can be dealt with after the pressures of an opening. Often the playwright's self-critical energies are at their most intense at this time, making the dramaturg's continued involvement with the play crucial. (This is true immediately following workshops as well.) At this time the playwright's "inner critic" might be carping the loudest, and the dramaturg can help him turn the carping into creative options and plans for future revisions. Also, at this time the dramaturg can free himself to become a critic, one who "writes an open letter" to the playwright, creating a way of thinking critically about problems, solutions, the next writing phase, and the workshop or production as an experiment, now completed and in the past, that has produced findings about the play.

## Dramaturgy and "the Autonomy of Play"

In one of the finest theoretical statements about the nature of production dramaturgy, Helmut Schäfer speaks of the dramaturg as a theatre worker caught inevitably between, on the one hand, systematic and speakable ideas and, on the other hand, the inarticulate autonomy of "play" that goes on (or ought to go on) in rehearsals.[11] In intervening in the playwright's relations to his project (or play) and process, as well as in the director's relation to those things, the new-play dramaturg tries to stimulate the playwright's own "play" in his work. Sometimes he does this through the discussion of concepts, but at all times he strives to translate concepts into bases for creative action, and to interpret the results of that action in terms that can be liberating to the writer, rather than reductive or paralyzing.[12] The dramaturg can do this by focusing on the relationship between *how* and *what* a writer is writing; between this and what the writer yearns to write; and between all these things and the workshop or production process's effects upon them. Such a focus is not a guarantee of dramaturgical success, but it is the special province of the dramaturg, defining him as a necessary collaborator who is central to the art of making drama.

1994

# Notes

1 Arthur Ballet, "Playwrights for Tomorrow: The Work of the Office for Advanced Drama Research," *Theatre Quarterly*, 8, No. 29 (1978), p. 15. This same essay appears in abbreviated form in *Theater*, 9, No. 2 (1978), pp. 41-44, under the title "Fifteen Years of Reading New Plays: Reflections on the Closing of the Office for Advanced Drama Research." Ballet is of course talking about a traditional collaboration, in which a playwright writes a play that is in turn staged by a director. The present essay focuses on this kind of collaboration. Dramaturgy on new works created in alternative forms of collaboration is a separate subject that would have to be treated on its own.

2 To place the idea of a production as an embodiment or fulfillment of a play in its historical context, see Marvin Carlson, "Theatrical Performance: Illustration, Translation, Fulfillment, or Supplement?" *Theatre Journal*, 37, No. 1 (1985), pp. 5-11. The dramaturgical principles outlined in this essay can be applied to any of the theoretical approaches that Carlson discusses.

3 John Lutterbie, University Pre-Conference, Annual Conference of Literary Managers and Dramaturgs of the Americas, June 5, 1993.

4 For a survey and bibliography of "dramaturgism," see my "Political Dramaturgy: A Dramaturg's Re(View)," *The Drama Review*, 37, No. 2 (1993), pp. 56-79. Also see Dennis Brissett and Charles Edgley, "The Dramaturgical Perspective," in *Life as Theatre: A Dramaturgical Sourcebook*, eds. Brissett and Edgley, 2nd ed. (Hawthorne, New York: Aldine de Gruyter, 1990), pp. 1-46.

5 See, for example, Kenneth Burke, *A Grammar of Motives* (Berkeley: Univ. of California Press, 1969) and *A Rhetoric of Motives* (Berkeley: Univ. of California Press, 1969).

6 Bertolt Brecht, *Brecht on Theatre* (New York: Hill and Wang, 1964), ed. and trans. John Willett, pp. 93, 101, 140, 145, 173-174, 227. The Brechtian connection is no mere illustration: Brecht's "epic theatre" is designed to provoke awareness, in a symbolic interactionist way, of the *processes* by which social reality functions.

7 "Dramaturgy" derives from the ancient Greek "dramatourgos," which combines "dramat" ("action") and "ergos" ("work"). I'm indebted to Geoffrey Proehl of Villanova University for pointing out this root meaning of "dramaturgy" to me.

    David Copelin has spoken similarly of the dramaturg as maintaining an "informed subjectivity." See Copelin, "Ten Dramaturgical Myths,"

*Callboard* (Bay Area), June 1989, p. 7. Reprinted in *What Is Dramaturgy?*, pp. 17-23.

8 Cf. Edward Cohen's (misguided) notion that the dramaturg's "overall function" is "to hold the playwright's hand through the process. . . ." See Cohen, *Working on a New Play: A Play Development Handbook for Actors, Directors, Designers, and Playwrights* (New York: Prentice Hall, 1988), p. 32.

9 For my ideas about this approach to dramaturgy, I'm partly indebted to James Leverett, whose work I observed at the Iowa Playwrights' Workshop in the fall of 1990. Leverett spent a semester provoking Iowa playwrights towards clearer and deeper senses of their work, without ever *pronouncing* (it seemed to me) a critical judgment. Nevertheless, astute critical discrimination underlay every one of his probing questions and comments.

10 Copelin, p. 5.

11 Helmut Schäfer, "On the Necessary Non-Sense of Production Dramaturgy," *Theater*, 17, No. 3 (1986), pp. 57-58. "Theoretical considerations . . . have to gain a consciousness of their poverty in relation to artistic processes. . . . One experiences the autonomy of 'play' whose independence eludes the systematic, an autonomy which, compared to the conceptual, offers an instance of irrationality which cannot be grasped in words."

12 Cf. Lars Seeberg, "From Analysis to Production: Dramaturgy," in André Helbo *et al.*, ed., *Approaching Theatre* (Bloomington: Indiana Univ. Press, 1991), pp. 183-184. "The role of the dramaturg . . . is different from that of the external critic. He must not completely immobilize the intellect but apply his analysis non-reductively, attempting to analyze actively, opening instead of stiffening, explosively and not implosively."

# The Ghost Lights of Our Theaters: The Fate of Contemporary American Dramaturgs

Carol Rosen

I have a bleak news flash for would-be American "dramaturgs" and "literary managers," those students who still think that these terms are job titles rather than oxymorons. First, keep in mind that the dramaturg is probably the only member of the American university-theater production team who gets that esoteric joke in the opening sentence of this essay. And second, an opening sidebar: the dramaturg is also probably the only member of the American university production team who considers the dramaturg to be an indispensable member of the production team.

For a brief time, roughly spanning the era from the Vietnam War until the 1980s, universities spawned a glut of perpetual students transfixed by art. As always, graduate programs drew young scholars destined for academic careers, apprentice professors seeking graduate degrees in drama and in the sister arts for the traditional reasons: they were transfixed by art, impassioned with ideas, and devoted to teaching and to writing about theater's duality, its simultaneously ephemeral and eternal nature.

But for a while enrollments in graduate humanities programs were swelled by another kind of student. In the era bracketed by the Vietnam War at the start and by a plummeting economy at the end, a cultural phenomenon, a fad, emerged: the slacker generation, seeking escape from the world of clocks and calendars, found refuge in the oasis of academia. Tempermentally ill-suited for the academic careers toward which they were propelling themselves, but even more ill-suited for sensible, button-down lives, a whole generation of artists *manqués* went mind-surfing, perpetuating idealism, seeking secular salvation—and inventing jobs, too—in the areas of art and experimentation.

So while surplus French scholars whipped out their passports upon graduation and boarded planes, seeking to eke out a living abroad by leading tourists around quaint European villages, American theater intellectuals instead headed backstage and into the rehearsal hall, hoping to get hired as learned tour guides intent on a mission to fuse criticism with art, to influence the very cultural history about which they theorized.

As a backstage pass, they flashed their advanced degrees and expertise, as well as their most persuasive credential: their potential to match their European counterparts' well-documented contributions to the shape and felt meaning of modern drama. In the tradition of the revered European "production dramaturg," these freshly minted American dramaturgs-cum-literary managers would function as the director's right-hand *doppelgänger*, a visionary conscience and voice for the theater.

It all seemed to make sense. Everybody seemed slated to win on the deal. Theaters gained cachet as performance think tanks. And critics gained access to the inner circle of theater, the space in which plays are prepared and rehearsed in private. And then, to paraphrase O'Neill's most ominous curtain line, "We were all so happy . . . for a time."

Why did it go awry? What caused the severance of the ties between American regional and non-profit theaters with their dramaturgical converts from thought to action? And how did the profession of American dramaturg get catapulted in record time from high-profile trend to inside joke?

****

The simplest answer is that the dramaturg on the payroll was simply a fad that ran its course. As in all marketing strategies, a need had been invented, and then a way to fulfill that need profitably had been engineered to appear on the scene. In a classic mutual backscratching move, the whole enterprise offered considerable financial benefit to universities in tuition dollars, while the standard degree requirement of "internship at a professional theater" resulted in a steady stream of cheap or even free labor being supplied to theaters for apprenticeships.

When hard economic times hit, they cut deeply, both into the budgets of non-profit theaters *and* into the enrollment figures of graduate programs that had started to turn out "professional" dramaturgs. Budget cuts invariably target luxury items first. So, no wonder that the house dramaturg was clearly seen as more expendable than anyone else on the payroll, surely more expendable than anyone performing a hands-on production job vital to getting the show up, like, say, carpentry, or stage management, or acting, all of which require talent, training, and skill.

Some dramaturgs had already gained excellent reputations to trade on, of course, some as itinerant theatrical trouble-shooters, "script doctors" to be called in as consultants, while others made original and creative contributions to their home-base companies, particularly in the areas of repertory selection, script development, textual analysis, community outreach, and historico-critical research for production "concepts." But plenty of other dramaturgs had, by now, worn out their welcome, with their quirky tastes in plays and with their garbled patois of theater language and academic jargon, which was at best distracting and at worst intrusive.

When government subsidies tapered off, companies whose work was characterized by experimental styles or by potentially controversial subject matter found themselves positioned atop a First Amendment powder keg. And that powder keg was located squarely in the dramaturg's office, where the avant-garde and new-play development had been cultivated. No longer committed to supporting avant-garde experiments or to subsidizing the development of new plays, government agencies pulled back from arts spending, thereby denuding theater programs championing high-end esoterica or coaxing revisions from potential Eugene O'Neills. The government's preemptive strike, trumpeting its responsible spending and its "family values" to the arts community, coincidentally rendered dramaturgs and literary managers, the respective shepherds of such theater programs, obsolete.

Literary managers and dramaturgs across America felt the
tides shift. Budget cutbacks invariably targeted their offices, yet
business went on as usual. Seasons got chosen, plays got
mounted, contemporary American audiences continued to
encounter and even sometimes, perhaps serendipitously, to
embrace drama.

****

For a long time, this had been the idea: an American national
theatre, modelled after the Comédie Française, or the Berliner
Ensemble, or the Moscow Art Theatre. Certainly, American
theatre artists had been dreaming since Eugene O'Neill first
made us aware that American plays could be called dramatic
art. They had been dreaming of such a home base, at once a
museum and a laboratory, a steady job and a series of new
adventures, all housed under one roof filled with sympathetic
companions.

After World War I, the Provincetown Players, led by George
Graham Cook, Susan Glaspell, and the great designer Robert
Edmund Jones, emerged as what was in essence, though not in
name, of course, a dramaturg's hothouse, in which several
adventurous playwrights, inspired by Continental experiments
in style, thrived. Foremost among these playwrights was O'Neill,
then the young expressionist.

The Depression-era Group Theatre, devoted to Stanislavski
and to social reform, drew *its* youthful power from the charismatic leadership of Lee Strasberg, remembered with a mixture
of love and dread for his sharp eye and his sharp tongue, and
for his uncanny ability to catch every false note played before
him, relentlessly drilling actors with his mantras of public soli-
tude, intense concentration, sense memories, and given circumstances.

The Group Theatre was kept afloat for about a decade thanks
also to Cheryl Crawford's savvy as a producer, as well as to the
populist appeal of resident playwright Clifford Odets' gritty dialogue and melodramatic situations of compromised ideals.
Again, though no word like "dramaturg" was ever invoked, one
did in effect function. It was the great Harold Clurman, whose

chronicle of the Group Theatre's *Fervent Years* still stands as a model of how at once to document and poeticize the voyage undertaken by a collective whose destination was to fuse art with ideals. Clurman's text is a dramaturg's case study of a distinctly American theatre company, its conflicts, controversy, principles, and profits.

After World War II, the Actors' Studio inherited the puritanical acting style developed by the defunct Group Theatre. Heading the Playwrights' Unit, Clurman continued to encourage works-in-progress by Norman Mailer, Edward Albee, Michael Gazzo, and James Baldwin. The Studio "developed" new plays, and its emphasis on American naturalism gave rise to our own Chekhov: Tennessee Williams, who had the good luck to have his plays served in production by his own controversial Stanislavski: Elia Kazan. When a huge slum was demolished on Manhattan's West Side and Lincoln Center was constructed in its place, the Actors' Studio was certain that the time had come to fulfill that long-held hope and promise of an American national theater.

But meanwhile other efforts and hopes in this direction fizzled, while classic repertory companies simply continued in their mission to deliver the classics in solid productions to middle America. Examples of such ambitious, large-scale commitments include companies once headed by Tyrone Guthrie and Eva LeGallienne.

The Vivian Beaumont Theatre was never offered as a home base to the Actors' Studio, an "oversight" which puzzled Lee Strasberg for the rest of his life. Instead, the space has turned out to be the "hot potato" passed down along a whole string of outstanding artistic directors, each of whom bets he can turn it into the home of a National Theater of America. Among those who have been thwarted by the Vivian Beaumont, the "sword in the stone" of American theaters, are Jules Irving and Herbert Blau of San Francisco's Acting Company, Joseph Papp of the New York Shakespeare Festival, and Gregory Mosher of Chicago's Goodman Theater. Most recently, André Bishop, former head of Playwrights' Horizons, is at the helm, facing the challenges of filling the cavernous space and meeting the endless expenses run up by this white elephant of "kulture," located closer to the neon products of Broadway than to the real danger of the Off-Off Broadway avant-garde.

But we *could* argue that the quest for an American National Theater has had a happy ending, although a somewhat different ending from the one we had in mind. I would suggest that our national theater does exist, and it is not modelled on the Comédie Française, and it emphatically does *not* employ dramaturgs. If this is of any comfort, it tries to avoid hiring actors, too. It employs "imagineers" to build and control "animatrons."

I am, of course, identifying Disneyland as our de facto National Theater. Disneyland is the only place in America where I have stood in line for over two hours, along with 300 other smiling and patient ticket holders, eagerly anticipating a matinee. The entire "Magic Kingdom," a paradise of ersatz emotion and state-of-the-art stage technology, functions as our National Environmental Theater.

****

Generally speaking, then, here is where the strategy went awry (assuming there *was* a strategy for changing the entire structure and organization of American theater): instead of following the real tradition of their Continental and even pre-World War II American models (as I have just been sketching them), and carving out a particular niche for themselves—with concrete, tangible value to their theaters—these would-be American dramaturgs went straight for the ersatz trimmings that come with the territory. They lost sight of the horizon, too, glibly churning out result-oriented, generic mission statements, and too frequently backing away from their essential function, that of advocate.

Instead, preening occurred. No sooner had all these dramaturgs appeared on the scene, than they were all instantly busy making their presence felt and heard. It was like that scene at the school playground in Hitchcock's *The Birds,* when a nice, idyllic landscape suddenly turns ominous, crows perched and pecking everywhere. All these dramaturgs were instantly busy congratulating themselves on how much they could contribute to the future of American theater, zealously scribbling all over strangers' hopeless scripts, as if they were plumbers tackling a leaky faucet. Before you could say de-construct, interdisciplinary graduate degree programs in dramaturgy proliferated, resulting in even more sites where dramaturgs, pretty much ignored by practitioners of other theater arts, could confer, network, and hobnob among themselves, interviewing each other for the biannual journals in which they published their manifestos and mission statements.

Cut to the chase, i.e., to the operating budget of a non-profit regional theater, being pored over like the Dead Sea Scrolls by a desperate artistic director who is looking to cut corners. How can someone be necessary to the life of your theater if that person's function is inexplicable, let alone unpronounceable?

****

Some saw it coming. Some say it was over in a flash.

When they first arrived on the scene, dramaturgs had been full of hope, envisioning the vital role they could play on the production team. Sports metaphors abounded. Here are some: heady with a sense of themselves as potential coaches to the American theater team, dramaturgs became high-visibility public spokesmen for their organizations; some functioned as cheerleaders for their theaters; others operated as Monday-morning quarterbacks.

Here is another sports metaphor: at football games, sports commentators analyze strategies in miked banter throughout the game. How far could the logic of this model have led a high-profile dramaturg/critic-in-residence? Why not create a booth for the critic, analogous to the announcer's box above the football field, and let the in-house critic talk both before *and* during the performance, not just after the curtain falls and we all go home.

Then, with ominous regularity, dramaturg jokes started to surface and make the rounds.

At regional theaters, repertory companies, non-profit theaters all across America (and all these theaters overlap, too), the literary manager's job description is "resident highbrow." And as all highbrows know, in today's populist America, where it is the height of fashion to romanticize grunge and to scorn abstract discourse, at best this epithet is a term of grudging admiration and affectionate disparagement; at worst, it is a hostile sneer, an Artaudian act of aggression, a word hurled like a brick.

Another joke: the dramaturg is the Blanche DuBois of an American theater company. Noisy, opinionated, splashing poetry and literary allusions around like French perfume, she is perceived as a loose cannon living in a dream world and threatening the status quo of realism, holding things up by reminding everyone that the name of the streetcar is a metaphor, that the name of the last stop is an ironic mythological reference, and that the flower seller is a symbolic *memento mori*, whatever that is. The dramaturg is a pesky phantom of Stanley Kowalski's cultured nemesis, the dreaded "English teacher," the loopy wet blanket who spoils our fun.

American theater never did get past this idea of the dramaturg as dour researcher, the annoying expert with rigid opinions about pronunciation, period costumes, and sacred author's intentions:

> Actor to designer: How can you spot a dramaturg?
> Designer to actor: He's the one who knows where the library is.

Literary managers were sources of amusement, too. The post-Beckett generation of American playwrights was flourishing, and there was the related rise of Off-Off Broadway as well as the proliferation of non-profit regional theaters. With the advent of playwrights such as Albee, Lanford Wilson, Guare, Kopit, Terry, then Shepard, Rabe, Mamet, Norman, Henley . . . came a hope for the next O'Neill. Every brochure of every theater included in its forthcoming season a much heralded NAP (new American play) TBA (to be announced). The dramaturg now became a potential theatrical Maxwell Perkins, euphemistically called the "literary manager," scanning, speed-reading, fiddling with scripts that avalanched the office. A literary-manager joke:

> Designer to actor: How can you spot the literary manager?
> Actor to designer: He takes the playwright to lunch.

This impulse towards euphemism and redefinition was understandable. The word "dramaturg" itself has always been as offputting as are its muddy parameters of meaning. Sounding scatalogical enough to send undergraduates into uncontrollable guffaw-fits, it always sounds as if it includes a slur on scholars as "turgid." If dramaturgs are such whizzes at translation, always on the trail of *le mot juste* or always trying to come up with the perfect adaptation of Molière into colloquial Americanese, how come we never got around to translating our own ugly job title? Directors are not called *régisseurs,* and that is, by contrast, a euphonious word. But in America dramaturgs remain stubbornly untranslatable. That should have been a clue.

Are you laughing yet? Here's a riddle:

What does the literary manager do?
He talks to visitors all day, telling them what a literary manager does.
And after the performance, he talks to the audience, telling them what
    the play did.

With its circular logic and its premise that the literary manager (a.k.a. dramaturg) is a dispensable, longwinded goldbricker, this conundrum is typical of all the dramaturg jokes (and believe me, we've got a million of 'em). It is grounded in the very real quicksand of translation and definition that dramaturgs, learned lovers of *le mot juste* and multilingual adapters and translators that they all claim to be, should have foreseen.

****

But, of course, we never saw it coming. This sudden gaggle of dramaturgs, high-minded and naively enthusiastic, was oblivious to theater politics and to the business side of the show, both of which privilege territorial and charismatic leaders who, as the old saw goes, can "take the stage."

There really are just a handful of major regional repertory theaters in America—among them D.C.'s Arena, Minneapolis' Tyrone Guthrie Theatre, the New York Shakespeare Festival at the Public Theatre, and Houston's Alley Theatre—where geography and architecture held promise for large-scale, long-range, wide-scope planning. On staff at such theaters, an American

dramaturg might have at first expected to find an ideal opportunity to champion "lost" classics, to develop new scripts, to cultivate new constituencies for a mainstream regional repertory
theater. That was the idea.

So considerable energy was brought to the challenges of
these new positions, which also offered some more prosaic but
equally daunting tasks: organizing staff and volunteers to
develop and present works-in-progress, sorting mountains of
unsolicited scripts, and administering community outreach
programs, in addition to performing other administrative tasks.
However, it was not long before the creative elements of the
position clearly took a backseat to the mundane ones. Dramaturgs spent more time writing grant proposals (often to support their own salaries) than they did reading scripts and cruis-
ing rehearsals. With ever dwindling funds and increased efforts
required to write grant proposals, the dramaturg found himself
counted among "administrative staff" and excluded from the
"creative team." In fact, administrative responsibilities have
turned out to be the mainstay of this position in American theater, and although the invention of the euphemism "intern" has
helped to generate a steady stream of volunteer undergraduate
and graduate grunts into the field, the creative perks of the
dramaturg's job have been drowned in a sea of paper and public relations. The joke used to be that the dramaturg was the
one who knew where the library was. But today the joke is that
the dramaturg is the one who knows how to use the word pro-
cessor. Unsolicited scripts and press releases are now routinely
routed to the Literary Manager's office.

Over the course of a few years, literary managers at major
regional theaters—that is, major players in the field appointed to
what looked like plum positions—would steadily lose their
ground and sense of purpose. This was due to three serious difficulties faced by dramaturgs across the board:

(1) the resistance to production dramaturgs by American
    directors;
(2) a lack of consistency in funding sources; and
(3) product-conscious subscription audiences.

While literary managers at small, experimental theaters were being let go, or being kept on at token freelance rates, their counterparts at major regional theaters steadily lost power and cachet, too. Feeling clout slipping away, dramaturgs complained. They formed new organizations with lively acronyms, and they held conferences dedicated to tracing the slippage in their clout and in their paychecks. They also held symposia, giving papers and arguing with each other about the definition of the word "dramaturg" as well as about the future of their "profession" in America. Whenever possible, they comforted one another with learned references to the European tradition and to the high regard in which their profession is held abroad. Meanwhile many sought speaking engagements at universities, where each told a version of the journey and fate of contemporary American dramaturgy. The next generation of drama students attended this series of alternately learned, woeful, and witty solipsistic speakers, and then they pieced together their own mythologized versions of this true story.

****

The news is finally this:

The dust is settling. Now the post-'60s fad of putting scholars on the payroll is winding down. Now the "resident highbrow" is sometimes given a more modest title, more accurately reflecting his peripheral though valued role in the structure of the theater company (i.e., literary advisor rather than literary manager; dramaturgy consultant rather than production dramaturg). Along with all the tattered and molding ephemera cluttering the attics of theater scholars, dramaturgs are obsolete, rendered superfluous by contemporary American theaters, where tight money and post-culture populist audiences have redefined conventional expectations.

Why blame theaters for the end of culture, and for the rise of a brave-new-world sensory post-culture? Instead admire their tenacity as they hang on, trying to hype the old scripts as newspeak, looking for plays that require small casts and one set, and still hoping for a razzle-dazzle hit that makes the audience feel as if the theater could offer what John Osborne once called "lessons in feeling."

Accustomed to instant high drama, formulaic plots, and potent images hyping every sound—turning language into a rhythmic ur-dialect, a word-music launched by fast and furious visual stimuli—the MTV audience has little patience and few spare entertainment dollars to spend on traditional evenings at the theater, delighting in the aesthetic machinations and social conventions of a dinosaur civilization. Given their druthers, they will choose to see special effects and "real" dinosaurs onstage at an amusement park or on the screen at the mall cineplex. And they can't wait for "virtual reality" to be more widely available.

So theater companies—a different breed of dinosaur—try to follow the survival formula. They try to fill the opening slot with a play from one of the following categories: (1) relevant or suspenseful [crimes and trials], (2) titillating [sex and violence], or (3) vaguely sci-fi [*Time Machine*-based flashback/flashforward]. Given these categories, it is no surprise that among the most frequently produced plays at American regional, community, and university theaters have been those which—like *Equus*, *Cloud Nine*, and *M. Butterfly*—straddle two or three of these surefire audience-draw categories.

Other belt-tightening strategies that nod to the "dumbing down" of American theatre include planning seasons around jobbed-in directors who pack plays and strategies for production in their back pockets; and targeting audiences through focus groups, special-interest (i.e., self-help) programming, and educational tie-ins ("You read the book! You watched the miniseries! Now see the play! And meet the actors, too!"). What can we expect? These are last-ditch efforts, noble even, in the face of dwindling budgets and even more dwindling attention spans.

With the lifeboat, triage strategy in place, the dramaturg's dispensability is no longer even debatable. Budgets, audience preferences, and directors' skills being what they are, only a lunatic artistic director would keep a resident expert on *The Prince of Homburg* on the payroll. When we prioritize, we find that the odds of our mounting a production of a play with such a limited esoteric appeal (i.e., such a hard sell to our subscribers) are almost nil. If we do undertake such an ambitious project (but only in order to plug some cultural cachet into our grant proposals), you can be sure we will hire some hot director with a "high concept" version of the play set on the moon, and he will have to take care of the research "out of pocket."

****

For a student to enroll today in a course of training leading to a certificate of competence in "production dramaturgy" is therefore absurd. To study the dramaturgy trade, and then to seek placement as an unpaid *apprentice* to a master dramaturg, is even more absurd. The whole business is history. It is like studying to be a blacksmith. It is anachronistic.

But, as they used to write, take heart, gentle readers. Taking that degree is merely anachronistic; it isn't fatal. After all, if you are reading this book, you are *already* an anachronism of our prevailing post-culture anyway. And if you wish to serve the art of the stage in *any* capacity, then the study of dramaturgy—by which *I* mean the hands-on study of every aspect of dramatic structure—is invaluable. Training in dramaturgy, then, the rigorous analysis of all aspects of a theatrical event, both practical and theoretical, is vital to *everyone* who seeks a life in the theater. The greatest American theater historians and critics themselves have straddled the fence between theory and practice. George Pierce Baker, Alan Downer, Francis Fergusson, Eric Bentley, Robert Brustein, Bernard Beckerman, Stanley Kauffmann, Richard Gilman, Ruby Cohn, Richard Schechner, Jan Kott—all have been highly sensitive to the nuances of plays as those plays are energized by actors onstage in performance.

It was the Yale Drama School that first devised a strategy to retool the study of dramatic theory and criticism as a "professional" degree, putting its Ivy imprimatur on the dramaturg label. The first golden batches to emerge from the Yale program in dramaturgy (where they studied, most notably, under Stanley Kauffmann and Richard Gilman) included Ann Cattaneo, now dramaturg for André Bishop, Artistic Director of the Vivian Beaumont Theatre at Lincoln Center; Michael Feingold, today the senior theater critic for *The Village Voice*; Jonathan

Marks, currently a professor at Stanford and literary manager of San Francisco's American Conservatory Theatre; Russell Vandenbroucke, former literary manager of the Mark Taper Forum and currently artistic director of Chicago's Northlight Repertory Theatre; and Mark Bly, who himself has recently been appointed to the Yale Drama School faculty/Yale Repertory Theatre staff. Key dramaturgy positions at the major American regional theaters have all, at one time or another, been held by members of this group.

However, each of this handful of hybrid scholar-practitioners bearing the imprimatur of a major university has found his niche outside as well as inside the inhospitable rehearsal hall. As critics, directors, television producers, or professors of drama, all have found a way to earn a living from work related to their vocation. Theaters may pay a small fee for "research," or supply expenses, or even grant a clerk's salary for the administrative duties of the job—drawing up mailing lists, sending out flyers, putting together press kits—but, as Russell Vandenbroucke, former literary manager at the Mark Taper Forum, once joked, "No kid says, 'When I grow up I want to be a dramaturg.'" And here is the punchline: no one in America makes a killing, let alone a living, as a dramaturg. And no one ever will. A dinosaur of erudition in a system that does not know how—and does not *want* to know how—to use a dramaturg in production, the literary manager is regularly assigned to write program notes, not rehearsal notes. It was long ago noted that no American dramaturg has ever had the impact on a production to match the impact of a Kenneth Tynan or a Jan Kott. And no one ever will.

To clarify: there is nothing wrong with the training offered in dramaturgy programs per se. It is fine. But calling it dramaturgy as opposed to, say, dramatic theory and criticism, is to say that the emperor has new clothes. The many fine graduate programs that sprouted in this field are equally suited to training directors, actors, playwrights, designers, *et al*. Dramaturgy is, I would argue again, nothing more than a fancy term for dramatic structure. As we recruit students we should make this clear. For what we are really selling to potential M.F.A.s or Ph.D.s in drama is an honest devotion to criticism as a sister art, a way of broadening perspectives, a method of grasping and illuminating the mysteries of live performance. There is no need to give it a paint job and adjust the odometer: education in the history, theory, and practice of theater arts is the real thing and speaks for itself.

The promise of professional on-the-job training, of theatrical respectability, that we make to students rings false. To disguise the product—especially when the product has been recalled—is to generate dissatisfied customers, surprised to discover that they will, upon completing their degree, be competing with Ph.D.s in theater, English, and comparative literature for assistant professorships. Most will, if they are lucky, dramaturg "on the side," for a "token honorarium," and for the love of glimpsing a theatrical experience as it takes on its essential shape in rehearsal.

****

The best element of training in dramaturgy is being thrust into the melee, learning all aspects of theater from the inside out. In fact, if we really want to obliterate dramaturgs, we should apply complementary logic to the training of actors and directors and technicians and designers and managers of theaters: let them all be hybrids, with slashes in the job title. Let us train actors/dramaturgs, directors/dramaturgs, scenic artists/dramaturgs, managers/dramaturgs: let every theater artist consciously place himself in an historical context, and analyze his aesthetic principles in light of those championed during other periods and in other cultures.

We might ask, what if a text such as this were required reading for actors as well as for theoreticians? How might that alter the pitch, tone, and impact of theatrical enterprises in America? For one thing, it might elevate our emphasis on "behavior" to the level of world vision. For another, it might lead us into territory earlier camouflaged by walls erected under the old divisions. We might further ask, why are there no opera-turgs? or symphony-turgs? or ballet-turgs? The answer is obvious, but somewhat embarrassing to theater practitioners. In fields such as opera, classical music, and ballet, the practitioners are also the keepers of tradition, poised in the space between memory and immediacy, history and art.

Only in American theaters, and especially among theater students, do we find a widespread neo-romantic disdain for any and all "background" information. They consciously hold on to ignorance, and they avoid unsettling situations or discussions that might "hamper creativity and free expression." So American actors and directors in particular, long accustomed to exploring their senses and objectives in a vacuum, rationalize their ignorance of the tradition from which their art springs. Train actors and directors to know the world, and they will, perhaps heroically, learn how to dramatize that world. And all the remaining dramaturgs, weary of their odd-man-out status, looking for jobs that do not exist in America, will invent new counter-jobs.

For the kind of training I am promoting here presumes that all impassioned theater artists should consume everything about the theory and history of their craft, as well as its methods. In a landmark piece in the Fall 1978 Dramaturgy Issue of Yale's *Theater* journal, *New Yorker* theater critic John Lahr, formerly an audacious literary advisor at the Guthrie and Vivian Beaumont Theatres, put forth what is now a poignant argument for the crucial importance of the dramaturg to the theater. Lahr wrote:

> Somehow, being part of a production as well as support for a production eliminated the inevitable alienation of forever being in a position of no risk. I also found—and I think this is crucial for the development of dramatic criticism—that once inside the theater in the role of dramaturg, one's language for the discussion of theater becomes more concrete, more vivid and devoid of the litcrit sludge which sinks most critical writing.

Lahr's final recommendation, that it is vital for critics to involve themselves in the artistic process, still rings true, and I have never heard it said better. Here are his words:

> If theaters want better critics, they must open their doors to them. And find a way of making work for them inside the theater as well as outside it. It's the only way for both to grow. I think that critics must get their hands dirty; must learn about the craft from the inside so they can serve the art they purport to love.

I would suggest that this recommendation and a complementary recommendation are equally essential for students pursuing theatrical callings. While critics-in-training are getting their hands dirty so they can better serve the art they claim to love, their fellow students, practitioners-in-training, should be straining their eyes to read the voluminous literature of the theater.

And all those would-be production dramaturgs, stubbornly waiting "up against the fourth wall" for the American theater to make use of them, had better practice or experience this art from many different perspectives. If you truly believe your vocation is to serve as the "ghost light" of drama and its traditions, you should start by finding out what a ghost light is, and then you should see if, without it, you could find your way around a darkened theater.

1994

# IV

# DRAMATURGY IN ENGLAND

"It's the dramaturg's job to figure out what's happening beneath the structure of a rehearsal."

—David Copelin

# The Critic Comes Full Circle:
# An Interview with Kenneth Tynan

Editors of *Theatre Quarterly*

*In his first book of collected reviews,* He That Plays the King *(1950),
Kenneth Tynan championed a theatre of heroic acting—while in* Cur-
tains *(1961), containing his vintage* Observer *and* New Yorker
*reviews, he called for and gave coherence to a more socially-directed
drama. Recently he has combined his work as literary manager for
Britain's National Theatre with such independent enterprises as mas-
terminding the productions of* Soldiers *and* Oh! Calcutta!

## Function of the Critic

*Do you have regrets that you aren't any longer yourself writing criti-
cism?*

None at all. I did it for twelve years, and so did Max Beerbohm.
I think that's long enough. After that you are recording not
what is actually happening to your sensibility but what you think
ought to be happening to it, or what once happened to it. After
twelve years of seeing four or five plays a week your reactions
have been so trampled on that it takes years of convalesence.
You are left with a clear knowledge of what you liked, but the
vocabulary of disapproval has begun to pall. Suddenly you
become—at least I became—much more interested in concocting
the recipe than in being a rented palate.

*One sensed, reading some of your later reviews, especially when you
got back from America, that a sourer note was creeping in—the enthu-
siasm had gone, if you like. . . .*

Or rather had become confined to the things that one was
really keen about. One of those things was to be in touch with

theatre people. I find it's impossible to know what ought to be happening in the theatre unless I am in constant touch with the writers and the directors and the actors.

*But surely the critic is speaking for an audience that is not thus in touch. Mustn't both judge theatre by its end-product, the play as staged, which has nothing to do with the personalities of directors or actors or authors?*

The ignorance of the audience need not necessarily be shared by the critic. Now I say *necessarily*—there have been great critics who were participants, like Shaw, and great critics who cut themselves off completely from the theatre world. But for me it was necessary. Perhaps it was just that one wanted a little more influence over the menu, and to stop being a mere client in a restaurant that always served apple pie when you occasionally wanted oysters *au beurre blanc.*

*Did you begin to feel yourself writing for effect—writing maybe for a nice amusing column, rather than real solid comment?*

This is an aimless question. The solid comment might not get the readership unless you find the right hook of words. This bait of form takes your carp of truth.

*Do you feel you have more influence now, than you did as a critic?*

Oh yes, certainly. If I read a play now that I like, I can probably get it done, either in the commercial theatre or in the subsidized theatre. But if you're going to do that you really have to resign your job as a critic. When I first joined the National Theatre I saw no reason why I couldn't continue as a critic for a while, knowing myself to be totally incorruptible. But the West End theatre managers combined, and wrote to Sir Laurence saying they would not allow this, because they thought I might attack a play not because I disliked it but because I wanted it to close so that the National Theatre could hire an actress that was in it—that sort of devious motivation. I don't think I could have or would have gone on for longer than about a year anyway.

Also it's a question just of the boredom of writing to a deadline every week.

## Call to the National Theatre

*What were your reactions on being asked to be Literary Manager of the National Theatre?*

Well, obviously I knew what Sir Laurence was up to. He's an expert politician. Like Abraham Lincoln. In his first cabinet Lincoln included one of his most virulent opponents, and the man said, 'Why are you doing this, Mr. Lincoln?' and Lincoln said, 'Because I'd rather have you inside pissing out than outside pissing in.' But I'd known Larry for a long time, we'd had many conversations about what form a National Theatre should take. And another thing I think he knew was that there would be no direct competition between him and me—he would know from the first that I was not a contender for the job of being Director of the National Theatre. I am not an actor and I am not at the moment a director, so we would not find ourselves at loggerheads. He would also know that any advice I gave him would be disinterested, in that if a production is a success I don't get the praise and if it's a flop I don't get the blame. We complemented each other because he has all the practical skills that an actor and a director could have, and I presumably have the theoretical knowledge: where he was strong I was weak, and vice versa. He almost to a fault protests that he isn't an intellectual, and I almost to a fault protest that I'm not a participant. It's true that I've sometimes been nettled by his reluctance to delegate authority and he's been annoyed at my obtuseness and stubbornness and obduracy in pressing causes that he has no sympathy with: but we have never had any bad blood, so the combination has worked out rather well.

## Choosing the Repertoire

*How did you begin to tackle—even at the mechanical level—the problem of being confronted with the whole body of world drama, and from this choosing what was to be performed in the first season, the second season, and so on?*

Sometimes we sit and argue all night, and we draw up charts and make plans and issue little memos to each other. A little booklet was rather prettily printed, called *Some Plays,* which was simply my own list of all the plays in world drama that could possibly, conceivably be worth reviving in Britain in the second half of the twentieth century. Interestingly, it wasn't a very long list, although I did all I could to make it exhaustive and included everything that might have the least claim to revival. We use this as a reference book when we are planning the repertoire—it's an easy and portable way of finding out what plays John Lyly wrote, or Anzengruber, or Aphra Behn.

Sir Laurence takes the actors' point of view, and his tendency will always be to keep the ensemble together by looking for the right parts for them. My tendency has always been to look for the right plays and the right playwrights, and such differences as we've had have usually occurred when these two aims haven't overlapped, so that we sometimes find ourselves doing plays to make actors happy that were perhaps not plays we ought to have done, and sometimes we've done plays to make play-wrights happy or to make *me* happy that we oughtn't to have done. But on the whole the overlapping has been considerable, and greater I think than either of us expected when we first went into this.

The first thing we said to each other was that our policy should be to have no policy, except excellence in whatever we did, because one has seen so many artistic projects hoist on their own manifestoes. We just wanted to do something that ought to have been done fifty years ago in this country—to make the world repertoire available, the rare classics and the popular classics and the new work at the same time. There are enormous gaps of course. We've done just over fifty produc-tions, and there are perhaps six which I rather regret, and I'm sure there are a different six which Sir Laurence might regret.

*As productions, or as choices?*

As choices. And others, as productions. But on the whole it's been more successful than either of us ever dreamed, mainly because we promised nothing. We just said, we're going to do plays chosen from all periods, and we've tried to keep a balance, this awful balance between the available talent and the magnitude of the plays. Occasionally the play you want to do tremendously is a play you haven't got the right actors for, and the play you have got the right actors for is the play that you ought not to be doing. Now which of those two plays do you do? The great play badly, or the mediocre play marvellously?

*Which people have actually made these decisions?*

At first, John Dexter, Bill Gaskill, Sir Laurence, and me. That was the way it was until Bill left, and then it was John and Larry and me, and then it was Larry and me for a while and now it's Frank Dunlop and Larry and me—plus Derek Grainger, since last winter.

*You also have advisers who read scripts and give opinions on them?*

We have readers, and all of the twenty odd plays that we get each week *are* read, but it's very rarely that we get more than one that's worth even a second reading, and we've never I think put one on. We've either commissioned, or we've known the authors and said, can we have your next play? This is what happened in the case of Peter Nichols. It's simply a case of long, long all-night debates. And the difficulties involved in running a continuing, accumulating repertory are geometrically greater than those of running a seasonal repertory. You have to think of parts for an actor not only for one season but for the next season. You have to know that certain actors will be leaving you, so that if a production is to remain in the repertory other actors will have to take over their parts—and a continuing rep where a play may be in the repertory for five or six years means that the parts have to be re-rehearsed by lots of other actors.

When a new actor joins the company, it's part of his job to take over parts already played by other people. And the time needed to rehearse the replacements for these plays is enormous. We've found that we have to have somebody who does almost nothing else but work out the availability of our actors. I mean, how many hours per day can somebody re-rehearse this play, understudy that part, play a new part in this play, go to the Young Vic to do something on Saturday, then go on tour the following Monday to Newcastle? It's really a computer job, running a large company which has a continuing repertoire.

*And there are other considerations—a feeling, perhaps, that you're obliged to do a Shakespeare every so often, fit in a new play every so often, choose one to please the tourists . . . ?*

No, although the Arts Council originally wanted us to do far more Shakespeare than we do. But we've come to a sort of armed truce whereby we do one Shakespeare a year, usually about the time of Shakespeare's birthday. I would be surprised if we increased that proportion as long as we only occupy one theatre, because we can't afford to do more than about six new productions a year, and if more than one of them is Shakespeare I think that's disproportionate, so long as the Royal Shakespeare is doing about five or six a year. We do feel we ought to do at least one new play a year, yes, and of course at the Young Vic we shall be doing a lot more. The other five productions are where we have to decide, say, if we don't find a play for Miss X will she leave the company? She's a very talented actress: but have we had her in the company long enough, have we exhausted her particular abilities, can we stretch her any further, or would it be a kinder and more charitable thing for us to say to her, leave the nest for a couple of years, go and work in films, and come back to us later? Or, perhaps: this actor is a very good actor—is he really going to develop into a Macbeth? If he is, should we give him an intermediate part in—say—a Büchner play which will lead him in that direction? Or shall we keep him at the level of acting he is on now? He may leave the company if we do: can we afford to lose him, because he's playing in five other productions and will have to be replaced, and that will mean re-rehearsing the five other productions?

Those are the sort of considerations—they are really logistical things, just like running a factory. Considering Sir Laurence's seniority he keeps in very close touch, but there is on my part even after all these years, and I think on everybody else's, a sense of a gulf. He has done it all, seen it all, and we haven't. There is naturally a gap there that he does his best to bridge, but there is a certain feeling of awe and I think there always will be.

## Instant Mannerisms

*What ways are there of preventing a play that may be in the repertory for five or six seasons from going stale? How can actors be stopped from slipping into instant mannerisms, easy ways of getting laughs?*

We haven't found the answer to that. We do call re-rehearsals constantly. When a play has been out of the repertoire for even as little as three weeks we have a special dress rehearsal of it before we bring it back in, and new actors are constantly being rehearsed into important parts. But when a director comes back to a production after a year, say, in the States, almost inevitably he will call a rehearsal 'to take out the improvements.' It's a built-in hazard of theatre. All one can say is that whenever the actors know Sir Laurence is out front they tend to revert to the original performance, and we let it be known that he's out front quite often when he's in Brighton.

*Hasn't it been a weakness at the National since William Gaskill and John Dexter left that, although there is Sir Laurence to speak for the actors and yourself—well, to speak for the audiences, there has been no strong voice speaking from the director's point of view?*

When Frank Dunlop joined the company as administrative director the aim was that he should provide that voice. He is a marvellous enthusiast, but he is now throwing nearly all of his energy into the Young Vic and doing a tremendous job, so I think there is a gap for an associate director which we haven't filled.

## Director vs. Ensemble

*One result of this seems to have been that of late there have been a lot of productions by outside directors, which have sometimes achieved an excellence of their own, but seem to have worked against the grain of the ensemble that's been built up.*

But you see the word ensemble is getting to be a dangerous one. You must remember that in the Granville-Barker and Archer period of ensemble there was no film and no television. You can no longer in the English-speaking theatre have a permanent ensemble. You can in the German theatre because the film industry in Germany is non-existent, and there's less television than here. But the whole English-speaking market is competing for an English-speaking actor's talent.

*Even so, my impression is that more actors have remained for longer periods in the National Theatre's company than in, say, the Royal Shakespeare's, and that there is a strong rapport amongst these actors—yet nothing like the same sense of directorial continuity.*

Well, the Royal Shakespeare is much more a director's theatre, and this, parenthetically, may be the reason why I prefer the National as a place to work: there is not so much scope for a literary manager at the RSC as there is in an actors' theatre like ours. I've always been a great supporter of the bringing in of outside and indeed foreign directors as often as possible. But I was very sad when John Dexter left, because I think he's one of the top six English-speaking directors. He was a tremendous fire in the company's belly, and without him I think a certain impetus has been lost. Bill Gaskill always wanted to have his own company, and we all understood when he went to the Royal Court. But you're right, we do need directors. We have some very interesting young directors working with the Young Vic, and the question will be whether Frank Dunlop will let them graduate to the Old Vic or whether he'll hang on to them.

## Pitfalls of Commissioning

*Do you follow any particular guidelines in commissioning new plays? Is there any reluctance to accept commissions?*

We've tried asking authors of the stature of John Osborne to do adaptations of lesser-known classics, with varying success. But if I was a young author I would undoubtedly prefer to write for TV, because the seed I'd planted would tend to come up much more quickly. I'd finish my script in May, and it could well be seen nationwide in July. In a theatre that has to plan as far ahead as we do, it might not be seen for twelve or eighteen months, and I'd by then be that much older and have gone on to other things. This is a tremendous problem. One TV playwright whom I won't name said to me when I tried to commission a play from him, 'Why should I expose my work to the fangs of twelve critics in the national press after only nine hundred people have seen it? In television sixteen million people have seen it before the critics get their hands on it.' There, on television, he gets an untainted response.

Now in the theatre only the first-night audience has that untainted response. I see his point. Newspaper criticism *does* modify the consciousness of anyone who reads it. We've all seen this happen—the production that is raved about in the daily press is knocked in the Sundays and then rehabilitated in the weeklies. The Sunday critics write their piece having read what the daily critics have written. Similarly, the audience that goes after the opening night has read one or two reviews—they go knowing what the play's about, knowing what several people thought of it. The TV audiences haven't been got at in that way, and I can see why an author would regard this as a purer response.

All one can do in reply is to quote Peter Brook's remark in *The Empty Space* about the curious electricity of theatre—though this always makes it the most potentially dangerous of the arts where censorship is involved. And, of course, a play done in the National Theatre repertory with success suddenly gets done all over the world, film rights are in demand, and the author is established overnight. That happened with Tom Stoppard. At the moment we have a play I commissioned from Robert Shaw about the Cato Street conspiracy which is going to go on in the spring. It's very exciting—a completely political play, by the way.

*Did you choose the subject?*

No. Robert Shaw came to me and said, 'Look, I've been reading about the Cato Street conspiracy, do you think there's a play in it?' We talked about it, and I said, 'I do, please go ahead and write it.' Which he did. Then there's something else that is interesting us more and more—the need to integrate music and dance into our work somehow. *Guys and Dolls* was one part of that impulse, but had to be postponed because Sir Laurence was ill. So I thought, why don't we create our own musical? I was talking one evening to Adrian Mitchell, and I told him we wanted to bring song and dance into our work, and he said, 'Why don't I write my Blake play for you? I've always wanted the theatre to celebrate Blake.' So he has now written a play called *Tyger*. He calls it a cranky panto, and it is that. It's not about the life of Blake but about the ideas of Blake, and I think it is going to be a total theatrical experience such as is not possible in the other arts. So Adrian's coming into the theatre in that way, not as a translator as he was in the *Marat/Sade,* or as just a lyric writer as in *US,* but as a man with a total theatre concept. What else have we got coming? Victor Garcia, one of the most exciting directors in Europe, is doing the first major British production of an Arrabal play for us—and scenically that will represent a technological revolution at the Old Vic. Tom Stoppard's writing a new play for us. And I hope we'll have a chance to do one by Mike Weller, who wrote *Cancer.*

## Theatre without Identity

*Would you describe any writers as distinctively National Theatre playwrights, in the way that there are Royal Court playwrights or Aldwych playwrights?*

No. I would hate a playwright to come to us and say, 'I think I'm writing your sort of play.' That would really mean that we had failed to fulfill our brief. The Royal Court is entitled to have a special sort of play, the Royal Shakespeare is, Joan Littlewood is—but the moment *we* have a special sort of play then we're limiting ourselves too much. I think we have to leave all the doors open, whereas they're entitled to slam some.

*So this means that you have to suppress personal preferences to some extent in settling your repertoire—perhaps even bend over backwards to be catholic. . . .*

No, it means simply that the National Theatre has no preconceived identity, which is marvellous. . . .

*But* you *have an identity. Do you have to conceal it?*

Ah. *Officially* I have no identity. Of course, I would be very sad if a play that supported apartheid were done at the National Theatre, and I would do what I could to prevent it. Similarly, a play that supported the American action in Vietnam would be unlikely to find me rooting for it. And if a play that involved mass audience participation was proposed for the Old Vic I would probably vote against it. Of course, I might lose the vote in any of these instances. But I can't think of a play that's been critically applauded in the English theatre in the last ten years that we wouldn't have given very sympathetic consideration to.

### Failures and Abortions

*Have there been many failures in commissioning?*

Oh, several, which one wouldn't want to talk about. Where playwrights were given advances and didn't produce plays. But not more than you would find in the commercial theatre.

*I was thinking more of plays that actually did find their way onto your desk, but which were somehow not satisfactory.*

Well, there were two things. I was very keen at one time—still am—on documentary theatre, and we commissioned a play about the Cuba crisis from an American and an English author. The American had a nervous breakdown and unwisely, I think, we left the English author to complete it, forgetting that no Englishman can ever write dialogue for an American. And most of the people involved in the play *were* Americans. So that was something which was completed, and money paid for it, but was not right for performance. We also worked on the General Strike idea for a long time. That never quite worked out, and we passed it on to the Royal Shakespeare, and now years later it may be bearing fruit there. Oh, there have been quite a lot of abortions.

*Did you at any stage think that these are subjects we* must *do a play on?*

Oh yes, exactly that. Both Sir Laurence and I, when we went to Moscow with the National Theatre in 1966, saw *Ten Days That Shook the World,* and thought, why don't we do something like that? It was about that period that we were developing the play on Cuba and working on the General Strike idea, and these would have used all the techniques of film and mime and song, to illustrate historic events. But the nearest we've actually come to it is *H,* which was also a commissioned play and a flop. Not to my mind an artistic flop, but a critical flop.

*Was that your choice of subject?*

No, it was Charles Wood's subject. He said that while he was doing research for *The Charge of the Light Brigade* he had learnt a lot about what happened to many of the people involved immediately afterwards. A lot of them had served in India, and been caught up in the Indian Mutiny. He fascinated me, talking about it, so I said, for God's sake, write a play about it. And he did.

*Failures in production, rather than failures relating to the quality of the writing, often seem to come back to the problem of finding the style to fit a particular play. Fielding's little burlesque,* The Covent-Garden Tragedy, *in* Triple Bill, *for instance, seemed to me to fail because nobody really knew how to play a mock-heroic, burlesque style.*

Now this is a rather invidious thing to say. There is a theory that actors know more about how to make actors act than non-actors do. Sir Laurence being an actor and a director has a splendid and often rewarded faith in the ability of actors to direct. On that particular occasion, maybe because of the choice of subject or a failure to match subject and director, it didn't work. But I agree with you that in other circumstances it could have worked.

*This would seem to be one of the possible functions of a National The-atre, which as you say has to be catholic, and so is well placed to re-discover styles which have almost been forgotten. One of the empty rooms we've been talking about might be discovering how to comment within plays about what the theatre itself ought to be doing, or is doing badly, which is after all how burlesque operates. . . .*

Or something like what the Berliner Ensemble do in the *Mess-ingkauf Dialogues.* In fact when I first saw the *Messingkauf Dia-logues* I asked Helene Weigel if we could have the English rights and she said, 'You have not earned the right to do this yet.' She's quite correct. That is their personal credo and how they worked it out, and it's not our job to annex their discoveries as if they were our own.

*Of the range of plays that you've done, in which forms and which areas do you think you've had most success?*

I think we've been best at certain sorts of humane, ironic com-edy. That may be because it accords with the spirit of the age: the zeitgeist is not, I should have thought, sympathetic towards the totally tragic. The commonest intelligent response to the age in which we live seems to be an ironic one, since it's con-sonant with some sort of civilized poise. And the sort of talents we've nourished have tended to make a joke of it. I think that's absolutely natural. That kind of play, whether it's the intellec-tual irony of *Rosencrantz and Guildenstern Are Dead* or the rather more emotional ironies of *The National Health,* and comedy like *The Recruiting Officer* and *The Beaux' Stratagem,* those are things we've been really best in—plus sudden eruptions from Sir Lau-

rence, as in *Othello*. I think Maggie Smith's performance in *The
Beaux' Stratagem* is perhaps the most consummate bit of female
high comedy I've ever seen, and one knows that she wouldn't
have been able to do that if she hadn't played Desdemona, *The
Master Builder*, and so on. The Maggie Smith who came to the
National Theatre was a gauche girl. The Maggie Smith who's at
the National Theatre now is a fully mature and ripened actress.

### The Young Vic and the Future

*How far do you think the Young Vic will now take over this kind of
maturing work with actors and actresses for the parent company?*

You must remember that the Young Vic was entirely Frank
Dunlop's conception. He got the money, he found the site, he
got the architects, and he formed the company. I don't think
anybody else could have done it in the time. But it's not just a
place to fledge actors and playwrights, though it is partly that.
What Frank wants to do with it is to discover if there is a special
art form called young people's theatre—assuming there really is
a generation gap, how to express it theatrically, and to find
what it is that appeals to the under-twenty audience that is different from what the over-thirty audience likes. Is Jeff Nuttall
right when he says that those who came to puberty after the
thermo-nuclear bomb are a different sort of human being? Do
they need a different sort of stage entertainment? The Young
Vic is Frank's attempt to find out.

*My own hope when you gave up full-time criticism and went to the
National Theatre was that you would eventually write some latter-day
equivalent to what Lessing attempted in the* Hamburg Dramaturgy:
*recording the impressions of the critic in the theatre but not quite of
the theatre.*

Well, I'm writing a book on precisely those lines, about what
I've learnt in these last seven years of working on the other side
of theatre, both at the National Theatre and in the commercial
theatre with *Soldiers* and *Oh! Calcutta!* I may not want to publish

it until, or unless, I leave the National, because there's a certain element of inside information in it which one probably wouldn't want to publish if one were still there. Yes, one is making notes, a full record is being kept, but this isn't perhaps the time to publish it. To write about an organization that is still paying one's salary imposes certain restraints of vocabulary, however small the salary and however large the vocabulary.

*What kind of development do you personally anticipate taking place at the National Theatre over the next few years?*

The National Theatre has been in existence now for seven and a half years and a certain replenishment is I think necessary. It may be that there are people connected with the organization, myself included, who have been there too long. Peter Hall once said the maximum time that any ensemble should stay together without renewal was five years. I think that's an arbitrary figure, but it is true that one needs new directions, new infusions, every so often.

1970

# Literary Management at the National Theatre, London: An Interview with John Russell Brown

Richard Beacham

John Russell Brown has been an Associate Director and Literary Manager at the National Theatre of Great Britain since 1973. He has written many books on Shakespeare and contemporary theatre.

**Beacham:** Britain doesn't have a strong tradition of theatrical literary managers or dramaturgs. Do you see historically any rough equivalent in British theater for the type of work that you do here?

**Brown:** Not really. I think the first one was Kenneth Tynan when he was brought in by Olivier as the "Literary Manager" of the National Theatre. But the theater's always had contacts with universities. Barry Jackson at the Birmingham Rep was a very close personal friend of Professor Allardyce Nicoll. At the Malvern festivals along with late Bernard Shaw plays were revivals of strange plays like *Woman Killed with Kindness, Merry Devil of Edmonton, Jacob and Essau*: for all those Allardyce did act as a kind of dramaturg, literary adviser to Barry Jackson. I suppose that you could say Gilbert Murray, particularly for the Euripides translations, was a kind of literary adviser for Granville-Barker at the Court.

**Beacham:** Was Granville-Barker himself such as person?

**Brown:** Well, Granville-Barker was an actor, director, and playwright; he wasn't free for academic speculation or scholarly research; all that came later in his case. He moved towards being a critic and also acted as adviser to the Gielgud *Lear* in 1948.

**Beacham** Are you the only such figure on the scene today?

**Brown:** Oh no. The RSC followed suit and went through several literary advisers: Derek Sanford, John Holstrom, Jeremy Brooks, Ron Bryden. At present they have made a different sort of appointment which is concerned with new writing rather than with advice on the repertoire in general: Howard Davies is now their man for contacting young writers, but he is also in charge of the Warehouse studio theater in London.

**Beacham:** But is he particularly concerned with new plays?

**Brown:** Yes, indeed. Plays which are submitted to the RSC by new writers are sent automatically to Howard Davies, who has an assistant called Walter Donohue. The Royal Court has also had a literary adviser. They tend to change every two or three years and they employ dramatists—Ann Jellicoe, David Howarth, David Hare, and N. F. Simpson have all done this job; and I'm told that Richard Crane is about to take over.

**Beacham:** Outside of these major companies and the major subsidized national companies, how does the task get done?

**Brown:** The type of work that I do is usually done unofficially by friends at the local university and other personal contacts. Most of the repertory theaters in England haven't got the time or money for a regular appointment. Sometimes resident dramatists (under the Thames Television New Dramatists' Awards Scheme) are given the task of reading new plays when they come in. The Royal Court at one time had a circle of about 6 readers of plays, who were largely young dramatists or young directors that were on a kind of minimal payroll.

**Beacham:** Do you see the shape of the situation changing particularly—with companies undertaking to bring such people on to their staff?

**Brown:** If there was more money, that's one of the things that would happen. I'm not sure how high a priority it would be given, but theaters do get sent a large number of scripts and it is very difficult to handle that if you're the artistic director of a theater working with a very tight budget. The most economical way of coping is to use an assistant director, or resident drama-tist; and I suspect that failing a flood of new money this will continue to be the way most theaters will respond.

**Beacham:** Into what sort of categories does your work fall?

**Brown:** I've been talking chiefly about receiving new scripts but that's just a part of my job. I'm not a 'dramaturg' as that term is understood in Germany or Austria. I'm one of eight or nine associate directors of the NT, and my special task is to be in charge of the Script Department. As Associate Director, I'm a member of the Planning Committee of this theater meeting once a fortnight: here all aspects of the theater's policy are dis-cussed before decisions are made. So since early 1973 I've been involved in the development of the policy and program of the theater, together with other Associates and the Administrative Heads.

**Beacham:** Do you work directly with the company on produc-tions of which you're not actually the artistic director?

**Brown:** Not as a dramaturg. In Germany a dramaturg would do that. I can remember writing to the Stadt Theater in Vienna asking if I could meet my opposite number: and they replied by asking which of the five would I like to meet! Every production there has its allotted dramaturg. He is a kind of research man; he provides material for the program but he also researches for the director and attends all the rehearsals. In some cases his opinion is sought out constantly; sometimes his opinion is ignored.

**Beacham:** We found at Yale in fact that at first the actors tended to view this person with a good deal of suspicion, as a foreign body, but eventually they accepted him and found him useful.

**Brown:** I must say that I would hate to be a dramaturg in that sense. It's like standing around in a kitchen peering into other people's pots, or like back-seat driving. I think a director of a play ought to do his own research: he knows what he's looking for, if he's any good; and only he can recognize the unexpected detail that fits his work. He'd best do it himself. However I do get involved with some of our productions; it depends on the director. Some want to consult and ask particular questions, or to get informed response to work in progress.

**Beacham:** When considering the academic training and teaching in England, it strikes me and it strikes a lot of other American academics of similar backgrounds as remarkable that theater studies as such—criticism, theater history—haven't traditionally had a very strong part in the curriculum of British universities. Why is that?

**Brown:** I think one of the reasons is that North American universities developed theater departments partly in order to have a theater at all. It was a community theater service. There was so little theater in places like Bloomington, Indiana, or Champaign, Illinios, that the Arts Faculty felt the need not only to study the theater but actually to create it. It's one part of academic work which the local community can be invited to share. A theater on campus is also a social meeting point for both faculty and students, a subject for common debate and, very often, concern. North American universities were also more influenced by the example of Austria and Germany, where a tradition of theater research is much stronger in universities.

**Beacham:** What would you see as the most desirable relationship between higher education and theater?

**Brown:** The first university in this country which has a professional company under the same direction as the drama department will make a *major* change. Until that happens I don't see the connection between academic and professional theater being developed strongly. Academic theater insofar as it is a teaching facility has its own rhythms, its own intentions. Every year it goes back to base. It has to do plays which are suitable to the talents and academic development of students and faculty. It hasn't got a chance of saying "Look, here is a problem and this is what might be done" and, later, "These are the results." A department of local government, music, or engineering can respond in this way; a theater department can't. "What do you do about making a bridge that can stand this sort of stress, these conditions, and how do you build that bridge?" A department of engineering can make models and get subvention for full-scale tests. It isn't at all equivalent when a theater department has a brave shot at a problem text with the talents of miscellaneous students who are grouped together for a very short rehearsal period—especially when half of them don't really want to be involved in the project at all. The work gets nowhere. It's like trying to run a department of fine arts when you are only showing the students and the outside world what student drawings and paintings look like. It's ridiculous.

**Beacham:** Looking at the state of health of the British theater generally, would you characterize it as "in the pink," or "critical," or "sick unto death?"

**Brown:** Educational theater in schools and communities is a hugely important and only partly recognized force in theater which is likely to change the profession very considerably. New writing for theater has grown over the last ten years in quantity, if not in quality. The actor's profession has changed a great deal over the last ten years too: the actor's expectation. There's an outgoing restlessness in the profession now. Actors want to find new audiences, new ways of working that do not allow them to take refuge inside a theater but require them to travel around, to innovate, and to change their relationship to each other, their audience, their director, their management.

**Beacham:** Obviously, education offers one means of doing this.

**Brown:** Yes. But there are other signs of the same restlessness. Ian McKellen is going to head a company of actors doing middle-scale touring from the RSC. This will be something like the Actors' Company, but now it's happening inside one of the major subsidized companies. It's a sign of a quest for a new kind of confidence.

**Beacham:** Related to this, my next question is about the quality and quantity of new plays, new writing that you actually see come across your desk. What is it like and has it changed in the last few years; do you see an evolution of some sort?

**Brown:** I've been at the National Theatre since '73 and we have been getting more and more new plays of better quality that come here unsolicited. The young generation of playwrights, those around 25 years old, are using theater in adventurous ways.

**Beacham:** The obstacles, though, for a new playwright are still fairly formidable, aren't they?

**Brown:** I don't think so. Arts Council bursaries and royalty supplement their "contract writers" schemes; the Thames Television Dramatists' Award, the National Theatre's Resident Dramatist Scheme, and certain creative-writing fellowships in universities, have enormously increased the chances of somebody in their twenties working as a dramatist. All these awards have been started in the last ten years and this means that a new play done at somewhere like the Bush or the Traverse Theater, where it can play for three weeks to perhaps a hundred people each performance, can bring a writer £700 to £1000. That wasn't so five years ago. It wasn't so three years ago. It's become a much more viable profession. I don't think that necessarily will mean that writers become better, but the hard-luck story no longer holds good.

**Beacham:** I'm sure you're asked this last question repeatedly. The National Theatre has been an idea and a dream for a long time; how do you see it shaping up and what has its impact been now after its first year?

**Brown:** We've been hobbled by financial restrictions far greater than we anticipated. On account of the incomplete state of the building, we still have to use stone-age methods of scene-shifting because, for example, the marvellous turntable hydraulic lift in the Olivier doesn't work, and the hoists are not properly functional; and all that costs money. The theater is designed to have four or five plays with each set fully built, able to be shuffled onto the stage at the touch of a button on a computer; and that's just one of the things which was meant to be economical about this building, but it doesn't work, and until it does stage-handling is very expensive. It is also an expensive building in that it tries to be welcoming to its audiences.

The theater was designed for a scale of work that supplies productions not only for the three houses here, but also for extensive tours and the bringing in of visiting productions. We were geared for all that, but now there just isn't money to do it. The effect of the National Theatre can't be properly judged yet because the National Theatre isn't yet able to do fully the job it was designed to do and set out to do. It was meant to do ten plays a year in the Olivier, and at the moment we've cut down to five. In the Lyttelton we had hoped to have three seasons a year of four plays each, plus some visitors; but we've had to cut back to four or possibly five plays in a single year. The Cottesloe was meant to mount twenty productions a year and send them out around the country. We now have about ten new productions a year in the Cottesloe and half or a third of those have to be geared to the casting of the main-house plays. We're starting a series of workshop productions in the Cottesloe so that we can respond to plays that we have in hand and want to do, but cannot stage in a full-scale production. So, although it looks as though our subsidy is a lot of money—and it is a lot—a little more—perhaps 20% more—would really enable the National Theatre to do its proper job; and it could then be properly judged.

**Beacham:** Instead you get unhelpful articles in the press.

**Brown:** We have had helpful and unhelpful articles in the press. At first it was thought that subsidy to the National Theatre would reduce subsidy to other theaters; but that has been proved not to be the case. In fact the subsidy for theater in the provinces has gone up from twenty-odd percent to forty percent since we've been around; that's nothing but good, it seems to me.

The National Theatre ought to be established so that its full potential could become absolutely clear. We're already doing above 90% capacity business in our two main houses; the public is coming to the theater for exhibitions, music, short plays, and readings, as well as for full-scale productions of old and new plays; 1978 sees Edward Bond's *The Woman* as the first new play in the Olivier, plus a new Harold Pinter in the Lyttelton Theatre. But more is possible. The country should have a fully flying National Theatre in London and far more National Theatres in the center, theaters which serve the community and the profession with productions of new plays and the classical repertoire; theaters able to move into educational and community fields. There is a hell of a lot of work to do.

1978

# V

# DRAMATURGY IN EASTERN EUROPE

"The dramaturg is new to the American theatre,
but not to any other national theatre."

—Alain Piette

# Directors, Dramaturgs, and War in Poland: An Interview with Jan Kott

Rustom Bharucha,
Janice Paran, and Laurence Shyer

*The following discussion is excerpted from an interview with Jan Kott,
author of* Shakespeare Our Contemporary *(1964),* The Eating Of
The Gods *(1973), and other books.*

## I. Brook, Strehler, and the Burg Theater

**Jan, you have not written about your association with Peter
Brook or Giorgio Strehler in any way that would confirm this,
but would you say you served as their dramaturg? When did
you first begin to talk with Brook about *King Lear*?**
Peter Brook came to Warsaw in 1957 with his production of
*Titus Andronicus.* I was impressed by the production; it confirmed my thoughts that the cruel, Renaissance Shakespeare
was our contemporary. After seeing his production I took
Brook to the old town section of Warsaw . . . We had a quiet
conversation for three or four hours—it was our first and only
meeting not interrupted by telephone calls. It was the beginning of our conversations about *King Lear.* After that Peter
invited me to his London flat, where I stayed as a guest for two
weeks. He read the French version of my essay on *Lear* before
his production of the play. I remember that when we discussed
the play he was always working with his hands on a design of
the set. For Peter the production was first of all to be planned
in the set.

**Have you met with Brook about other productions since then?**

Not much. *Lear* was the first and last occasion that I was in
some way involved in one of his productions. But you should
know that Peter Brook is open to all kinds of influence. He is
highly eclectic, always looking for some kind of inspiration. The
written word, as well as paintings and other productions, are
for him *just* the inspiration. I cannot say I was his dramaturg. It
would be impossible to be a dramaturg for Peter. You can only
be a dramaturg in his dreams, if he dreams about you. At the
same time that he is open to influence, he is extremely independent.

One of Brook's greatest accomplishments in his *King Lear*
was the disintegration of the stage plateau. By the end of the
performance the surface of the stage had been eroded as after
an earthquake.

**This came from one of your ideas about the play?**
My idea had been that there had to be some sort of physical disintegration, and that this could be shown with higher and lower
platforms on the stage. [Editor's note: This conversation with
Brook is described in Kott's "Shakespearean Notebook" chapter
of *Shakespeare Our Contemporary*. Kott says he once tried to persuade Brook "to show how all characters of this drama
descended lower and lower. I wanted the early acts to be performed on a large plate placed high up on stage and to demonstrate physically, materially, visibly as it were, the disintegration
and descent. Brook did not need any of these naive
metaphors."]

**Brook's idea was not entirely different from yours?**
No, but Peter worked with the stage as the stage, which is part
of his greatness. One almost alchemical result of his experience
are the Bouffes Parisian productions, where the theater exists
as the relics or skeleton of a theater. You have a stage that is
partially "destroyed." One sees the seams or bare bones
beneath the surface. In his Paris productions of *The Cherry
Orchard* and *Carmen,* he used the basic structure of the
theater—the remnants of the theater—as part of the set.

**I understand he did the same thing in his *Timon of Athens*.**
He uses the theater's balconies and the public doors as elements in the set, ingeniously opening up the setting more than
so-called "environmental theater," because he employs the fundamental structure of the theater as the theatrical environment.
The stage works as a metaphor for the actions, perhaps as it did
in ancient Greek theater and at the Globe, when elements of
the stage changed into a palace or a forest. It was not necessary
for Brook to have painted scenery in *Carmen*; the arena for bull-
fighting was located behind one of the doors, for example. This
style began in *King Lear*, where the stage plateau was rendered
"naked."

**In *A Midsummer Night's Dream* Brook used the stage as stage,
too.**
Yes. If you recall, in the last act the theater house (audience
space) is fully lit. That established another kind of relationship
between the stage and the audience; the audience under the
lights became part of the stage world. While the actors watched
the comedy of *Pyramus and Thisbe*, the audience watched the
larger comedy in a relation parallel to that on stage. This was
an extremely ingenious construction of theater within theater.

**What do you admire most about Brook?**
The greatest difference between him and other directors is that
he is working with the text. He wants to have a great text performed, and not to create it himself. (There have been exceptions to this in his work.) There is a marvelous line in Hegel:
"You have to meet your fate; but you have to meet your fate as
your friend and your enemy." For Peter the great texts are both
his friends and his enemies. He is fighting the text, but he is
also fighting for the text. (He is performing Shakespeare as he
actively resists it.)
   Once when I was serving as a dramaturg in Vienna, in a lecture I said: "We have to perform the classics in such a way that
we rape them, but rape them with love." It is a relationship built
out of both violence and respect. It is a relationship where one
is both friend and enemy.

**Have other essays you wrote about Shakespeare influenced
Brook?**
My chapter on *A Midsummer Night's Dream,* particularly the
emphasis on the sexual meeting between Titania and Bottom,
influenced Brook's production of the play. The chapter inspired
many productions, but I was probably wrong in what I said
there.

Ultimately it was my book, more than any meeting with directors, which influenced productions. There are exceptions; two
or three times in Poland I worked on productions with directors who were friends of mine. But I am not a professional
man, and if I have been an animus, a spirit of enlightenment—it
has been in influencing or reshaping, recreating the theatrical
imagination of the directors, designers, actors.

**You also discussed *The Tempest* with Giorgio Strehler prior to
his production of the play in Milan.**
Yes, that was the first time abroad that I worked as an unpaid
dramaturg, in two ten-day sessions. Strehler is a genius, but one
completely different from Brook. Brook is like a big cat, always
watching you; not talking, but taking. You don't really have a
conversation with Brook; he is always questioning, but he does
not give you an answer.

Giorgio is quite different. He asked me to come and talk with
him, but then he did almost all the talking himself. He asks a
question and gives his own answer immediately.

My greatest experience with Giorgio was in Rome, before we
worked together. He arrived there with a Goldoni play. Before
the performance he rehearsed with his actors for a few hours in
the afternoon. He invited about 40 or 50 friends and critics to
watch the rehearsal. He ended rehearsing with his face to the
audience and his back to the actors. This was the first time I
ever saw a director rehearsing as if he were a performer.

Strehler is a marvelous person, but difficult to work with. He
could not begin to work before 1 a.m., which was rather late for
me. Also, for him working together is always a ritual or cere-
mony. He has 10 to 15 collaborators, assistant directors; his
wife assists too, and everything has to be a show.

In Giorgio's vision, the paradise still exists, at least as a promise; it is almost impossible for him to make something tragic, pessimistic or hopeless. While the ending of *The Tempest* is bitter in my reading of it, Giorgio did everything he could to change the ending to preserve some hope for Prospero, for spectators; for himself, for us . . .

**Did you discuss that with him?**
Yes, but it was like talking to the wall. He identified himself with Prospero, and Prospero's loss would be a personal failure to him. After Prospero throws away his staff, a stagehand in the orchestra pit would give it back to him in Strehler's production.

At times I was the only one who was able to say "No" to him. If he didn't listen to me, at least I partially convinced him, and he partially convinced me, because his knowledge of the theater is so great.

One of my ideas for his *Tempest* was that Caliban should be beautiful, young, fascinating. They say he is dirty because he is a Negro and a slave; but he could be fascinating. I thought the role should be played by a beautiful, young black actor. Finally, I guess Giorgio was right; he thought a "savage" in the theater should be a white man playing a "Nigger." He chose to have a white actor playing a black Caliban and it worked quite well . . .

**Did you see Strehler's *Re Lear*?**
Yes. His production, which he did after reading my essay, was to my mind the most faithful to my book: extremely cruel. And the same actress, Ottavia Piccolo, played both Cordelia and the Fool.

Strehler has excellent intuition, as well as great knowledge of *commedia dell'arte* and Renaissance theater, and dialects and lighting. He is probably one of the greatest artists of lighting in the modern theater. He once spent 4 or 5 hours changing lights for *The Tempest*, with his lighting director and Miranda and Fernando on stage. It was one of the most marvelous nights I've had in the theater, watching him light sunsets, or the beginning of the world, with the young actor and actress on stage in flesh-colored costumes, so that they resembled Adam and Eve. It was

almost like a trance or hallucination, a beautiful use of the theater by Strehler for his own delight.

**In 1976 you were a guest dramaturg at the Burg Theater in
Vienna. What did you do there?**
That is a beautiful story. Kafka could have written it. First of all,
I don't speak German; the Burg Theater knew this when they
first interviewed me. Did they believe that I would learn the
language after a few months in Vienna? Anyway they hired me,
and paid me a handsome salary for my six-month residency.
They gave me a wonderful office, with automatic doors, so no
one could enter or leave without my pushing a button. The
office had three or four telephones, a kitchen, and a bathroom
with a hidden window through which I could see the interior of
the theater.

In the kitchen I had a supply of cognac and vodka. They
brought me coffee twice a day. I was astonished that after two
or three weeks there no one had asked for me—neither the
directors, nor the Intendant, nor the actors. I asked for meetings at times, but I was almost completely alone. And each
morning at ten they brought me a stack of German newspapers.
So I adjusted to my situation after a few weeks; I had my salary,
my telephones, the German newspapers, and Viennese coffee.

After five or six weeks, I was surprised to hear someone
knocking on my door. A bouquet of flowers was being delivered, but it was not for me; the card was addressed to my predecessor as dramaturg at the Burg Theater. When I called the
main office, they said he was one floor above me. I decided to
visit him when I learned this, and discovered he had an office
like mine, with perhaps one less telephone and a smaller
kitchen.

When I told him about my situation, with no one calling me,
and so on, he said: "You should be very happy, because you
receive the German newspapers when they're new; when I
receive mine they're a week old."

A few months after this meeting, when I was about to leave
Vienna, I again went to pay my respects to my predecessor, and
he said: "It would be good if you could go and see *my* predecessor; he is on the third floor." So I met him, a very old man with

a long beard, seated in a beautiful office. He was surprised to see me. I was the first one to visit him in almost a year. He said he received his German newspapers a month after they were published. And he had only two telephones, but no one called him anyway.

So we had three generations of dramaturgs at the Burg Theater, each on his own floor.

**Didn't the Burg Theater initially invite you there to change things, to introduce innovations?**
Yes, they did; but they did not show any willingness to change once I was there. When I proposed any change, they would say: "This is impossible." Either the audience could not change, or the actors, or someone else. Anyway, it was pleasant to stay in Vienna, and the *Kaffee mit Schlag* was excellent.

## II. Poland Before and After December 13th

**You have worked as a dramaturg in Poland?**
Yes, I worked at various theaters as a literary advisor for several years; I was also writing regular reviews at the time. I figure I have spent somewhere between one third and one half of my life in theaters, either onstage or off. Most of my friends have been directors, designers, and actors. I was almost never seriously tempted to write or direct plays myself, although I did direct three or four times when I was in San Francisco. One particularly successful production experience in Poland was *The Misanthrope*; I wrote a prose adaptation of it to be performed in modern dress. It ran for hundreds of performances and was even translated into Serbo-Croatian. The poster was very gratifying; it read *"Misanthrope–Molière–Kott."*

**What do you make of Grotowski's current work? He was one of the great visionaries of the modern theater, and now he is running workshops and exercises, not rigorous as in his earlier work, but concerned instead with communication—very mystical it seems.**
Grotowski understood quite well that the ultimate achievement of his career was *Apocalypsis cum Figuris*, and that the best way

for him to continue was to stop working in that way and do
something completely different. He looked instead to create
paratheatrical experiences in rituals of meeting, mating, and so
on. I couldn't take it entirely seriously—to me, it was like adults
playing boy scout: hiking to the forest, building fires, etc. It was
very useful for the Polish government, however; many of the
participants paid in hard currency for the privilege of spending
a night in the woods with Grotowski, or the Polish ritualistic
gods and not-so-ritualistic girls. There are always two sides to
mystical experiences.

**It does seem that theater today lacks the urgency, the vitality
that it had a generation ago.**
Yes, things are different. For the first ten or fifteen years after
the war in Poland, the situation was special. There were very
few movies, because of the scarcity of hard currency to import
them. The theater was relatively cheap; a ticket cost less than a
pack of cigarettes. Theater was an important part of our lives,
more so than any time before or since, and it always presents
special opportunities in times of political repression. Something
in theater's nature makes it relevant to the political arena, even
in plays that aren't political like *Waiting for Godot*. That was an
especially significant play, perfectly suited to the circumstances;
it was Waiting for Communism. Also, at that time in Warsaw,
there was an active political and artistic intelligentsia for whom
the theater was a reflection of the times. It didn't even really
matter what was onstage; the audience found in it connections
to their own lives.

**You are one of the few critics of theater and dramatic litera-
ture who are not embarrassed to relate texts and productions
very personally to events of your own life. For instance, you
have discussed the oppositions, and Bernardine's "refusal to
die," in *Measure for Measure* in relation to your own experience in the war. Can you tell that story?**
It was in the last weeks of the guerilla campaign in Poland, after
the Warsaw uprising. The situation was very bad, everything
was being destroyed. The regiment to which I belonged was
trying to cross the Vistula River to escape the German army,

and we counted on the Hungarians' help. We had worked out
an arrangement with the Hungarian soldiers, who were the
Germans' allies. They gave us arms in exchange for American
twenty-dollar (gold) coins. We had a lot of American money,
because the Americans parachuted belts packed with gold coins.
You could live a month on a single coin—it was a lot of money.
Anyway, our regiment bought submachine guns from the Hungarians and they told us that they would insure our passage
across the river. I don't know if what happened next was a mistake, a change in plans from German headquarters, or a
betrayal, but when we got to the river, we were met not by the
Hungarians but by an army of S.S. We fought them for four
days and nights; we were completely circled. Our regiment con-
sisted of about 180 men with four machine guns among us. The
fighting was very heavy—we tried desperately to escape. We had
nothing to eat or drink in all that time and we lost about a
dozen men. Finally, on the fifth night, we managed to escape.
We marched about 20-25 kilometers and encamped at last. My
captain assigned me to the night watch. It was extremely difficult—I was terribly tired, as we all were, having been fighting
nonstop for days—and I fell asleep in the early hours of the
morning. Another officer discovered me. Falling asleep on
guard duty was a very serious offense during the war. A military
court was held the next day and I was sentenced to be shot. The
tribunal was held at six a.m.; I was to be shot at one. As I
remember, I went back to sleep after the sentencing. I was still
exhausted and slept like a log. About noon, my captain came to
see me. "Janek," he said to me, "I'm sorry, we're all extremely
sorry, but what can I do? There is no other way. Now there is
an old military custom that, if you are going to be shot, you can
have a final request—a bottle of vodka, a girl, or a priest. Janek,
because we all love you, we'll make an exception for you: you
can have all three." I was still so tired I had only one wish—to be
allowed to sleep up to the time of the execution. No girl, no
priest, no vodka—well, maybe that, just before the shot. No one
could believe I was so cold-blooded. Half an hour later medics
were sent in. They discovered I was running a very high fever;
in fact, I had typhus. When they realized I was ill, they were put
in a rather embarrassing position. You can't put a sick man to

death, it's against procedure. A man must be in good health to
die. Later, a new trial was held and I was absolved of my crime.
In fact, because they were ashamed of having earlier convicted
me, they awarded me the highest military honors and sent me
back to the hospital.

**It's a little like *The Prince of Homburg*. Do you feel events like
that have influenced your view of the theater?**
Yes, I think I am somewhat different from many of my colleagues in that respect, and not just as a critic but as a teacher.
For me, there is not a great difference between books and life,
between dramatic literature or criticism and basic human experiences: fighting, eating, sleeping, making love, travelling, and
so on. They are not separate but the same, and they provide
mutual enrichment; books enrich human experience and
human experience enriches books. My life may seem out of the
ordinary to an American scholar—I was a guerilla, involved in
the Party and in the underground and so on—but to a Polish
man of my generation these experiences are quite routine.
Because of my background, I think I do have some understanding of the "cruel world," of the tragic experiences in drama,
though it is sometimes revealed through the most trivial events.
For many scholars, however, I think there is not this same connection between literature or the drama and their lives. The
lovely scene they see on stage or read in a book is nothing like
their own love scenes in bed—it's not the same world at all. Perhaps they are too embarrassed to allow their own experiences
to shed light on a dramatic character's.

The story of Cressida, for example, is connected to something important in my own life. Cressida's story is the same as
Juliet's: each was able to spend only one night, her first night,
with the man she loved before they were separated, before the
world intervened to part them. To understand Cressida's behavior, to relate it to probable behavior in "real life," it is necessary
to look at it from her viewpoint: if the world is made in so devil-
ish a way that a girl can sleep with the man she loves only one
night in her life before they are separated, then there are only
two solutions: one, tragic, is suicide—that is Juliet's solution; the
second one is to become a whore. That is Cressida's. There is

no other, if you really understand what it is to be a young girl who loses her lover after her first night of lovemaking.

I once taught a course to a group of young guerillas in Warsaw; they were from the Communist party, from the People's Army. They performed very dangerous tasks, terrorist attacks against the Gestapo; they were very heroic. Among my students was a young couple: she was a poet, he was a clever, beautiful boy. In this time that I knew them, they made love for the first time. He was killed the same week. A few weeks later, this beautiful young girl, who had been so innocent, began sleeping around. Later, when I read *Troilus and Cressida*, I understood it because of that girl.

**What do you think of the situation in Poland now?**
The last time I was in Poland was in December of 1981. It was for the first independent congress of culture sponsored by Solidarity. On the third day of the congress the coup took place; the congress was dissolved and many of the participants were arrested and put into isolation camps. I left Poland one week later.

When I returned to this country, I was asked what things were like in Warsaw. The situation there gets worse and worse; to my mind, it's hopeless for years to come. Of course in Poland, these things move in cycles, up and down, with a rebirth of hope every eight to ten years. Now history seems to be accelerating and perhaps we'll have a new reason to hope in another five or six years, but for the time being, there is little reason to think so. The current situation has changed my plans completely. I had hoped to return to Poland to renew my teaching career there. I had been fired from the University of Warsaw during the years of repression, then reinstated by a new Rector under Solidarity's influence. Now *that* new Rector has been fired, everything has changed again, and a new cycle of repression has begun. Like the Grand Mechanism.

1983

# The Dramaturg in Yugoslavia

Sanja Ivić

The role of the dramaturg, as well as of the dramaturgy team (usually each theater is equipped with two or three individual dramaturgs), is similar in every theater in Yugoslavia. At the HNK (Hrvatsko Narodno Kazaliste), one of the oldest national theater institutions in the country, the dramaturg has played a substantial role for some time. In the 1985-1986 season, the theater celebrates its 125th anniversary; during those years it has had many distinguished dramaturgs on the staff. At present the HNK employs a small dramaturgy team composed of two young experts and a chief who coordinates their work with the manager of the Department of Drama. We are also at the point of creating a dramaturgy team for Opera and Ballet, in addition to the existing one which works with Drama.

## The Role of the Dramaturg

The *first* task of dramaturgs is to read all the plays or dramatizations submitted to the theater. At the same time they are obliged to answer all queries made by writers before and after the process of selecting the repertoire. The theater is an international institution; thus we think that a basic prerequisite for such work is the knowledge of foreign languages. Such knowledge of languages provides the opportunity for dramaturgs to propose a wide variety of interesting plays, both domestic and foreign, whether translated or not. Our small staff of dramaturgs speaks and reads seven languages: English, French, German, Italian, Russian, Latin, and classical Greek.

The second task of dramaturgs is to propose a repertoire, that is to say, to create the repertoire in cooperation with directors, actors, and managers. Each considered text is submitted to a brief critique and analysis of characters, situations, etc., and reasons for or against putting the play on the stage are debated (of course, this is not done without consulting the directors or actors who are most likely to be involved). HNK is a repertory theater: the repertoire must be fixed five years in advance. Naturally, there is always the possibility of changing the repertories for its two theaters, one involving the main stage (shared with Opera and Ballet) and the other involving a small stage which is reserved for modern and avant-garde plays.

With these two tasks in mind, the dramaturg strives to contribute to the creative work of the theater. But there are many other activities which supplement his basic work. One such primary task is to accumulate as much information as possible about other theaters in Yugoslavia and abroad.

The dramaturg keeps abreast of all important festivals in Yugoslavia and Europe. He also tries to be informed about theatrical projects in the United States and, if there is anything interesting, he does his best to acquire the text. Thanks to our Archives Department, which maintains a collection of theater magazines and reviews, we have a general idea of the repertoires of various theaters in Europe. We are lucky that some of our directors, choreographers, and scenographers work occasionally in European and American theaters, and can provide us with current information. We also maintain good relations with all the national theaters in Yugoslavia (in some cases we exchange the more interesting plays), and in the future we intend to do the same with other theaters abroad. The members of the dramaturgy staff also take part in national and international congresses (in July our young dramaturg gave a lecture on Sophocles' *Antigone* in Greece). As part of this activity HNK is currently investigating the possibilities of professional scholarships in foreign countries.

During the last two years a dramaturg was assigned to every drama production in our theater. Since that type of work is very demanding, all three men on the dramaturgy team were involved. During rehearsals of the production with the director and the theater staff, the other members of the dramaturgy team also did regular readings, analyses, etc. Such an arrangement means that each member of our dramaturgy team can be a dramaturg on one production. He can be chosen to participate by the director or by the chief manager of Drama. When he is chosen to be a member of the production staff (usually a few months prior to rehearsals) he immediately begins to collect material. He is obliged to introduce to his director all interesting materials pertaining not only to the text, but also to the time and the customs, together with various pertinent details, information about the author, comparative studies of other plays or authors, and cultural research. He proposes cuts to the text; he can also invite experts from various universities or other specialized institutions to provide cultural information. Of course, this is done in consultation with the director. The director then chooses from this material items of interest to him and instructs his dramaturg to undertake further research. The dramaturg also collaborates with the set and costume designers. Naturally, he is very much involved with the actors, and often prepares material for study by each of them. To give a more detailed picture of the dramaturg's efforts in preparing a drama for the stage, a description of the work that went into the play *The Master and Margarita*, by M. A. Bulgakov, will be useful.

### The Master and Margarita— ### A Dramatization of the Novel ### by M. A. Bulgakov

The dramatization was done by a visiting director, Horea Popescu, in collaboration with his Romanian dramaturg, Andrea Baleanu.

The dramatization had been written in Romanian; then it was translated into Serbo-Croatian.

The translated text was compared to the original and proofread by our dramaturg and two assistant directors.

Communication with the Romanian director (who was also a stage designer) was in French.

Work on the scenario was divided into several parts. One group concentrated on *Pontius Pilatus* (that part of the novel which describes the crucifixion of Jesus Christ). Literature included the following:

1. *The Bible* (with a chronology of all events between 63 B.C. and 123 A.D.).
2. John Buchan's *Augustus* (London: A. P. Watt & Son, 1937).

3. André Aymard and Jeannine Auboyer's *Histoire Générale des Civilizations* (Paris: Press Universitaires de France, 1980).
4. Max Cary's *A History of Rome Down to the Reign of Constantine* (New York: St. Martin's Press, 1954).
5. Flavius Josephus' *De Bello Iudaico,* Libri septem (Florence: Bartolommeo di Libri, 1493).
6. Several back copies of the *National Geographic* with articles on Jerusalem.

A second group concentrated on *Woland* (the devil's part of the text). The literature was:

1. Vladimir Bayer's *Ugovor s Davlom,* or *Contract with the Devil* (Zagreb, 1969), about the trials of wizards and witches in Europe.
2. Jacques Bril's *Lilirh ou la Mère Obscure* (Paris: Payot, 1981).
3. Carlo Ginzburg's *I Benandanti: Stregoneria e culti agrari tra Cinquecento e Seicento* (Torino: G. Einaudi, 1979).
4. Jean Chevalier and Alain Gheerbrant's *Dictionnaire des Symboles* (Paris: R. Laffont, 1969).

A third group was concerned with the citizens of Moscow in the 1930s. For them we suggested the following literature about life in the USSR during the 1920s and 1930s:

1. Isaac Deutscher's *The Prophet Unarmed: Trotsky, 1921-1929* (London: Oxford University Press, 1959).
2. Aleksandar Flaker's *Pojmovnik Ruske Avangarde,* or *On the Russian Avant-Garde* (Zagreb, 1984).

For the background to the character of Ivan Bezdomny the only books suggested were the two novels by Ilia Ilf and Evgenii Petrov, *The Twelve Chairs* (1934) and *The Golden Calf* (1932).

For the actor playing the Master, we assigned various chapters from Sören Kierkegaard's *Sickness Unto Death* (translation: Beograd, 1974).

The actress playing Margarita was obliged to read *Vestice i njihov svet,* or *Witches and Their World* (Beograd, 1979), translated from Julio Caro Baroja's *Las Brujas y su Mundo* (Madrid, 1961). The last two performers also were given excerpts from

Thomas S. Szasz's *The Manufacture of Madness: A Comparative Study of the Inquisition and the Mental Health Movement* (New York: Harper & Row, 1970).

We had many consultations with several professors from the universities, for example, with a professor of Russian literature, Aleksandar Flaker, with a professor of comparative literature, Milivoj Solar, and with other experts from the Faculty of Arts and Sciences in Zagreb.

To facilitate the director's work as a set designer our dramaturg gave him a *Catalogue de l'exposition Paris-Moscou organisée par le Ministère de la Culture de l'URSS* (Moscou et le Centre Georges Pompidou, Paris, 1979), and also Aleksander Flaker's book on the Russian avant-garde, full of illustrations, affiches, and various materials from that period in the USSR.

The *Catalogue Paris-Moscou* also helped the costume designer. In addition, for costumes the dramaturg delineated descriptions of clothing from the novel.

The composer was also helped by the dramaturg (who, by chance, had majored in music).

For this enormous project with almost 40 actors, 30 stagehands, a mass of costumes (over 200), numerous changes of scenery (30 scenes), and an hour and a half of music (recorded as well as live music), the entire staff was completely immersed in work for almost four months. It would have been impossible to do this without the organization which the dramaturg's staff helped to provide. The final version of the production lasted four hours and was a great success.

But the dramaturg has one more important task—advertising. For each premiere the dramaturg must compose all announcements for TV, press, and radio. He is also obliged to provide materials for the program. For this kind of work a dramaturg is highly appreciated as a consultant with imagination and invention. He can be of enormous help to the director and actors and can make the process of staging a play much easier.

The role of the dramaturg in our theater does not differ from that of a literary advisor. The qualifications for a dramaturg are varied. Study of literature and the theory of drama, combined with a fundamental knowledge of music and the history of art, is essential. Above all, he must possess an enormous ability to provide new information and brief, understandable analyses. Further, he must have strong nerves, a positive bearing, and a sense for public relations. Such qualifications require several years of study and a certain amount of life-experience. Our dramaturgy staff includes two young ladies who are very keen for the heat of battle—but are often cooled by a chief with more than twenty years of experience in the theater.

In Yugoslavia there are six Academies of Dramatic Art, and each has a special department for training dramaturgs. Students not only specialize in theater, but during their four years of study can also choose one of several other specializations: film, TV, or radio. We cannot say that we are just beginning to train dramaturgs in Yugoslavia, but in some ways we are still pioneers. Therefore we are sure that the dramaturg has a bright future in our country. Many fields of theater are still left unexplored and, of course, the dramaturg is the one to explore them.

Our two young members of the dramaturg's staff have completed the following studies:

1. Department of Arts and Sciences (comparative literature, Latin and Greek languages, Yugoslavian literature, and philosophy).
2. The Academy of Dramatic Arts, IIIrd degree in the Department of Arts and Sciences (literature).

Both of the departments have programs which last four years. Our two dramaturgs studied simultaneously in the departments and finished in six years. Judging by this experience a qualified dramaturg can begin work at the age of 24 or 25. Our opinion is that such work in the theater should not be in the hands of the overly young, but if someone is going to work as a dramaturg, the sooner he begins the better.

We can all agree that this century is seeing only the beginning of an explosion of computers, video, and communication technology of all kinds. But we are equally certain that the theater has always needed a person with knowledge, imagination, and a love of the arts, and especially needs one now.

1986

# The Program as Performance Text

Nicholas Rzhevsky

The dramaturg's traditional job of preparing programs was given new dimensions in the Taganka Theater during the 1970s and 1980s. Emphasis, in this leading Moscow avant-garde company, was shifted from the secondary background material usually offered the audience to the use of printed images and words as organic parts of the performance. Such devices reflected a longstanding commitment at the Taganka to find new ways of integrating the written text into the stage action. Without going to the hieroglyphic extremes of Artaud, the resulting performance programs were often reminiscent of the Cruel Theater's attempt to make words a physical presence, to merge ideas and action, and to eliminate the distance between the written script and the affective life of the stage.

In his two Western productions of Dostoevsky's *Crime and Punishment* and *The Possessed,* Yury Liubimov, the founder of the theater, extended this performance strategy by providing spectators with school children's essays on Raskolnikov, and by handing out Stavrogin's Confession during intermission. The second play, in particular, demonstrated the director's typical creative response to literature. Stavrogin's Confession, of course, was not included in the first editions of the novel, just as its text was not included in the performance proper. In both instances the primary importance of the confession in understanding Stavrogin's motivations was given a peculiar emphasis by its ostensible exclusion from the work (although in Dostoevsky's case the exclusion played a stronger role since it forced substantial changes in the chapters that followed).

The dramaturgical activity that shaped such printed material—including, as in Poland, theater posters—involved intensive collaboration among director, set designer, actors, literary consultants, and other theater personnel. Particularly important was the contribution of David Borovsky, the Taganka's former set designer (now at the Contemporary Theater) who, in addition to strong visual images, often insisted on the inclusion of the original written text in the theater's promotions or communications. The poster for *Boris Godunov* (a play shut down by government order in 1983), as designed by Borovsky, thus included the opening lines spoken by Borotynsky and Shuisky; in another instance the title of the play based on Mayakovsky's poem "Listen!" became part of the exterior wall of the theater, sending an unmistakable call to the Moscow citizenry.

The following remarks pertain to nine representative programs. A uniting image on all Taganka literature, it must be said, is the theater's bright red emblem, which for each production suggests different meanings and different affective correlatives.

## 1.

*Ten Days That Shook the World* (1965). The performance of John Reed's novel opens with rehearsal exercises by the entire cast. The stage activity is interrupted by a shot as a scroll, held by two actors, is unrolled for the audience downstage center. It reads: "A Folk Performance in Two Parts with Pantomime, a Circus, Buffoonery, and Shooting. Based on Motifs from John Reed's Book." The same text is given in the program, under the title. The Taganka emblem at the top of the program, of course, carries the obvious revolutionary connotations, as does a long statement from N. Krupskaya printed immediately below. At the end of the performance, a reproduction of a historical document announcing Lenin's revolution is passed out to the audience. The interesting theatrical factor here is that confirmation, even a form of immortalization, of a historical event—after a performance resplendent with many styles of theater—is seen to be the natural purview of the written word.

## 2.

*Comrade, Believe* (1973). This production, based on Pushkin's correspondence, is introduced to the audience in the form of a letter. The program metaphor is more subtle than it might seem at first glance; the letter openly refers to the censorship which has haunted Russian letters from Pushkin's time to the present day, and it has a black border, in commemoration of the poet and in condemnation of a society that rejects its most talented writers. The contemporary reference, of course, is explicit in the bitterly ironic title (it was permitted only because the words were indeed written by Pushkin).

### 3.

*The Dawns Are Quiet Here* (1971). The Taganka emblem takes on memorial connotations in this program. The names of the five martyr-like heroines of the play are printed in large commemorative block letters. The red emblem is repeated at the end of the performance in memorial torches lit in the theater foyer.

### 4.

*Listen!* (1967). In this program—as in the program of *The Master and Margarita*—the Taganka emblem carries connotations of artistic creativity. The subtitle "A Poetic Performance—Love, War, Revolution, Art" notes organizing motifs of the script, which are entirely taken from Mayakovsky's poem. The different motifs, in turn, suggest the complexity of Mayakovsky and a primary performance strategy, since the poet is played by five different actors.

### 5.

*A Tale of Inspection* (1978). The famous Gogol profile shown on this program suggests the biographical issues which figure in the writer's works and the production's use of them. The agonizing creative responsibilities of the artist—delineated in the episodes based on "The Portrait"—are here illustrated in a peculiar interjection of the theatrical present. Before producing *A Tale of Inspection*, Liubimov and his colleagues, the composer Alfred Schnitke and Gennady Rozhdestvensky, had been soundly lambasted in *Pravda* and other Soviet publications for their work on Tchaikovsky's *Queen of Spades*. That production—originally scheduled for the Paris Opera—eventually was forbidden by the Soviet authorities. Rozhdestvensky and Schnitke, at the time of the *Tale of Inspection* premiere, were in disfavor and Liubimov's inclusion of their names in his program was more a signal of creative and moral support rather than an acknowledgment of their participation in the actual performance. (Rozhdestvensky, who is listed as "conductor," could hardly have directed an orchestra at the Taganka since there was no orchestra to direct.) Nevertheless, the interjection of names not related to the performance of Gogol does carry direct implications for the production. The principle at work is aesthetic solidarity and independence in the face of outside pressures. The production, like the credits, indicates support for the individual behind the creative act and reflects ways of honoring his talent. In Liubimov's *A Tale of Inspection*, a major stage imperative is to rediscover the man whom Chizhevsky labeled "the Uncommon Gogol" and who has been hidden under thick layers of subsequent interpretation, as in the Moscow Art Theater's production of *Dead Souls*.

## 6.

*The Exchange* (1977). The program for Yury Trifonov's work is probably the most original and best known in the Taganka repertoire. It is based on an application form for the exchange of an apartment in Moscow. As noted by Michael McLain, this method of listing characters, actors, and production personnel "implies the connection between the compromised, trapped Dmitriev and [Liubimov's] theatre company."[1] The principal tenant is thus listed as Liubimov, while the theater's housing authority is bleakly indicated to be the RSFSR Ministry of Culture. The official blank form denotes the endless bureaucratic procedures which are a part of Soviet society and the kind of utilitarian attitudes which undermine moral and theatrical sensibilities.

### 7.

*The House on the Embankment* (1980). This program came out of a second collaboration between Trifonov and Liubimov. David Borovsky's design is clear: the huge "DOM" (House) dominates the "embankment," as does the real apartment building which Trifonov describes in his story. The program design reflects the stage design. The production features a huge glass wall which covers the proscenium space from top to bottom and towers threateningly over the audience. The actors play from behind this glass wall, and occasionally break out to the stalls. If the official blank form of the first Trifonov work signaled the exchange of emotions and moral commitments for calculation and compromise, the wall and program in this instance indicate the bleak sociopolitical features of the writer's landscape. Liubimov joins Trifonov in exposing and literally foregrounding threats and barriers to friendship, love, and courage. The red emblem, here as in the other Taganka programs, still represents moral-aesthetic commitments, but it is simultaneously a pessimistic, even satiric sign of the theater's sociopolitical views. The change in possible denotations, of course, reflects the change in the theater's and Liubimov's attitudes from the time when *Ten Days That Shook the World* was being rehearsed to the premiere of *The House on the Embankment* in 1980.

### 8.

*The Master and Margarita* (1977). The red emblem of this program again affirms aesthetic and creative values and relates to the torch used in the production as well as to Woland's remarks that "manuscripts do not burn." Bulgakov's photograph is one of those held up and applauded by the actors during their curtain call, in homage to the writer's own survival and creative insolence in the face of Stalin's terror.

**9.**

*The Three Sisters* (1981). An underlying premise of this production is that Chekhov has become boring and meaningless through the endless theatrical production of his plays. Liubimov's stage version takes a metatheatrical tack—by use of a stage within a stage, for example—and the printed repetition of "Anton Pavlovich Chekhov" fourteen times on the program cover is in keeping with this approach. Deliberate shocks to the audience's expectation of the humdrum—such as the opening moment when the theater wall comes down and the three sisters finally get to see Moscow—are provided, among other instances in the description of the production as "A Performance in 2 Acts." The same metatheatrical reminders and proddings are given in the printed list of characters and actors. It is headed by famous Chekhovian actors of the past, including Kachalov as Tuzenbach and Popova as Irina. Kachalov, Popova, and Lursky do appear in the performance by means of their recorded voices. And the comparison of their dialogue with those of the Taganka actors, as one might expect, is not always to the benefit of past acting and speaking technique.

1986

# Notes

1  Michael McLain, "Trifonov's *The Exchange* at Liubimov's Taganka," *Slavic and East European Arts*, 3, No. 1 (1985), p. 166.

# VI

# A DRAMATURGY
# BIBLIOGRAPHY

"The dramaturg is, first and foremost, a resource."

—Jonathan Marks

# A Dramaturgy Bibliography

Allison, Ralph. "England's National Theater: An Interview with Kenneth Tynan." *Performance*, 1, No. 4 (Sept.-Oct. 1972), pp. 77-86.

Anderson, Douglas. "The Dream Machine: Thirty Years of New Play Development in America." *The Drama Review* (T119), 32, No. 3 (Fall 1988), pp. 55-84.

Ballet, Arthur. "Fifteen Years of Reading New Plays: Reflections on the Closing of the Office for Advanced Drama Research." *Theater*, 9, No. 2 (Spring 1978), pp. 41-44.

———. "Playwrights for Tomorrow: The Work of the Office for Advanced Drama Research." *Theatre Quarterly*, 8, No. 29 (Spring 1978), pp. 12-28.

Bank, Rosemarie K. "Interpreters, Dramaturgs, and Process Critics: A New Configuration for American Theatre." In *The 1980 Winners*. Ed. Roger Gross. A monograph published by the U.C.T.A. Program in Theory and Criticism of the American Theatre Association, 1981, pp. 11-16.

———. "Shaping the Script: Commission Produces a Bibliography of Dramaturgy." *Theatre News* (American Theatre Association), 15, No. 1 (Jan.-Feb. 1983), p. 6.

Barba, Eugenio. "The Nature of Dramaturgy." *New Theatre Quarterly*, 1, No. 1 (Feb. 1985), pp. 75-78.

Bennetts, Leslie. "Stage Conference Asks What Is a Dramaturge?" *New York Times*, 23 June 1983, Sec. C, p. 15.

Berc, Shelley. "Theatre in Boston: Lee Breuer's *Lulu*." *Theater*, 12, No. 3 (Summer-Fall 1981), pp. 69-77.

Booth, Susan V. "Dramaturg in Search of an Axis." *American Theatre*, 7, No. 6 (Sept. 1990), pp. 62-63.

Borreca, Art. "Political Dramaturgy: A Dramaturg's (Re)View." *The Drama Review* (T138), 37, No. 2 (Summer 1993), pp. 56-79.

Brown, John Russell. "Green Room: My Job at the National." *Plays and Players*, 25 (April 1978), pp. 10-11.

Bryden, Ronald. "Dear Miss Farthingale, Thank You for Your Tragedy. . . ." *New York Times*, 7 December 1975, Sec. 2, p. 1.

*Canadian Theatre Review*, CTR 8 (Fall 1975). This issue is devoted to dramaturgy and criticism:
Don Rubin, "The Critical Response," pp. 6-16
Philip Weissman, "Psychoanalyzing the Critic," pp. 17-23
Mary Humphrey Baldridge, "Canada's Critical Dilemma," pp. 24-26
David McCaughna, "Nathan Cohen in Retrospect," pp. 27-36
Ingmar Holm, Selem Petar, Harold Clurman, Carlos Tindemans, and Mendel Kohansky, "Training the Critic," pp. 37-42
Peter Hay, "Dramaturgy: Requiem for an Unborn Profession," pp. 43-46
Ernst Schumacher, "Brecht as Critic," pp. 47-54
David Watmough, "The Audience as Critic," pp. 55-58

Castagno, Paul. "Informing the New Dramaturgy: Critical Theory to Creative Process." *Theatre Topics*, 3, No. 1 (1993), pp. 29-42.

Cattaneo, Ann. "Institutionalizing the Blind Date: The Theatre and the Playwright." *Performing Arts Journal* (PAJ 24), 8, No. 3 (1984), pp. 100-104.

Cohen, Edward. *Working on a New Play: A Play Development Handbook for Actors, Directors, Designers, and Playwrights*. New York: Prentice-Hall, 1988.

Cook, Judith. "John Russell Brown: Head of Script Development." In *The National Theatre*. London: Harrap, 1976, pp. 67-72.

Copelin, David. "Ten Dramaturgical Myths." *Callboard* (Bay Area), June 1989, pp. 5, 7, 9.

Cottrell, John. *Laurence Olivier*. Englewood Cliffs, New Jersey: Prentice-Hall, 1975, pp. 329-331, 348-352, 364, 373-374. (On Kenneth Tynan's tenure as Literary Manager at the National Theatre.)

Davis, Ken, and William Hutchings. "Playing a New Role: The English Professor as Dramaturg." *College English*, 46, No. 6 (Oct. 1984), pp. 560-569.

"Directors, Dramaturgs, and War in Poland: An Interview with Jan Kott." Conducted by Rustom Bharucha, Janice Paran, and Laurence Shyer. *Theater*, 14, No. 2 (Spring 1983), pp. 27-31.

*The Drama Review* (T85), 24, No. 1 (March 1980). The German theatre issue, which discusses dramaturgs in various articles:
Arno Paul, "The West German Theatre Miracle: A Structural Analysis," pp. 3-24
John Rouse, "The Sophocles/Hölderlin *Antigone* and the System," pp. 25-38
Richard Riddell, "The German *Raum*," pp. 39-52
Volker Canaris, "Peter Zadek and *Hamlet*," pp. 53-62
Raimund Hoghe, "The Theatre of Pina Bausch," pp. 63-74
Brigitte Kueppers, "Max Reinhardt's *Sumurun*," pp. 75-84
Mel Gordon, "Lothar Schreyer and the Sturmbühne," pp. 85-102
Glen Gadberry, "The Thingspiel: Das Frankenburger Würfelspiel," pp. 103-114
Carl Weber, "Brecht in Eclipse?", pp. 115-124

"Dramaturgy and Physics: Panel Discussion Moderated by James Leverett, with James C. Nicola, Richard Dresser,

Morgan Jenness, and Tim Sanford." *Journal of Stage Directors and Choreographers*, 5, No. 1 (Summer 1991), pp. 4-21.

Elwood, William R. "Preliminary Notes on the German Dramaturg and American Theater." *Modern Drama*, 13, No. 3 (Dec. 1970), pp. 254-258.

Esslin, Martin. "Giving Playwrights Experience." *West Coast Plays*, 2 (1978), pp. 211-216.

Fjelde, Rolf. "Lost in Translation." *Theatre Communications*, 6, No. 2 (Feb. 1984), pp. 1-4.

Granville-Barker, Harley. *The Exemplary Theatre*. London: Sidgwick & Jackson, 1922, pp. 185-192. (On the qualifications and powers of a playreader.)

——. *A National Theatre*. London: Sidgwick & Jackson, 1930, pp. 40-42. (On the qualifications and responsibilities of the literary manager.)

Hay, Peter. "The Eugene O'Neill Theatre Center." *Canadian Theatre Review*, CTR 21 (Winter 1979), pp. 17-26. (Discusses the role of dramaturgs at the O'Neill and explores whether Canada should implement a similar play development center.)

——. "American Dramaturgy: A Critical Re-Appraisal." *Performing Arts Journal*, 7, No. 3 (1983), pp. 7-24.

——. Letter to the Editor of "Arts and Leisure" (in response to Terence McNally's article "From Page to Stage: How a Playwright Guards His Vision," 7 Dec. 1986). *New York Times*, 8 Feb. 1987, Sec. 2, pp. 19, 40.

Helbo, André, *et al.*, ed. *Approaching Theatre*. Bloomington: Indiana Univ. Press, 1991. (Originally published as *Théâtre: Modes d'approche* in 1987 by Editions Labor, Brussels. Contains such articles as Patrice Pavis, "Dramaturgy and Specificity of the Media," pp. 24-28; Lars Seeberg, "From Analysis to Production: Dramaturgy," pp. 174-184; and André Helbo, J. Dines Johansen, Patrice Pavis, and

Lars Seeberg, "*As You Like It*: A Dramaturgic Analysis," pp. 209-223.)

Hornby, Richard. *Script into Performance: A Structuralist View of Play Production*. Austin: University of Texas Press, 1977, pp. 63, 197-199. (On the dramaturg and "dramaturgical criticism.")

"John Lahr: Critic-at-Guthrie Theatre Rehearsals." *Variety*, 16 Oct. 1968, p. 2.

Kott, Jan. "The Dramaturg." *New Theatre Quarterly*, 6, No. 21 (Feb. 1990), pp. 3-4.

Lahr, John. "Green Room: I Lost It at the Theatre." *Plays and Players*, 20, No. 4 (Jan. 1973), pp. 12-13. (Lahr discusses his experiences as literary advisor to the Repertory Theater of Lincoln Center.)

Leverett, James. "Dramaturgs and Literary Managers: A Major Conference to Define the Role." *Theatre Communications*, 2 (March 1981), pp. 4-5.

Levine, Mindy. "How Does a Literary Manager Manage?" *Theatre Times* (Alliance of Resident Theatres), Feb. 1983.

*LMDA Newsletter*. A publication of Literary Managers and Dramaturgs of the Americas, Box 355 CASTA, CUNY Grad Center, 33 West 42 St., New York, N.Y. 10036; telephone (212) 642-2657.

Loup, Alfred J. "Vienna's Burgtheater in the 1970s." *Theatre Journal*, 32, No. 1 (March 1980), pp. 54-70. (A discussion of the policies and practices of the dramaturgs and artistic directors of this theatre during the decade.)

Maes, Nancy. "Drama-what? Dramaturg—The Behind-the-Scenes Interpreter." *Chicago Tribune*, 23 May 1986, Sec. 7, pp. 5, 10.

Marowitz, Charles. "The Dramaturg's Lament." *American Theatre*, 6, No. 7 (Oct. 1989), p. 9.

McKenna, Maryn. "The Dramaturg: Towards a New Job Description." *Dramatics*, 58, No. 8 (April 1987), pp. 28-31.

McNally, Terence. "From Page to Stage: How a Playwright Guards His Vision." *New York Times*, 7 Dec. 1986, Sec. 2, pp. 1, 26.

Price, Anthony. "The Freedom of the German Repertoire." *Modern Drama*, 13, No. 3 (Dec. 1970), pp. 237-246. (A discussion of the functions of the German dramaturg and the practice of rewriting plays.)

Schechter, Joel. "Lessing, Jugglers, and Dramaturgs." *Yale/Theatre*, 7, No. 1 (1975), pp. 93-103.

———. "American Dramaturgs." *The Drama Review* (T70), 20, No. 2 (June 1976), pp. 88-92.

———. "Heiner Müller and Other East German Dramaturgs." *Yale/Theatre*, 8, Nos. 2 & 3 (Spring 1977), pp. 152-154.

Shyer, Laurence. "Writers, Dramaturgs, and Texts: Maita Niscemi, Heiner Müller, Annette Michelson." In his *Robert Wilson and His Collaborators*. New York: Theatre Communications Group, 1989, pp. 87-152.

Skopnik, Günter. "An Unusual Person: Der Dramaturg." *World Theatre*, 9, No. 3 (Autumn 1960), pp. 233-238.

*Slavic and East European Arts*, 4, No. 1 (Spring 1986). Issue devoted to dramaturgs and dramaturgy:
Ileana Berlogea, "The Role of the Dramaturg in Contemporary Romanian Theater," pp. 7-13
Sanja Ivić, "The Dramaturg in Yugoslavia," pp. 15-20
Kazimierz Braun, "I Love Literature, Great Poetry, and the Keen Intelligence of Writers," pp. 21-25
Andrzej Makarewicz, "The Dramaturg: Dreams and Reality," pp. 27-30
Zdeněk Hedbávný, "Dramaturgs in Czechoslovakia," pp. 31-34
Judith Szántó, "Dramaturgs in Hungary," pp. 35-40

Aleco Mintchev, "The Dramaturg in the Theatres of Bulgaria," pp. 41-44

Klaus Voelker, "Responsibilities and Functions of the Dramaturg in West Germany," pp. 45-48

Ernst Schumacher, "The Power and Impotence of the Dramaturg: The Image of a Profession and Its Problematic Nature," pp. 49-54

Russell E. Brown, "Bertolt Brecht as Dramaturg," pp. 55-60

Alf Sjöberg, "Sensuality in Brecht," pp. 61-67

C. J. Gianakaris, "The American View: The Future for Dramaturgs on U.S. Campuses," pp. 69-81

Felicia Hardison Londré, "A Note on Soviet Dramaturgs," pp. 83-84

Alexey Kazantsev, "Soviet Dramaturgy Today," pp. 85-95

Nicholas Rzhevsky, "The Program as Performance Text," pp. 97-101

E. J. Czerwinski, "Józef Szajna's *Replika*: Expanding the Scope of Dramaturgy," pp. 115-119

*Theater*, 10, No. 1 (Fall 1978). This issue is devoted to dramaturgy:

Laurence Shyer, "America's First Literary Manager: John Corbin at the New Theatre," pp. 8-14

"Dramaturgs in America: Eleven Statements," pp. 15-30 (Statements by Jonathan Alper, André Bishop, Oscar Brownstein, Ann Cattaneo, Barbara Field, John Lahr, Steve Lawson, Jonathan Marks, Bonnie Marranca, Mira Rafalowicz, and Douglas Wager)

William Kleb, "Dramaturgy at A.C.T.: An Interview with Dennis Powers and William Ball of the American Conservatory Theatre," pp. 31-36

Richard Beacham, "Literary Management at the National Theatre, London: An Interview with John Russell Brown," pp. 38-42

Carol Rosen, "Literary Management at the RSC Warehouse, London: An Interview with Walter Donohue," pp. 43-46

Martin Esslin, "The Role of the Dramaturg in European Theater," pp. 48-50

Henning Rischbieter, "Dramaturgy in Berlin: An Interview with Ernst Wendt," pp. 51-52

Reinhardt Stumm, "Dramaturgy in Stuttgart: An Interview with Hermann Beil," pp. 53-56

Joel Schechter, "Brecht and Other Dramaturgs," pp. 57-59

Laurence Shyer, "Playreaders, Dramaturgs, and Literary Managers: A Bibliography," pp. 60-62

*Theater*, 17, No. 3 (Summer-Fall 1986). This issue is devoted to dramaturgy:

Mark Bly, "American Production Dramaturgs: An Introduction and Seven Interviews," pp. 5-42

Introduction, pp. 5-6

"Dramaturgy at the Eureka: An Interview with Oskar Eustis," pp. 7-12

"Dramaturgy at the Mark Taper Forum: An Interview with Russell Vandenbroucke," pp. 13-18

"Dramaturgy at the Magic and the O'Neill: An Interview with Martin Esslin," pp. 19-24

"Dramaturgy at Second Stage and the Phoenix: An Interview with Ann Cattaneo," pp. 25-28

"Dramaturgy at Large: An Interview with Arthur Ballet," pp. 29-32

"Dramaturgy at the Yale Rep: An Interview with Gitta Honegger," pp. 33-37

"Dramaturgy at the Brooklyn Academy of Music: An Interview with Richard Nelson," pp. 38-42

David Moore, Jr., "Dramaturgy at the Guthrie: An Interview with Mark Bly," pp. 43-50

Linda Walsh Jenkins and Richard Pettengill, "Dramaturgy at the Court and Wisdom Bridge," pp. 51-55

Alexis Greene, "A Note on Literary Managers and Dramaturgs of America," p. 56

Helmut Schäfer, "On the Necessary Non-Sense of Production Dramaturgy," pp. 57-58

Mark Lord, "Sweepstakes for a Vision: 'Classics in Context' in Context," pp. 59-62

Trousdell, Richard. "New Writers, New Plays: A Dramaturg Measures What's Wrong (and Right) with Them." *Theatre News* (American Theatre Association), 17, No. 4 (March-April 1985), pp. 2, 12.

Tynan, Kenneth. "The Critic Comes Full Circle." *Theatre Quarterly*, 1, No. 2 (April-June 1971), pp. 37-48. (An interview in which Tynan, Literary Manager of the National Theatre, comments on his appointment, the company's choice of repertory, his collaboration with Olivier, script readers, the commissioning of new plays, and his intention to chronicle his years at the National Theatre.)

——. *The Sound of Two Hands Clapping*. London: Jonathan Cape, 1975, pp. 119-140. (The development of the National Theatre's productions of *The Recruiting Officer* in 1963 and *Othello* in 1964 is described by the Literary Manager.)

Valine, Robert. "The Mark Taper Forum's New Play Program." *West Coast Plays*, 1 (1977), pp. 141-149. (An interview with David Copelin, Literary Manager of the Mark Taper Forum in Los Angeles.)

White, George. "The O'Neill Experience: A Practical Experiment in Helping New Writers." *Theatre Quarterly*, 4, No. 15 (Aug.-Oct. 1974), pp. 32-53. A year-by-year chronicle of the National Playwrights' Conference, containing the following articles:
George White, "The National Playwrights' Conference at the O'Neill Center, 1965-1973," pp. 32-36, 38, 40, 42, 44-52
Dan Sullivan, "Los Angeles Drama Critic Learns From the Learners," p. 35
Israel Horovitz, "Successful Playwright Tells How It All Began," p. 37
Robert Gordon, "A Playwright on When It Works," p. 39
Arthur H. Ballet, "OADR [Office for Advanced Drama Research] Director—a Friend of the Family," p. 41

Martin Esslin, "Head of BBC Radio Drama Reacts as Dramaturg," p. 43
Fred Gaines, "A Playwright on When It Doesn't Work," p. 47
"O'Neill Plays and Playwrights: 1966-1973," p. 53

Wolff-Wilkinson, Lila. "Production Dramaturgy as the Core of the Liberal Arts Theatre Program." *Theatre Topics*, 3, No. 1 (March 1993), pp. 1-5.

Zipes, Jack. "Utopia as the Past Conserved: An Interview with Peter Stein and Dieter Sturm of the Schaubühne am Halleschen Ufer." *Theater*, 9, No. 1 (Fall 1977), pp. 50-57. (A conversation with the director and dramaturg of Berlin's leading theater.)